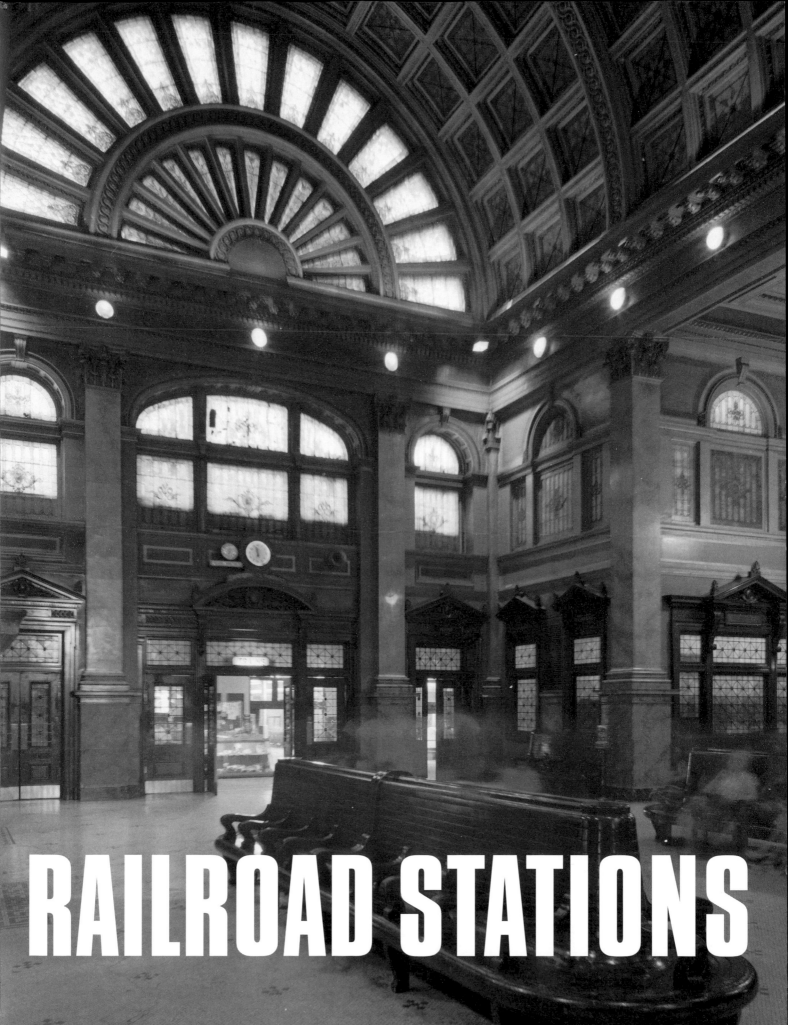

RAILROAD STATIONS

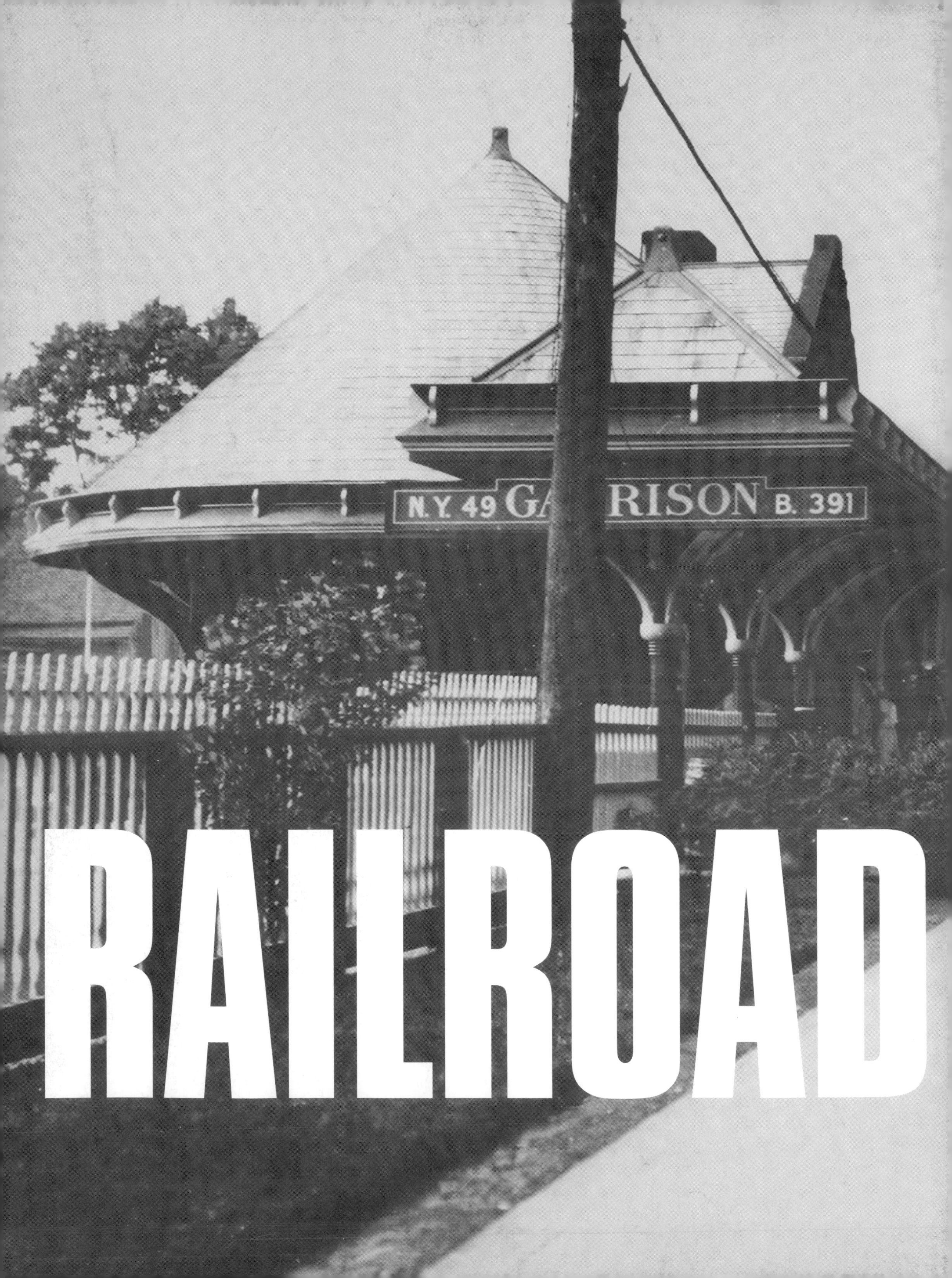

N.Y. 49 GARRISON B. 391

RAILROAD

NORTON/LIBRARY OF CONGRESS VISUAL SOURCEBOOKS IN ARCHITECTURE, DESIGN, AND ENGINEERING

DAVID NAYLOR

W. W. Norton & Company, New York and London | Library of Congress, Washington, D.C.

STATIONS
The Buildings That Linked the Nation

This publication was made possible in part through a generous contribution from the Union Station Redevelopment Corporation.

For information about special discounts for bulk purchases, please contact W. W. Norton Special Sales at specialsales@wwnorton.com or 800-233-4830.

Book design by Kristina Kachele Design llc
Composition by Ken Gross
Index by Robert Elwood
Manufacturing by Edwards Brothers, Ann Arbor
Production Manager: Leeann Graham

Library of Congress Cataloging-in-Publication Data

Naylor, David, 1955–
Railroad stations: the buildings that linked the nation / David Naylor.
p. cm. — (Norton/Library of Congress visual sourcebooks in architecture, design, and engineering)
Includes bibliographical references and index.
ISBN 978-0-393-73164-4 (hardcover)
1. Railroad stations—United States.
2. Architecture—United States. I. Title.

NA6311.N39 2011
725'.310973—dc22   2010037267

ISBN 13: 978-0-393-73164-4

W. W. Norton & Company, Inc., 500 Fifth Avenue, New York, N.Y. 10110
www.wwnorton.com
W. W. Norton & Company Ltd., Castle House, 75/76 Wells St., London W1T 3QT

0 9 8 7 6 5 4 3 2 1

Acknowledgments

Heartfelt thanks to all who have helped over the long haul in the production of this book, foremost to Nancy N. Green and her literate editors, Andrea Costella Dawson, Kristen Holt-Browning, and Vani Kannan at W. W. Norton; to C. Ford Peatross and his merry band of librarians in the Prints and Photographs Division at the Library of Congress; to Patricia L. Price for all her work in unearthing and selecting a great many of the images in this book, and also to her boss, Allan Greenberg, with his large conference table, along with his wise and witty insights; to favorite neighbors Linda Brandon and Gayle Poirier; to aids to mental health Ann, Mike, and Kevin; to David Carol, formerly of Amtrak, who often treated me to a burger lunch at D.C.'s Union Station Bar & Grill; and most of all to Amy Bloom for her great gift of hospitality a few Metro stops up the line. Thanks to others who have kindly offered a roof and a power outlet: Hannah Boulton; Elizabeth Graff; Ron and Heidi Morse with their Baja Gang, and especially Beanhead buddy Susan Reed; plus Deirdre and Michele back home in the Berkshires. Some families have been helpful and patient, to the point where I cannot thank them enough: the Ellings (particularly Ray and Jo, Diane and Gene, who now knows the photos as well as I do); the Smith family (Jack and Theresa, Laura and Kyle); the Minnix family (Jay and Mary, Cara and Diana); the Terry-Patrick family (Grant and Susan, Morgan and Will); and the Maddexes (Diane, Robert, Ali, and Lucien, the Pirate King); along with my own family. This book is dedicated to fathers, here and departed, most especially those of Patricia, Jeff, and Grant, and my own, Charles Arthur Naylor, who gave me so much support and lived to see the book completed.

The Center for Architecture, Design and Engineering and the Publishing Office of the Library of Congress are pleased to join with W. W. Norton & Company to publish the pioneering series of the Norton / Library of Congress Visual Sourcebooks in Architecture, Design, and Engineering

Based on the unparalleled collections of the Library of Congress, this series of handsomely illustrated books draws from the collections of the nation's oldest federal cultural institution and the largest library in the world, with more than 130 million items on approximately 530 miles of bookshelves. The collections include more than 19 million books, 2.7 million recordings, 12 million photographs, 4.8 million maps, and 58 million manuscripts.

The subjects of architecture, design, and engineering are threaded throughout the rich fabric of this vast archive, and the books in this new series will serve not only to introduce researchers to the illustrations selected by their authors, but also to build pathways to adjacent and related materials, and even entire archives—to millions of photographs, drawings, prints, views, maps, rare publications, and written information in the general and special collections of the Library of Congress, much of it unavailable elsewhere.

Each volume serves as an entry to the collections, providing a treasury of select visual material, much of it in the public domain, for students, scholars, teachers, researchers, historians of art, architecture, design, technology, and practicing architects, engineers, and designers of all kinds.

Supplementing this volume, an online portfolio of all the images in this book is available for browsing and downloading at *www.wwnorton.com/npb/loc/railroadstations*. It offers a direct link to the Library's online, searchable catalogs and image files, including the hundreds of thousands of high-resolution photographs and measured drawings, and data files in the Historic American Buildings Survey, Historic American Engineering Records, and the recently inaugurated Historic American Landscape Survey. The Library's Web site has rapidly become one of the most popular and valuable locations on the Internet, experiencing over 3.7 billion hits a year and serving audiences ranging from school children to the most advanced scholars throughout the world, with a potential usefulness that has only begun to be explored.

Among the subjects to be covered in this series are building types, building materials and details; historical periods and movements; landscape architecture and garden design; interior and ornamental design and furnishings; and industrial design. *Railroad Stations* is an excellent exemplar of the goals and possibilities on which this series is based.

JAMES H. BILLINGTON
THE LIBRARIAN OF CONGRESS

The introduction to this book provides an overview of the history and evolution of railroad stations in the United States. It is a view that is broad and inspired by the depth and quality of the resources of the Library of Congress. The balance of the book, containing 794 images, is organized into nine sections that focus on specific aspects and representations of railroad stations in history. Figure-number prefixes designate the section.

Short captions give the essential identifying information, where known: subject, location, creator(s) of the image, date, and Library of Congress call number, which can be used to find the image online. Below is a list of the collections from which the images in the book were drawn.

ADE	Architecture, Design, and Engineering Drawing Series
BIOG FILE	Bibliographical File Series
CD	Cartoon Drawing Series
DETR (formerly DPCC)	Detroit Publishing Company Collection
DIG	Digital File from Original Print
FSA	Farm Security Administration
Gen. Coll.	General Collections
HABS	Historic American Buildings Survey
HAER	Historic American Engineering Record
LC	Library of Congress
NYWTS-BIOG	New York World Telegram & Sun Newspaper Photograph Collection, sub-series Biographical
P&P	Prints & Photographs Division
PAN SUBJECT	Panoramic Photographs Collection, sub-series Subject
PAN US GEOG	Panoramic Photographs Collection, sub-series Geography
PGA	Popular Graphic Arts
POS	Posters: Artist Posters
STEREO PRES FILE	Stereograph Series, sub-series Presidential
STEREO U.S. GEOG FILE	Stereograph Series, sub-series U.S. Geography
SWANN	Swann Collection of Caricature and Cartoon
U.S. GEOG FILE	Geographic File Series
WC	Wittemann Collection

CONTENTS

Introduction: Building the American Railroad, 9

Mid-Atlantic Region I
(Maryland, Delaware,
West Virginia), 63

Mid-Atlantic Region II
(Pennsylvania, Ohio), 91

Mid-Atlantic Region III
(New Jersey, New York),
133

New England, 175

The South, 197

The Midwest, 243

The Northern Plains and
the Northwest, 275

The Central Plains and the
Rockies, 289

The Southwest, 303

Bibliography, 327

About the Online Portfolio, 329

Index, 331

BUILDING THE AMERICAN RAILROAD

For a set of buildings that all have performed the same function, with roughly the same layout and patterns of circulation, the variety of railroad stations produced across America is astonishing. No direct model existed for the building type that developed during the mid-nineteenth century. As a result stylistic character varied widely. But this matter goes far beyond style. For example, travelers today can find Spanish Mission treatments at stations in the expected regions of Florida, Texas, and California—but also in unexpected places such as Boise, Idaho. Nineteenth-century American architecture was awash in stylistic revivals. There were obvious distinctions between big-city stations along the eastern seaboard and frontier stations in the western territories, but over time the chief differences were in size and complexity. By any other measure the western buildings were often just as handsome, if not quite as elaborate, as the eastern ones.

What all these stations had in common for that first century of the railroads was a sense of their centrality in the communities they served. Almost overnight the railway lines spread across the nation's maps and assumed a key role in its national development. As historian Anne M. Lyden has noted, just as the railroad supplanted the role of the ocean-going ships of the eighteenth century, the trains in turn gave way in the twentieth century to airplanes, the new "transcontinental carrier."[1] Still, for an entire century the train was king. Decisions about where to lay the tracks and build the stations helped chart our nation's rise as an industrial power and affected the course of the Civil War. Trains enabled us to cross and eventually settle the western territories. We matured as a country in tune with our rail system.

IN-001. Washington Terminal Station—gate in train fence showing train sign set for departure of "Royal Limited," Washington, D.C. Unidentified photographer, early 1900s. P&P, LOT 12334, LC-USZ62-991605.

IN-002

IN THE COURSE OF HUMAN EVENTS

Few buildings have had to withstand more of a daily beating—constant comings and goings—than railroad stations. For over a century the station buildings formed a constant backdrop for events both commonplace and extraordinary: arrivals and departures became special when relatives visited over the holidays, or when some VIP came to town, or with someone's first trip on a train. In decades long past, public lecturers and evangelists would go from town to town, often holding rallies right at the railway stations (IN-002). In our modern Jet Age this is pure nostalgia, but for generations presidential campaigns conducted as whistle-stop tours were an American institution (IN-003–IN-004). Many other presidential moments of a more somber nature were also linked with rail stations (IN-005–IN-007). Most poignant of all departures have been those of American soldiers, from the time of the Civil War to the present day. With each new world conflict many of our nation's wartime troop movements have begun and ended at the depot (IN-008–IN-010). Then there were the times that station buildings became stories in their own right. Like all buildings, stations are subject to both natural and manmade disasters (IN-011–IN-013). No matter how solid the railroad buildings appeared, even they were not impervious to damage. Anytime a station was forced to close down, the disruption to people's lives could be substantial, much as with airports today.

IN-003

IN-004

IN-003. President Theodore Roosevelt speaking from his train, Colorado Springs, Colorado. Stereograph by H. C. White Company, 1905. P&P,STEREO PRES FILE,LC-DIG-PPMsca-18927 from LC-USZ62-102864.

IN-004. President Franklin D. Roosevelt leaving Washington, D.C., for Florida, waving goodbye from the rear of his private car on the Atlantic Coast Line Presidential Special Railroad, Washington, D.C. Acme Newspictures, Incorporated, 1934. P&P,NYWTS-BIOG,LC-USZ62-128758.

IN-005. The attack on President James Garfield's life—Mrs. Smith supporting the President while awaiting the arrival of the ambulance, Washington, D.C. Engraving by Berghaus & Upham for *Frank Leslie's Illustrated Newspaper*, vol. 52, no. 1346 (July 1881): 325. P&P,AP2.L52 1881,LC-USZ62-77908.

The attack, by Charles J. Guiteau, took place at Washington's Baltimore & Potomac Station. President Garfield succumbed to the gunshot injuries two and a half months later.

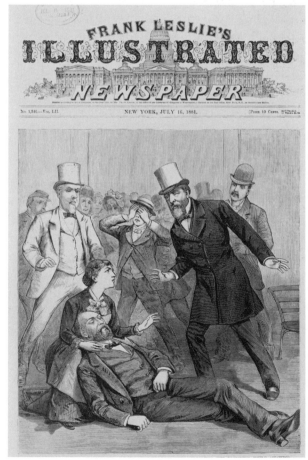

IN-005

IN-006

IN-007

IN-006. President Lincoln's funeral car, Alexandria, Virginia. Andrew J. Russell, photographer, 1865. P&P,LOT 11486-C,no.3,LC-DIG-ppmsca-08259.

IN-007. Hundreds of people gathered before a large-screen television in New York's Grand Central Terminal to watch coverage of President Kennedy's funeral, New York, New York. NYWTS/AP, November 1963. P&P,NYWTS-BIOG,LC-USZ62-132900.

IN-008

IN-008. Roosevelt's Rough Riders' arrival, Tampa, Florida. B. L. Singley (Keystone View Company), photographer, ca. 1898. P&P,STEREO PRES FILE,LC-USZ62-6228.

IN-009. Soldiers of the First Division enjoying a watermelon feast near the Union Station, Washington, D.C. Stereograph by Keystone View Company, ca. 1919. P&P,STEREO U.S. GEOG FILE,LC-USZ62-106123.

IN-010. Pennsylvania Railroad Station, New York, New York. Marjory Collins, photographer, August 1942. P&P,LC-USW3-006961-E.

For the northeastern United States, Pennsylvania Station was a major staging point for soldiers headed for Europe. Eventually war bond sales, USO booths, and special information stands for servicemen and servicewomen bordered the concourse.

IN-009

IN-010

IN-011

IN-011. Accident at the Michigan Central Railroad Depot, November 12, 1906, Detroit, Michigan. DETR, November 1906. P&P,LC-D4-19780.

IN-012. Ruins of the B&O Roundhouse after tornado of 1896, East St. Louis, Illinois. William Schiller, photographer, 1896. P&P,LOT 9646,LC-USZ62-63604.

IN-013. Bird's-eye view of Delaware flood, March 29, 1913, Delaware, Ohio. Fuller & Harmount, March 1913. P&P,PAN US GEOG-Ohio no. 30 (E size).

IN-012

IN-013

IN-014

Trains and rail stations rarely play such momentous roles in present-day America, but they did help make us who we have become in the world. At no time was the rail system more pivotal than during the Civil War. The previously untested capacity to move troops, and to re-supply them with food and munitions, was a key determinant in the Union victory. By 1860, just prior to the war, American rail companies had laid roughly 30,000 miles of track—two-thirds of it in the more industrialized northern states.[2] This logistical advantage for the North was offset over the first half of the war by strategies developed by the Southern generals. Beauregard and Jackson had quickly learned that wherever Union forces were poised to attack, the South's limited armies could be shifted by train to strengthen their counterattacks. Only after Grant took over the Union armies were measures introduced to stretch the Confederate forces and neutralize their speedy movements.

The Civil War was the first American conflict to be documented for widespread publication. Nascent photojournalists Matthew Brady and Andrew J. Russell recorded battles and troop movements, as well as the war's toll on many railroad properties. (IN-014–IN-015). Other scenes of the war were carefully rendered for *Frank Leslie's Illustrated Newspaper* (IN-016). The images produced by Currier & Ives generally had a more editorial bent (IN-017). Gradually some attention focused on the newly freed former slaves in the South, many of them looking to head north for safety and, for some, to join the Northern forces (IN-018).

IN-015

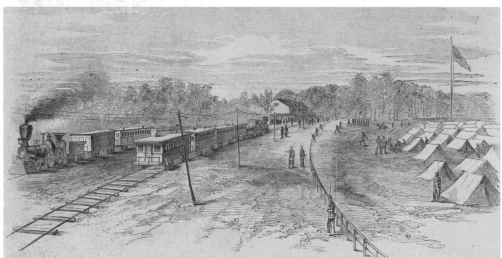

IN-016

IN-017

THE OLD BULL DOG ON THE RIGHT TRACK.

IN-015. Railroad depot, Petersburg, Virginia. Andrew J. Russell, photographer, April 1865. P&P,LOT 11486-C,no. 15,LC-DIG-ppmsca-08271.

IN-016. Annapolis Junction, on the Washington branch of the Baltimore & Ohio Railroad, in possession of the troops of the United States government, Annapolis Junction, Maryland. Engraving for *Frank Leslie's Illustrated Newspaper* (June 1861): 39. P&P,AP2.L52 1861 Case Y,LC-USZ62-90547.

IN-017. "The old bull dog on the right track." Lithograph by Currier & Ives, ca. 1864. P&P,PGA-Currier & Ives-Old bull dog . . . , LC-USZ62-8626.

Summarized as "An election year cartoon measuring Democratic candidate McClellan's military failures against the recent successes of his successor, Ulysses S. Grant. At right Grant, portrayed as a bulldog wearing a collar labeled 'Lieut. General' and his epaulets, sits pugnaciously on the tracks of the 'Weldon Railroad,' a Confederate supply route. He looks to Republican presidential incumbent Abraham Lincoln and boasts 'I'm bound to take it.' Grant refers to the city of Richmond, here represented by a doghouse, in which cowers Confederate president Jefferson Davis. Davis, flanked by his own generals Lee and Beauregard, remarks, 'You aint got this kennel yet old fellow!' and so on . . ."

IN-018. African American workers standing on railroad tracks in front of a storage facility, possibly at Geisboro cavalry depot, Geisboro, South Carolina. Andrew J. Russell, photographer, ca. 1861–1865. P&P,LOT 11486-G,no. 18,LC-DIG-ppmsca-11733.

Ultimately the photographers focused on scenes of destruction, of both troops and property, as Union forces pushed their way across the Confederate states (IN-019–IN-020). The cities that served as major railheads were most heavily affected. These included Richmond, Nashville, Charleston, and—as immortalized, if fictionalized, in the classic 1939 film *Gone with the Wind*—Atlanta (IN-021–IN-022). At the Atlanta station Northern troops rested for what came to be known as Sherman's March to the Sea. Some of the soldiers passed the time by tearing up the tracks. They set the ties ablaze to heat up the iron rails, which in turn the soldiers bent to form so-called Sherman's Bowties. On their departure the Union troops left the Atlanta station in shambles (IN-023–IN-024).

IN-019

IN-020

IN-019. Destruction of the railroad bridge over the Potomac, at Harper's Ferry, by the rebels, June 15, 1861, Harper's Ferry, West Virginia. Engraving in *Harper's Weekly*, vol. 5 (July 1861): 429. P&P,AP2.H32 1861 Case Y,LC-USZ62-75924. (See IN-031.)

IN-020. View of town and railroad bridge in ruins, Harper's Ferry, West Virginia. C. O. Bostwick, photographer, ca. 1861. P&P,LC-B8171-7649.

IN-021. Ruins of Richmond & Petersburg Railroad Depot (destroyed locomotive shown), Richmond, Virginia. Unidentified photographer, April 1865. P&P,LC-B811-3260,LC-DIG-cwpb-0279.

IN-022. Railroad yard and depot with locomotives; the Capitol in the distance, Nashville, Tennessee. George N. Barnard, photographer, 1864. P&P,LC-8611-2651,LC-B8171-2651.

IN-021

IN-022

IN-023

IN-023. Sherman's men destroying railroad, Atlanta, Georgia. George N. Barnard, photographer, 1864. P&P,LC-B811,3630B.

IN-024. Ruins of depot, blown up on Sherman's departure, Atlanta, Georgia. George N. Barnard, photographer, 1864. P&P,LC-B811-2715,LC-DIG-cwpb-02226.

As the official photographer of the Chief Engineer's Office, George N. Barnard recorded the capture of Atlanta and the subsequent three-month period during which Sherman's forces were reprovisioned for their March to the Sea. Having captured the munitions center of the Confederate army in September 1864, Sherman's army set fire to both the munitions and, through proximity, the railroad depot on their departure two and a half months later.

IN-024

IN-025. Across the continent, "Westward the Course of Empire Takes Its Way." J. M. Ives, delineator, drawn by F. F. Palmer, lithograph for Currier & Ives, ca. 1868. P&P,PGA-Currier & Ives-Across the Continent . . . (D size),LC-USZ62-1.

CROSSING THE CONTINENT, EXPANDING OUR HORIZONS

Once the Civil War was over, the country began to look again at its western territories, still largely unexplored. As rail lines pushed toward the Pacific, the rail stations served as outposts marking the frontiers of settlement. Just five years after the war ended, one of America's greatest nineteenth-century triumphs occurred with the completion of the first transcontinental rail line at Promontory, Utah (IN-026–IN-027).

The scheme to cross the country by rail had been in the works since the California Gold Rush of 1849. Five major surveys were conducted, in roughly parallel lines between the nation's northern and southern borders, looking for the best route. Abraham Lincoln set things in final motion by signing the Railroad Act of 1862. The winning route was that of Theodore Judah, chief engineer for the Central Pacific. His path across the Sierras eastward from Sacramento ultimately joined with Grenville Dodge's route for the Union Pacific westward from Omaha. The chief beneficiaries of the route were the four Sacramento merchants who funded Judah's survey: Leland Stanford, Mark Hopkins, Charles Crocker, and Colis P. Huntington.

IN-026

IN-027

IN-026. Ceremony at "the wedding of the rails," May 10, 1869, Promontory Point, Utah. Unidentified photographer, May 1869. P&P,LOT 8772,LC-USZ62-59794.

IN-027. "Does not such a meeting make amends?" Engraving for *Frank Leslie's Illustrated Newspaper* (May 1869): 176. P&P,AP2.L52 Case Y,LC-USZC4-747.

IN-028. Fall View, Niagara, New York. DETR, ca. 1900. P&P,LOT 12697,no. 27 (OSF),LC-USZC4-124191.

New routes to the West made settlement easier and more rapid. New railroad stations were essential to that process. Still, it took decades before there was any significant population growth in the region. For the time being, stations were designed to serve a new class of tourists who were drawn to look at the reported wonders of the western interior. Rail companies promoted these natural wonders, mainly by means of pamphlets filled with tinted images and hyperbolic prose.

The scale of such promotions was unprecedented in America, but these were not the first efforts to exploit the railroads' tourist potential. As early as the 1840s a plan envisioned building a line from New York City up to the Niagara River at the falls. By 1855 the first trains were arriving (IN-028). By the turn of the twentieth century Henry Flagler was looking to bring his fellow New Yorkers south to Florida for the winter. He went so far as to hire the firm of Carrère & Hastings, architects for the main branch of the New York Public Library, to create a luxury hotel at St. Augustine, Florida, to house the southbound travelers. Ultimately, for the period 1912–1935, Flagler ran his Overseas Railroad all the way to Key West (IN-029).

IN-029. Arrival of first train at Key West, Florida, over sea, Florida–East Coast Railroad, January 22, 1912, Key West, Florida. Unidentified photographer, January 1912. P&P,PAN US GEOG-Florida no. 31 (E size),LC-USZ62-127312.

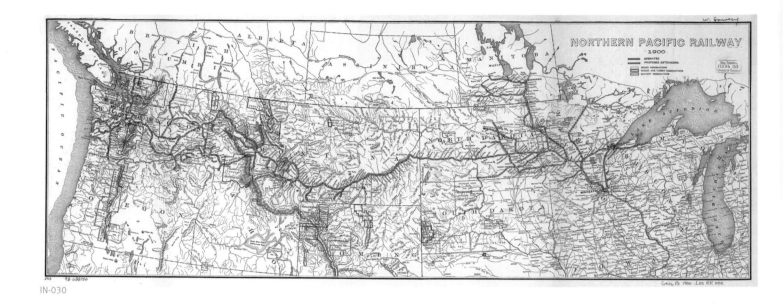

IN-030

These eastern efforts were minor compared to the plans to induce a grand-scale, western tourist boom designed to show off the lands that would become America's first national parks. As the Northern Pacific Railway crossed Montana it was well positioned to give easy access to what eventually became Glacier National Park (IN-034–IN-035). Initially more significant was the railway line's relative proximity to the world's first national park, at Yellowstone, founded in 1872.

In 1903 Northern Pacific completed a spur line from Cinnabar, Montana, to the town of Gardiner, just across the border from Wyoming and the national park. Architect Robert C. Reamer (1873–1936) had just finished designing a new hotel at the geyser basin, the Old Faithful Inn.[3] The railway company put Reamer back to work on a rail station for Gardiner (IN-036), along with a monumental entry portal to the parklands. A Yellowstone National Park Association publication issued a dozen years later was as effusive about the Gardiner structures as it was about the geysers: it mentioned "[the] passenger station built of great logs from the Western Montana forests . . . within 100 yards of the 'gate' to the 'Wonderland of the World.' . . . [and] the $10,000 official lava arch marking the boundary and the entrance to the great national park, the cornerstone of which was laid by President Roosevelt"[4] (IN-033).

The lava arch was not the first huge rock pile to be erected by the railroads in the American West. Back in 1880 the Union Pacific Railroad had hired architect Henry Hobson Richardson (1836–1886) to design a stonework monument to honor his fellow Massachusetts notable, railroadman Oakes Ames. The monument was placed a short distance from Laramie, Wyoming, to mark the highest point of the transcontinental line — at least until the tracks were moved in 1918 (IN-034).

IN-031

IN-030. Northern Pacific Railway Map, 1900. G4126.P3 1900 .L55 RR 502.

IN-031. An emblem on a Chicago & Great Western Railroad freight car, San Bernardino, California. Jack Delano, photographer, March 1943. P&P, LC-USW3-021561-E.

IN-032. "Gardner Station," Yellowstone National Park, Gardiner, Montana. Unidentified photographer, ca. 1913. P&P,US GEOG FILE-Wyoming-Yellowstone National Park,LC-USZ62-92912.

Park concessionaires operated the stagecoaches at the station in Gardiner under the guidance of the Northern Pacific Railway. The stagecoaches delivered passengers to the various lodges scattered across Yellowstone Park—from Mammoth, to the lake, to the geyser basin.

IN-033. Gateway entrance to Yellowstone National Park, U.S.A. American Stereoscopic Company, ca. 1904. P&P,LOT 11959-10,LC-USZ62-101056.

IN-034

IN-034. Ames Monument, Interstate 80, Laramie, Albany County, Wyoming. Unidentified photographer, before 1974. P&P,HABS,WYO,1-LARAM,1-3.

Oakes Ames had a highly questionable role in the completion of the Union Pacific Railway line across the West. The questionable aspect involved his assumption of control of Credit Mobilier stock and its discounted sale to members of the U.S. Congress in an attempt to influence their votes. Oakes died in 1873 following an official condemnation by Congress. Ten years later the State of Massachusetts authorized $65,000 to be spent on hiring eighty-five "skilled and semi-skilled workers" to build the monument in Wyoming.

At Gardiner, placing the station right at the edge of the park was of major importance for the builders of the Old Faithful Inn. Reamer made great use of local stone and (perhaps unbelievable to modern environmental sensibilities) cut down huge swaths of the forests surrounding the geyser basin to build both the inn and the rail station. Still, much of the building materials had to be brought in over long distances by rail.[5] Redwood shakes came from California, while furniture and hardware arrived from the eastern states.

Even as the Old Faithful Inn went up, plans were afoot for a comparable lodge at the Grand Canyon in Arizona. The Santa Fe Railroad had run a spur line in 1901 to the South Rim of the canyon. By 1905 architect Charles Whittlesey's (1884–1921) El Tovar Lodge was completed with ninety-five rooms, some not even 100 feet from the canyon's edge. The Santa Fe built its own rail terminus for El Tovar (IN-035). The spur line to the terminal made it unnecessary for park visitors to endure a bumpy twenty-hour ride in a horse-drawn carriage to reach the canyon, as was previously the case. Instead the trains delivered guests to a point that was just a short walk from the lodge and the canyon scenery.

El Tovar was originally operated by the Fred Harvey Company. Proprietor Frederick Henry Harvey had come to America from London at age fifteen in 1850, and he found his calling in 1876 when he took over a restaurant at the back of a depot in Omaha, Nebraska. His business ultimately grew to encompass forty-seven Harvey Houses along the rail lines as well as thirty dining cars[6] (IN-036). Flocks of uniformed

IN-035. Railway station and El Tovar Hotel, facing WNW, Grand Canyon National Park, Coconino County, Arizona. Brian C. Grogan, photographer, 1994. P&P,HAER,ARIZ,3-GRACAN,10-8.

IN-036. Fred Harvey Eating House and Santa Fe Station, Chanute, Kansas. Unidentified photographer, ca. 1900. P&P,LC-USZ62-118086.

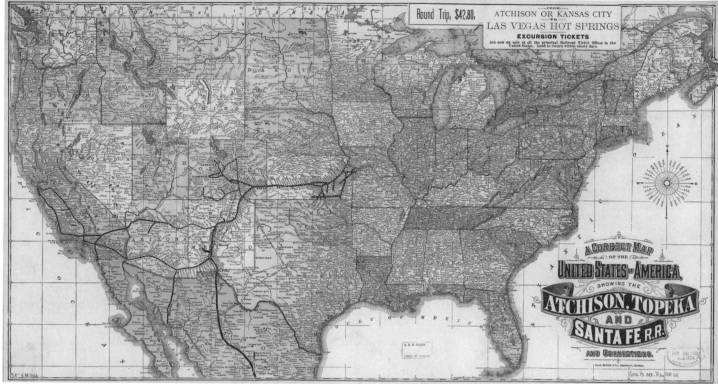

IN-037

IN-037. A correct map of the U.S. showing the Atchison, Topeka & Santa Fe Railroad and connections. Chicago, Rand McNally & Company, 1888.

Harvey Girls staffed his operations. The lives of these exemplary servers received full Hollywood treatment in the 1946 MGM Judy Garland vehicle appropriately titled *The Harvey Girls*. After helping to save the fictional western town of Sandrock (constructed on a MGM backlot), Judy launches into the Academy Award–winning song "The Atchison Topeka and the Santa Fe," as she and a puffing locomotive depart the station (IN-037).

The operations at El Tovar were likely not as dramatic as the events depicted in the movie, but they certainly were as stylish. The girls were all topnotch, as would befit respondents to the ad that solicited them: "young women of good character, attractive and intelligent, 18 to 30 . . . a salary of $17.50 per month, plus room and board."7

UPGRADING THE SYSTEM IN SCOPE AND STATURE

The emergence of the railways came at a time when the nation was roughly half a century old. There was as yet little attention given to the architectural treatment of buildings beyond churches and seats of government, aside from the houses of the wealthy (a familiar pattern across world cultures). The railway station, not yet the civic centerpiece it would become, seemed to fit an entirely different category of utilitarian buildings. Likewise, the great iron horse served foremost as a workhorse, a mechanical conveyance designed to support America's second great national revolution—the

IN-038. Mount Clare Station, 500 block West Pratt Street, Baltimore, Independent City, Maryland. E. H. Pickering, photographer, August 1936. P&P,HABS,MD,4-BALT,51-1.

The notes indicate the following (while inaccurately dating Mount Clare ahead of the Ellicott City station): "This building erected 1830 is the first passenger and freight station in America and the oldest in the world at the time of its use. Trains were hauled by horses between Baltimore and Ellicott Mills. . . . The first telegraph message sent from this building to Washington, May 24, 1844, 'What hath God wrought?' "

expansion of its fledgling national economy. America's first common carrier railroad, the Baltimore & Ohio, was part iron and part horse. The B&O, as chartered in 1827, began operations with cars pulled by horses over its first miles of roadbed. According to Joe Walsh in *The American Railroad*, "By 1839, the railroad had completed 13 miles of track, from Baltimore to Ellicott City"; steam locomotives only entered the picture in 1835.[8] As a result, the flagship Mount Clare Station (IN-038) that the B&O built near the center of Baltimore included stalls for horses in its passenger car shop (IN-039–IN-040). The car shop, complete with modifications for mechanical rail, was a forerunner of the roundhouse that developed later for stations to house spare locomotive engines (IN-041).

As for nomenclature, one can make some distinctions between the terms "station" and "depot." At first stations were simply the points along a rail line where horses and, later, locomotives required servicing. The station was primarily the place itself, whereas any structure put up to handle company business (freight operations, the ticketing and sheltering of passengers) was labeled a depot. Over time people used the two names interchangeably.

IN-039

IN-040

IN-039. Detail view of feeding trough inside horse stall, Baltimore & Ohio Railroad, Mount Clare Shops, south side of Pratt Street between Carey & Poppleton streets, Baltimore, Independent City, Maryland. William Edmund Barrett, photographer, 1976. P&P,HAER,MD,4-BALT,127A-9.

IN-040. View of 3-1/2 story, center-pedimented section of stables, looking east, Baltimore & Ohio Railroad, Mount Clare Shops, south side of Pratt Street between Carey & Poppleton streets, Baltimore, Independent City, Maryland. William Edmund Barrett, photographer, 1976. P&P,HAER,MD,4-BALT,127A-4.

IN-041. Elevation, Baltimore & Ohio Railroad, Mount Clare Passenger Car Shop, southwest corner of Pratt & Poppleton streets, Baltimore, Independent City, Maryland. P&P,HAER,MD,4-BALT,127-,sheet no. 2.

The circular car shop has a diameter of 235 feet and a clerestory ring around its roof that measures 100 feet in diameter. The shop building, which comprises twenty-two stalls, was completed in February 1884. Complete locomotives were assembled for B&O at these shops until just a few years following the end of World War II.

MOUNT CLARE CIRCULAR CAR SHOP, 1884.   MOUNT CLARE STATION, 1880.   PRINT SHOP, 1891.

DRAWN BY: ERIC N. DELONY · 1972
B & O RAILROAD SURVEY
OFFICE OF ARCHEOLOGY AND HISTORIC PRESERVATION
UNDER DIRECTION OF THE NATIONAL PARK SERVICE.
UNITED STATES DEPARTMENT OF THE INTERIOR.

NAME AND LOCATION OF STRUCTURE
B&O RR: MOUNT CLARE PASSENGER CAR SHOP c.1883-84
SW CORNER OF PRATT & POPPLETON STS.

BALTIMORE
INDEPENDENT CITY
MARYLAND

RECORD NO.
MD
6

HISTORIC AMERICAN
ENGINEERING RECORD
SHEET 2 OF 3 SHEETS

IN-041

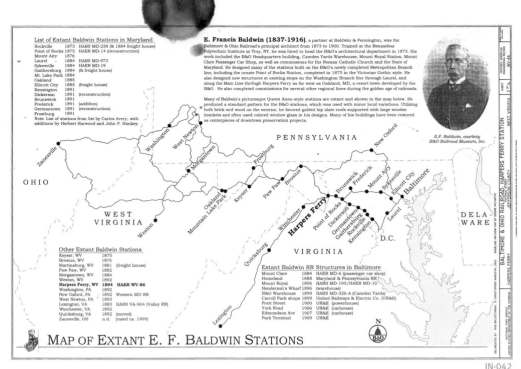

DELINEATED BY: ROB BRUDISTONEBA & CHRISTOPHER MARESTON 2002

NATIONAL PARK SERVICE
UNITED STATES DEPARTMENT OF THE INTERIOR

BASELINE ARCHIVE MAP BY DEBRA MCCARTY

HISTORIC AMERICAN
ENGINEERING RECORD
WV-86

SHEET 3 OF 14

WEST VIRGINIA

BALTIMORE & OHIO RAILROAD, HARPERS FERRY STATION
POTOMAC STREET
JEFFERSON COUNTY
HARPERS FERRY

List of Extant Baldwin Stations in Maryland

Rockville	1873	HABS MD-238 (& 1884 freight house)
Point of Rocks	1875	HAER MD-14 (reconstruction)
Mount Airy	1876	
Laurel	1884	HABS MD-973
Sykesville	1884	HAER MD-19
Gaithersburg	1884	(& freight house)
Mt. Lake Park	1884	
Oakland	1885	
Ellicott City	1885	(freight house)
Kensington	1891	
Dickerson	1891	(reconstruction)
Brunswick	1891	
Frederick	1891	(addition)
Germantown	1891	(reconstruction)
Frostburg	1891	

Note: List of stations from list by Carlos Avery, with additions by Herbert Harwood and John P. Hankey.

E. Francis Baldwin (1837-1916), a partner at Baldwin & Pennington, was the Baltimore & Ohio Railroad's principal architect from 1873 to 1900. Trained at the Rensselaer Polytechnic Institute in Troy, NY, he was hired to head the B&O's architectural department in 1873. His work included the B&O Headquarters building, Camden Yards Warehouse, Mount Royal Station, Mount Clare Passenger Car Shop, as well as commissions for the Roman Catholic Church and the State of Maryland. He designed many of the stations built on the B&O's newly completed Metropolitan Branch line, including the ornate Point of Rocks Station, completed in 1875 in the Victorian Gothic style. He also designed new structures at existing stops on the Washington Branch line through Laurel, and along the Main Line through Harpers Ferry as far west as Oakland, MD, a resort town developed by the B&O. He also completed commissions for several other regional lines during the golden age of railroads.

Many of Baldwin's picturesque Queen Anne-style stations are extant and shown in the map below. He produced a standard pattern for the B&O stations, which was used with minor local variations. Utilizing both brick and wood on the exterior, he favored gabled hip slate roofs supported with large wooden brackets and often used colored window glass in his designs. Many of his buildings have been restored as centerpieces of downtown preservation projects.

E.F. Baldwin, courtesy B&O Railroad Museum, Inc.

PENNSYLVANIA

OHIO

WEST VIRGINIA

VIRGINIA

D.C.

DELAWARE

Other Extant Baldwin Stations

Keyser, WV	1875	
Brosius, WV	1876	
Martinsburg, WV	1881	(freight house)
Paw Paw, WV	1882	
Morgantown, WV	1884	
Weston, WV	1892	
Harpers Ferry, WV	**1894**	**HAER WV-86**
Washington, PA	1892	
New Oxford, PA	1892	Western MD RR
West Newton, PA	1893	
Lexington, VA	1883	HABS VA-904 (Valley RR)
Winchester, VA	1892	
Quicksburg, VA	1892	(moved)
Zanesville, OH	n.d.	(razed ca. 1999)

Extant Baldwin RR Structures in Baltimore

Mount Clare	1884	HAER MD-6 (passenger car shop)
Homeland	1888	Maryland & Pennsylvania RR
Mount Royal	1896	HABS MD-193/HAER MD-10
Henderson's Wharf	1896	(warehouse)
B&O Warehouse	1899	HABS MD-326-A (Camden Yards)
Carroll Park shops	1899	United Railways & Electric Co. (UR&E)
Pratt Street	1900	UR&E (powerhouse)
York Road	1906	UR&E (carhouse)
Edmondson Ave	1907	UR&E (carhouse)
Park Terminal	1909	UR&E

MAP OF EXTANT E. F. BALDWIN STATIONS

IN-042

IN-042. Map of extant E. F. Baldwin stations, Baltimore & Ohio Railroad, Harper's Ferry Station, Potomac Street, Harper's Ferry, Jefferson County, West Virginia. P&P,HAER,WV-86,sheet no. 3.

IN-043. View of station showing tracks, Baltimore & Ohio Railroad, Point of Rocks Station, near State Route 28, Point of Rocks, Frederick County, Maryland. Jack E. Boucher and William E. Barrett, photographers, 1970. P&P,HAER,MD,11-PORO,1-1.

IN-043

As new rail lines took shape a corresponding need emerged for architects to design appropriate new station buildings. The country's first rail company was also the first to hire someone to do this work on a permanent basis. In 1873 E. Francis Baldwin (1837–1916) officially became chief architect for the B&O Railroad (IN-042). Shortly thereafter Baldwin designed what remains the best known of his stations, the Victorian Gothic brickpile of the Point of Rocks Station (IN-043). Completed in 1875, the steeple-topped station still sits at the junction of the B&O's main line from Baltimore and its branch line from Washington, D.C., at the point where they continue as one line west to Ohio.

IN-044

IN-044. East staircase, Baltimore &
Ohio Railroad Station, Twenty-fourth
and Chestnut streets, Philadelphia,
Philadelphia County, Pennsylvania. Cervin
Robinson, photographer, October 1959.
P&P,HABS,PA,51-PHILA,405-6.

Furness's attention to detail was pervasive
and always noteworthy, as visible here as at
his masterpiece, the Philadelphia Academy
of Fine Arts.

Once the B&O extended its line into Pennsylvania, another major architect, Frank
Furness (1839–1912), was hired to build stations in Philadelphia (IN-044) and Pittsburgh.
Furness also designed stations, in his idiosyncratic fashion, for the Reading Railroad
and the Pennsylvania Railroad, in Center City Philadelphia, along the city's suburban
Main Line, and in nearby Delaware. Moreover, Furness built the Bryn Mawr Hotel in
1890 for the Pennsylvania Railroad. Today the hotel survives as the centerpiece of the
Baldwin School, a preparatory school for girls located in Bryn Mawr, Pennsylvania.

IN-045. South and east façades showing porte cochère, Boston & Albany Railroad Station, Auburndale, Middlesex County, Massachusetts. Cervin Robinson, photographer, June 1959. P&P,HABS,MASS,9-AUB,1-1.

The Auburndale station was the first of several that H. H. Richardson built for the Boston & Albany Railroad.

IN-046. Railroad station, Ice Glen Mountain in background, Stockbridge, Massachusetts. WC, ca. 1910. P&P,LC-USZ62-46872.

The Stockbridge station later gained a barrel-vault roof running the length of the platform.

IN-045

IN-046

In Massachusetts during the 1870s and 1880s, Henry Hobson Richardson built a half-dozen small stations using the massive stones and heavy timbers that he often preferred for his buildings (IN-045). These stations, built mostly for the Boston & Albany Railroad, were scattered west from Boston across the center of the state. New York–based McKim, Mead, & White—the country's elite firm following Richardson's death in 1886—also built in stone for the Stockbridge Station in far western Massachusetts (IN-046). This was a more delicate variation on the Richardsonian model, and an unlikely prelude to the firm's best-known railroad building, New York City's Pennsylvania Station (1910; see 3-089–3-109).

THE STRIDE OF A CENTURY.

IN-047

The firm of Reed & Stem of St. Paul, Minnesota, designed the beautifully domed Union Station in Tacoma, Washington ((1911); see 7-028–7-029), and also was credited with the initial layout for the twentieth-century reincarnation of Grand Central Terminal in New York (1913; see 3-076–3-088). Execution of the terminal's centerpiece, the grandest of all grand concourses, however, is attributed to Whitney Warren (1864–1943), chief architect for the firm of Warren & Wetmore (and not incidentally the cousin of New York Central Railroad chairman William Vanderbilt). Most likely, without the participation of both firms neither the beauty nor the utility of Grand Central would have been fully realized. The sense of needing to strike a balance between aesthetic and functional concerns has long been deemed essential for any building to be considered a masterpiece. With their complex building programs, railroad stations are no exception.

Before the construction of the two New York giants of Penn Station and Grand Central, prior to the turn of the century an event took place in Chicago that had major ramifications for station design, as well as for the course of American architecture overall. The 1893 World's Columbian Exposition was a monumental undertaking. It was much larger than preceding fairs, including Philadelphia's Centennial Exposition of 1876 (IN-047–IN-048). The overall increase in scale was evident in the extent of the railroad infrastructure required in Chicago (IN-049). The nearly impossible job of plan-

IN-048

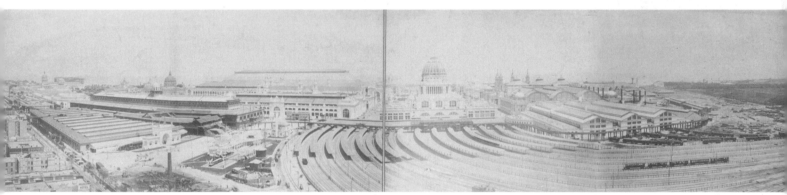

IN-049

IN-050

ning and building the 1893 fair was entrusted to Chicago's leading architectural firm of the day, Burnham & Root.[9] John Wellborn Root (1850–1891) did not survive to see the fair opened, but his ideas, together with those of the American landscape genius Frederick Law Olmsted, helped Daniel H. Burnham (1864–1912) (IN-050) guide a collaboration of the country's most prominent architects to build and run a successful exposition.

As Chief of Construction, Burnham delegated the design of the fair's railroad station to Charles Atwood (1849–1896). Burnham later designed a number of stations himself, including two masterworks, Pittsburgh's Pennsylvania Railroad Station and Union Station in Washington, D.C. Architectural historian Kristen Schaffer has described Union Station's stately presence as "a grand vestibule to the city" and has noted as an equal virtue that the building "solves the functional problems of moving large numbers of people to large numbers of trains."[10] Thus Burnham was making great use of the

IN-051. Union Station, Worcester, Massachusetts. DETR, ca. 1906. P&P,LC-D4-18898.

IN-051

lessons learned at the exposition in Chicago. Atwood had designed the fair's terminal to handle up to thirty thousand passengers per day on trains covering thirty-five tracks under a triple shed. Correspondingly, the operator of all those trains, the Illinois Central Railroad, built a new station on the edge of the Chicago Loop at a cost of $1.8 million, over the ten months prior to the Exposition's opening (see 9-031–9-032).

To a large degree the atmosphere of the fair was dominated by its central Court of Honor, nicknamed "The White City" (the Midway Plaisance served as the far less sober counterbalance to the main court). While Burnham was undoubtedly the master overseer of the exposition, its architectural godfather was Richard Morris Hunt (1827–1895), the designer of its domed Administration Building. Hunt had spent much of his youth in Europe and was the first American architect to attend the reputable École des Beaux-Arts in Paris. In this he preceded the (by-then) deceased Richardson, as well as Atwood and many of the other architects who built at the World's Columbian Exposition. And so it came to pass, with something resembling a religious fervor, that an architectural legacy was handed down from the architects at the fair to set a standard that practitioners all across America would follow for decades afterwards. From the previously dominant Richardsonian variations on Romanesque themes, the country moved on to a Beaux-Arts classicism, informally considered an American Renaissance. The overhaul was best exemplified by the City Beautiful movement as championed by Daniel Burnham in Chicago, and later in other cities from Washington and Cleveland to San Francisco.

IN-052

All American architects felt this tidal pull, not least the designers of railroad stations. (Perhaps this explains in part why, as objectors to the classical revival, such preeminent architects as Louis Sullivan and Frank Lloyd Wright were never called on to design rail stations.) The time was ripe for this major transformation in station design, as the year 1893 also saw completion of the Great Northern tracks across the Northwest, the last of the five original transcontinental lines. The attitudinal shift in design is evident when one compares the original Union Station of 1875 in Worcester, Massachusetts, with the station built in 1912 to replace it. The earlier station reflected the predominant nineteenth-century approach, focusing on the building's utilitarian aspects. Behind the great clock tower (just as emblematic of American railroad stations of the period as the headhouse hotel was for European stations), the enclosed public spaces of the earlier Worcester station building were overshadowed by the immense spread of the train shed. In contrast, the current Union Station presents a far more resolved composition. The body of the new building is the central waiting room, covered by a set of stained glass barrel vaults. Flanking this core volume are a pair of towers and a lower roof, modestly sized but lavishly coated in ornamental terra cotta. The earlier version was an imposing representative of industrial growth, powerful almost to the point of grimness. The later station building is a well-groomed citizen of the modern world. Here, and for America as a whole, the pattern set at the 1893 World's Columbian Exposition could been seen as bearing fruit (IN-051–IN-052).

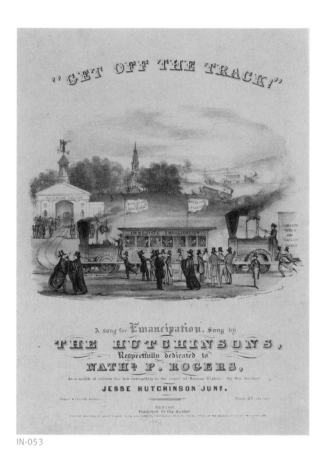

IN-053

A PLACE IN THE CULTURE

As an unmistakable part of our national heritage, the railroads influenced many aspects of cultural life in America. Working on the railroad lines was a common musical theme, from the slave era on into the twentieth century (IN-053). Songs by such popular artists as Flatt & Scruggs, Johnny Cash, James Taylor, and Arlo Guthrie testify to the abiding power of train imagery.

In terms of visual culture, American artists have not produced anything quite so famous as Monet's painting of the Gare St. Lazare. The quintessential artist of the American commonplace, Edward Hopper, seems never to have made a painting of a railroad station. The nearest Hopper came to a station painting was the brightly hued "Railroad Sunset" of 1929, on display at the Whitney Museum in New York and showing a single forlorn switching tower. Among artists whose subjects have included railroad stations was O. E. Berninghaus, who portrayed an adobe station in El Ortiz, New Mexico (IN-054). Watercolorist Irvin Jolliver often painted great locomotives and rail cars, seen at rest before a variety of stations located around the Pacific Northwest, during the last quarter of the twentieth century.

On occasion, editorial cartoonists have incorporated train stations into their output, though mainly for their symbolic value (IN-055). There were also times when major

IN-054. El Ortiz Station, El Ortiz, New Mexico. DETR, O. E. Berninghaus, artist, Lamy, New Mexico. P&P,LC-D417-1771.

IN-055. "Design for a Union Station." Luther Daniels Bradley, artist, October 1907. P&P,SWANN-no. 1718 (B size),LC-USZ62-84052.

According to the notes, "From 1906–07 the holdings and business practices of railroad administrator and financier Edward Henry Harriman became the focus of an investigation by the Interstate Commerce Commission. The committee charged that Harriman's use of Union Pacific resources (the company of which he was president since 1903) to invest in the stocks, bonds, and securities of competing railways, was an unlawful attempt to squelch competition and gain control of the market." The drawing is an unambiguous swipe at railroad magnate Harriman and his voracious appetite for swallowing up his competitors.

PITTSBURGH in the BEGINNING

FORT PRINCE GEORGE
Established February 17, 1754.
MODERN PITTSBURGH
IS SERVED BY THE
PENNSYLVANIA RAILROAD

IN-056

IN-056. "Pittsburgh in the Beginning." Color offset by N. C. (Newell Converse) Wyeth, ca. 1931. P&P,POS-US. W93,no. 3 (C size),LC-USZC2-732.

Wyeth's poster for Pittsburgh depicts "Fort Prince George established February 17, 1754," further noting that "Modern Pittsburgh is served by the Pennsylvania Railroad."

artists produced work directly for the railway companies, as when N. C. Wyeth did a set of four posters in 1931 promoting tourism for the Pennsylvania Railroad Company (IN-056). On some occasions artwork was produced inside some stations. Among the most spectacular was the photomural lifted into place in 1941 by the Farm Security Administration to support the purchase of defense bonds. This monumental construction covered an entire wall inside the concourse of the Grand Central Terminal (IN-057–IN-060).

IN-057. Preparing the defense bond sales photomural, designed by the Farm Security Administration, to be installed in the Grand Central Terminal, in the shop of a contractor. Mounting central panel on the homesote board with flour paste, New York, New York. Edwin Rosskam, photographer, 1941. P&P,LC-USF34-014673-D.

IN-058. Defense bond display, Grand Central Terminal, New York, New York. Arthur Rothstein, photographer, 1941. P&P,LC-USF34-012884-D.

IN-059. War bond mural, Grand Central Terminal, New York, New York. Arthur Rothstein, photographer, 1941. P&P,LC-USF34-024494-D.

The mural comprised twenty-two photographs selected from the Farm Security Administration Collection.

IN-060. Crowd watching the installation of the defense bond mural, Grand Central Terminal, New York, New York. Edwin Rosskam, photographer, 1941. P&P,LC-USF34-012886-D.

IN-058

IN-057

IN-059

IN-060

IN-061

IN-062

At times the trains themselves were wonderful works of art—particularly the locomotives (IN-061). There was also a long tradition of custom-designed sleeper cars. The Pullman Company of Chicago became the most famous mass producer of these luxury staterooms in the late nineteenth century (IN-062).

Throughout the twentieth century our trains and train stations were most conspicuous in popular culture in the movies. This was the case from the start, with the first narrative film, *The Great Train Robbery* (1903). Still in the era of silent pictures, a reluctant

IN-064

IN-063. Cary Grant and Eva Marie Saint in *North by Northwest*. Loew's Incorporated. (MGM), 1959. P&P,NYWTS-SUBJ/GEOG-Movies-Plays-Nm-Nz,LC-USZ62-127526.

The scene portrayed in this still from *North by Northwest* shows Cary Grant reaching down for Eva Marie Saint's hand along one of the faces at Mount Rushmore, the climactic moment of the movie. Back inside Grand Central, the ticket seller at one of the main floor ticket windows wasn't fooled by the sunglasses-wearing fugitive-adman Roger Thornhill (Cary Grant) in his attempt to purchase a sleeping car ticket to Chicago.

IN-064. West balcony, main concourse, Grand Central Terminal, New York, New York. DETR, ca. 1910. P&P,LC-D4-72980.

soldier is chased by military police all around San Diego's Santa Fe Station in *Tell it to the Marines* (1926). More recently, in 2003, the Los Angeles Union Passenger Terminal made lengthy cameos in both the feature film *Seabiscuit* and the documentary film *My Architect*. Given the proximity of the terminal to Hollywood, it has been a convenient location for filmmakers, most notably in the film noir era.

Alfred Hitchcock used the West Coast rail lines when he made a film of Patricia Highsmith's novel, *Strangers on a Train,* in 1953, but he moved production east, at least for the start of *North by Northwest* (1959; IN-063). Manhattan adman and alleged murderer Roger Thornhill (played by Cary Grant) has a tough time at a Grand Central ticket window, trying to book a sleeping car compartment to Chicago (IN-064). Once he gets there (with considerable help from Eva Marie Saint) his scenes of shaving in the Chicago Union Station men's room show Grant at his comic best. Grant was not the only one who failed to get a ticket at Grand Central. Ginger Rogers struck out as well while trying to pass as a child in *The Major and the Minor* (1942). Elizabeth Taylor fared better across town at Pennsylvania Station, arranging for her honeymoon travels with her new husband before calling her dad (Spencer Tracey) in *The Father of the Bride* (1950). Five years later Tracey made his own train trip in *Bad Day at Black Rock* (1955). The film begins and ends with his arrival and departure aboard a Streamliner at the title town's train station, a rudimentary shack for the telegraph operator.

Even at our present juncture when car and plane travel are so dominant, station buildings do manage to get work in the movie business. Nevertheless the cultural currency of railroad stations has slipped considerably from its zenith. At the dawn of the twentieth century train travel was high style, often novel and exciting. After World War II the automobile started to supplant the trains as the favored means of travel. The interstate highway system, begun in the 1950s, accelerated the changeover. The 1960s saw the rise of road movie. The most memorable of these, from *Easy Rider* (1969) to *Thelma and Louise* (1991), say a good deal about the times in which they were made. The dream of the open road is indispensable to their plots. The feel is different nowadays for train pictures, but not lost. Their heyday has passed but movies set on the rails were once every bit as compelling as road movies—as fifty years of film history can attest.

The railroads also had a major impact on the way we keep time in this country. Stations along the rail lines came to serve as timepieces for their communities. From the start, the railroads were out to make the trains run on time. As the rail lines spread across the maps, with trains traveling ever-greater distances, the relative precision of time became an issue. What all those tall station clock towers tended to show their communities was the local solar, or sun, time. The idea of switching to meridian-based time zones was controversial in the United States throughout most of the nineteenth century. It took a Canadian engineer, Sir Sandford Fleming, to persuade the railroads to adopt the idea of time zones in 1883, as initially proposed by American Charles Dowd in 1872. The plan became official nationwide with the Standard Time Act of 1918.

IN-065. Railroad depot, Grand Island, Nebraska. John Vachon, photographer, October 1938. P&P,LC-USF33-001328-M2.

IN-066. Timetable, Santa Fe railroad station, San Augustine, Texas. Russell Lee, photographer, April 1939. P&P,LC-USF33-012136-M3.

IN-067. Face of the regulator clock in President's office, Central of Georgia Railway, Gray Building, 227 West Broad Street, Savannah, Chatham County, Georgia. Jack Boucher, photographer, August 1976. P&P,HAER,GA,26-SAV,57A-14.

Even with the acceptance of Standard Time, oddities in world train travel have persisted. These include trains traveling during the changeover from Standard to Daylight Time: generally, westbound trains pause for an hour while passing from one time zone to the next. Still, time standardization helped coordinate train schedules for all stations, from the smallest depot to the busiest union station. The complexity of the larger operations finds echoes in modern air traffic control facilities. The difference lies in the technology at hand (IN-065, IN-066). Rail stations in the golden age of trains did not have computers. The clock was the critical element. With it, the railroads had time on their side (IN-067).

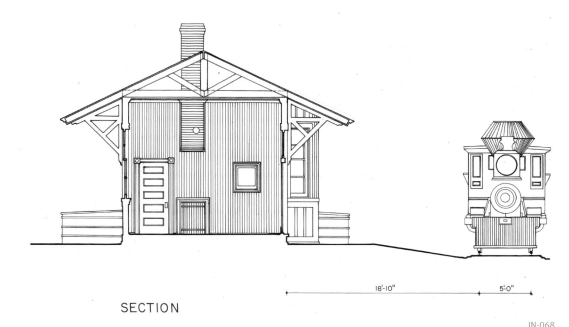

SECTION

18'-10"   5'-0"

IN-068. Section with locomotive, Chesapeake & Ohio Railway Station, U.S. Route 250 & Chesapeake & Ohio Railroad, Shadwell, Albemarle County, Virginia. F. J. Cabell, delineator. P&P, sheet no. 5.

IN-069. Clock and tower, Union Pacific Passenger Station, 121 West Fifteenth Street, Cheyenne, Laramie County, Wyoming. Unidentified photographer, 1974. P&P,HABS,WYO,11-CHEY,5-10.

ELEMENTS OF STATION ARCHITECTURE

From the earliest days of train travel all that was necessary to be called a passenger station was a canopy or simple shed, with perhaps a stove inside, set along the tracks. In a pinch a whistle-stop might do without even these rudimentary structures. Over time most stations—especially those in cities—gained more than one set of tracks, with trains and passengers coming through at all hours of the day and night.

Everything at a station was designed for comfort and efficiency, keeping in mind the best possible circulation of the maximum number of travelers. Names for the public rooms in rail stations match those used most often in ship terminals and airports: "waiting rooms" and "lounges," "concourses," "gates," and "platforms." The parts of larger stations, designed to house and service train cars and locomotives, employ a language more particular to the railways alone: "roundhouses" and "turntables," along with "watering stations" and "coaling stations."

The configuration of tracks relative to the station building proper also produced railroad-specific terminology. Those cases where the train stops at a station, and then continues on in the same direction, are "through stations." Where the set or sets of track reach a full, dead-end stop at a station (most often called a terminal for this reason), these are "stub-end stations." As ever, there was some leeway in this labeling. Many of the major city stations, especially union stations involving a number of different railway companies, were hybrids of the two station types. However, the need to distinguish between types has faded as American rail travel has been drastically reduced for most of the country (IN-068–IN-096).

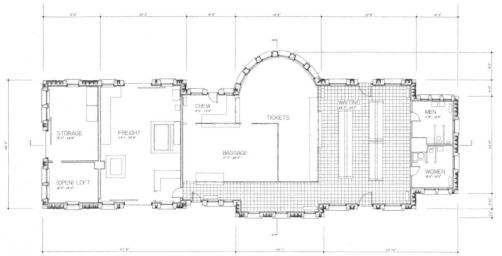

IN-070

IN-070. Floor plan, Junction City Depot, 410 East Tenth Street, Junction City, Geary County, Kansas. P&P, sheet no. 3.

IN-071. Negro waiting room, St. Louis, San Francisco Railroad Station, Perry, Noble County, Oklahoma. Frederick Schirrmacher, photographer, July 1975. P&P, HABS, OKLA, 52-PERRY, 2-5.

IN-072. Waiting room, from south, Erie Railway, Middletown Station, James Street, Middletown, Orange County, New York. Jack Boucher, photographer, July 1971. P&P, HAER, NY, 36-MID, 1-5.

IN-071

IN-072

IN-073

IN-074

IN-073. Detail of ticket window, Erie Railway, Middletown Station, James Street, Middletown, Orange County, New York. Jack Boucher, photographer, July 1971. P&P, HAER, NY, 36-MID, 1-7.

George F. Archer's design for the relatively small Middletown Station (1897) shows a remarkable ability to incorporate the standard features of larger stations without any sacrifice in comfort.

IN-074. Interior of ticket lobby, shows grilles around heat outlets, clerestory, and ceiling lights, Union Station, Washington, D.C. P&P, LOT 12334, LC-USZ62-91731.

IN-075. Arrival board, reception hall, Los Angeles Union passenger terminal, tracks & shed, 800 North Alameda Street, Los Angeles, Los Angeles County, California. Dick Whittington, photographer, May 1939. P&P,HABS,CAL,19-LOSAN,64-A-54.

IN-076. View showing concourse and entrances to the main waiting room, Grand Central Station, New York, New York. *The Inland Architect & New Record*, volume 38, no. 2 (September 1901). P&P,U.S. GEOG FILE,LC-USZ62-56923.

Note the clerestory section of sheds at top.

IN-075

IN-076

IN-077. View showing concourse elevation and access to platform and trains, Pennsylvania Railroad, Harrisburg station & trainshed, Market & South Fourth streets, Harrisburg, Dauphin County, Pennsylvania. F. Harlan Hambright, photographer, August 1981. P&P,HAER,PA,22-HARBU,23-31.

IN-078. Second level of the Delaware, Lackawanna & Western Railroad train shed looking east; Delaware, Lackawanna & Western Railroad, Lackawanna Terminal, Main Street & Buffalo River, Buffalo, Erie County, New York. Jack Boucher, photographer, 1971. P&P,HAER,NY,15-BUF,22-12.

Bumper at terminus of track shows right foreground with boarding platform between tracks; this view shows steel and reinforced concrete roof designed by Lincoln Bush. Bush, Chief Engineer for the Lackawanna Railroad, created the Bush shed in 1905. He simplified the manner in which trackside passengers could access cover and improved ventilation around the platform areas.

IN-077

IN-078

IN-079. Interior, train shed, Grand Central Station, 201 West Harrison Street (corner of West Harrison & South Wells streets), Chicago, Cook County, Illinois. Cervin Robinson, photographer, July 1963. P&P,HABS,ILL,16-CHIG,18-2.

IN-080. Elevation/section, train shed details, Grand Central Station, 201 West Harrison Street (corner of West Harrison & South Wells streets), Chicago, Cook County, Illinois. P&P,sheet no. 3.

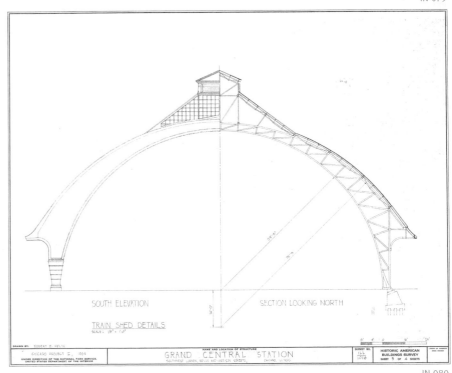

IN-081

IN-083

IN-082

IN-081. Detail of canopy, Los Angeles Union passenger terminal, tracks, & shed, 800 North Alameda Street, Los Angeles, Los Angeles County, California. Julius Shulman, photographer, October 1981. P&P,HABS,CAL,19-LOSAN,64-A-4.

IN-082. Exterior of ticket booth bay window on north (trackside) elevation, Boston & Albany Railroad Station, Waverly Street, Framingham, Middlesex County, Massachusetts. Cervin Robinson, photographer, November 1959. P&P,HABS,MASS,9-FRAM,10-3.

IN-083. Ticket wickets, northwest side of concourse, Cincinnati Union Terminal, 1301 Western Avenue, Cincinnati, Hamilton County, Ohio. Caleb Faux, photographer, July 1981. P&P,HABS,OHIO,31-CINT,29-11.

IN-084

MOUNTAIN GROVE

IN-085

IN-086

IN-087

IN-084. Baggage room entrance, west bay, front, Southern Pacific passenger station, 601 East Madison Street, Brownsville, Cameron County, Texas. Bill Engdahl/Hedrich-Blessing, photographer, 1979. P&P,HABS,TEX,31-BROWN,15-10.

The decorative features covering the exterior of Brownsville's Southern Pacific Station are of cast stone.

IN-085. Maurice Livingston works for Southern Express Company (began at fifteen years), Mountain Grove, Missouri. Lewis W. Hine, photographer, August 1916. P&P,LOT 7483,v.2,no.4457,LC-DIG-nclc-05112.

IN-086. Electric baggage truck operated by baggage porter, Union Station, Washington, D.C. P&P,LOT 12334,LC-USZ62-91729.

IN-087. Baggage area, Union Pacific passenger station, 121 West Fifteenth Street, Cheyenne, Laramie County, Wyoming. Unidentified photographer, 1974. P&P,HABS,WYO,11-CHEY,5-16.

IN-088

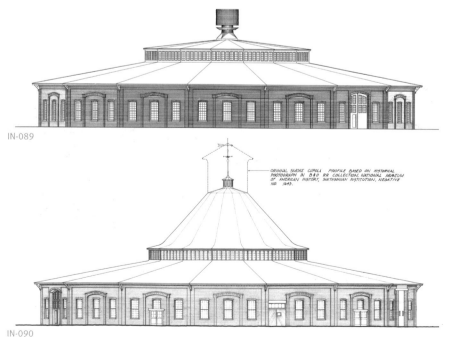

IN-089

ORIGINAL SMOKE CUPOLA PROFILE BASED ON HISTORICAL
PHOTOGRAPH IN B&O RR COLLECTION, NATIONAL MUSEUM
OF AMERICAN HISTORY, SMITHSONIAN INSTITUTION, NEGATIVE
NO. 1643.

IN-090

IN-088. Aerial view of shops complex looking east showing west and east roundhouses, frog and switch shop, and machine shop, Baltimore & Ohio Railroad, Martinsburg Repair Shops, west side of Tuscarora Creek opposite east end of Race & Martin streets, Martinsburg, Berkeley County, West Virginia. William Edmund Barrett, photographer, 1970. P&P,HAER,WVA,2-MART,1-1.

IN-089. Southeast elevation, Baltimore & Ohio Railroad, Martinsburg East Roundhouse, east end of Race & Martin streets, Martinsburg, Berkeley County, West Virginia. P&P,sheet no. 2.

IN-090. North elevation, Baltimore & Ohio Railroad, Martinsburg West Roundhouse, east end of Race & Martin streets, Martinsburg, Berkeley County, West Virginia. P&P,sheet no. 2.

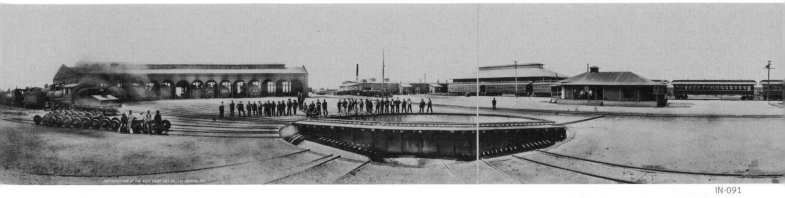

IN-091. Round house & shops, Douglas, Arizona. West Coast Art, ca. 1909. P&P,PAN US GEOG,LC-USZ62-62772.

IN-092. View of Grafton from Thayer, Northwestern Virginia (B&O) Railroad, Grafton Machine Shop & Foundry, U.S. 119 east of Tygart Valley River, Grafton, Taylor County, West Virginia. Unidentified photographer, 1876. P&P,HAER,WVA,46-GRAFT,1-2.

IN-093. View of bell-cut roof, Baltimore & Ohio Railroad, Martinsburg West Roundhouse, east end of Race & Martin streets, Martinsburg, Berkeley County, West Virginia. William Edmund Barrett, photographer, 1970. P&P,HAER,WVA,2-MART,1A-3.

IN-094. View looking northeast, Baltimore & Ohio Railroad, Martinsburg West Roundhouse, east end of Race & Martin streets, Martinsburg, Berkeley County, West Virginia. William Edmund Barrett, photographer, 1970. P&P, HAER,WVA,2-MART,1A-2.

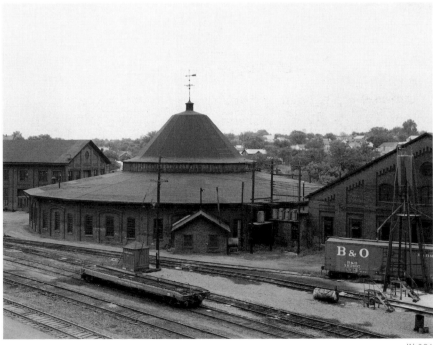

IN-095

IN-095. Coal chutes, Wymore, Nebraska. J. Martz, photographer, ca. 1910. P&P,LC-USZ62-98922.

IN-096. One of the Chicago & Northwestern Railroad's "400" fleet of locomotives lined up for coal and water at a coaling station, Chicago, Illinois. Jack Delano, photographer, December 1942. P&P,LC-USW33-014778-D.

IN-096

IN-097

IN-098

IN-097. View from inside train shed showing cherry picker and photographer (Jack Boucher) at work, Central of Georgia Railway, passenger station, & train shed, corner of Louisville (Railroad) Road & West Broad Street, Savannah, Chatham County, Georgia. Unidentified photographer, August 1976. P&P,HAER,GA,26-SAV,56-39.

IN-098. Jack Delano, Farm Security Administration/Office of War Information photographer, full-length portrait, holding camera, standing on front of locomotive. Unidentified photographer, ca. 1943. P&P,LC-USZ62-120966.

ABOUT THE IMAGES

The illustrations in this book depict railroad stations from nearly all fifty states and Puerto Rico. Regional groupings primarily reflect how the railway companies routed their lines across the country. For example, the first three sections treat portions of the Mid-Atlantic region, home to the great founding American railroads: the Baltimore & Ohio Railroad, the Pennsylvania Railroad, the Boston & Albany Railroad, and, later, the New York Central Railroad. Stations built for the principal railroads of the South, the Midwest, and the western states dominate their regional sections in turn.

Many of the images are the work of some of the best-known architectural photographers in this country—Cervin Robinson, Marion Post Wolcott, Carol Highsmith, and Jet Lowe. The conditions under which they did their job were sometimes grueling and sometimes precarious. In the course of his work for the Historic American Building Survey, Jack Boucher had to catch a ride in a cherry picker to record details at a rail yard in Savannah, Georgia. Later in his career Boucher spent a few days in a helicopter tracing the route of the main tracks from Washington, D.C., to Boston. Jack Delano followed a more conventional route in the course of logging thousands of miles, riding the rails back and forth from Chicago to California, to do his job for the Farm Security Administration. Delano photographed nearly every aspect of the railroad business, featuring locomotives and stations but also conductors and baggage handlers, and even the great workshops and coaling stations that kept the trains in operation. The work of Delano, Boucher, and the others, along with some photographs whose makers have been lost to time, consitutes an unmatchable picture of the legacy of our nation's railroad stations (IN-097–IN-108).

Throughout the process of selecting and cataloging these images, the aim has been to showcase as great a variety of stations and depots as possible. Some potential inclusions persisted in falling outside the scope of this book, no matter how wonderful the images. For example, the Monongahela Incline Plane in Pittsburgh has a pair of terminals—one each at the upside and downside ends of its pair of railroad tracks (IN-109–IN-111). The Incline has been transporting passengers since it opened in 1870. Its major disqualification: it is a cable car system. It is no railway, although the appeal of its stations is undeniable.

IN-099

IN-099. Detail of dome interior, looking east, Cincinnati Union Terminal, 1301 Western Avenue, Cincinnati, Hamilton County, Ohio. Caleb Faux, photographer, July 1981. P&P,HABS,OHIO,31-CINT,29-10.

IN-100. Detail of concourse roof, Pennsylvania Station, 370 Seventh Avenue, West Thirty-first–Thirty-third streets, New York, New York County, New York. Edward Popko, photographer, 1965. P&P,HABS,NY,31-NEYO,78-21.

IN-100

IN-101. View of west façade, Delaware, Lackawanna & Western Railroad, Vestal passenger and freight station, North Main Street, Vestal, Broome County, New York. Jack Boucher, photographer, July 1971. P&P,HAER,NY,4-VES,1-3.

IN-102. Model airplanes decorate the ceiling of the train concourses at Union Station, Chicago, Illinois. Jack Delano, photographer, February 1943. P&P,LC-USW3-015950-D.

IN-103. Little boy who is very interested in the model airplanes on the ceiling of the Union Station, Chicago, Illinois. Jack Delano, photographer, February 1943. P&P,LC-USW3-015881-D.

Before he set out to photograph the railroad facilities of the midwestern and southwestern states for the Farm Security Administration, Jack Delano found plenty to interest him inside Chicago's Union Station—such as the astonishing model airplane display.

IN-101

IN-103

IN-102

IN-104

IN-105

IN-104. Two trains with airplane overhead at the White Sulphur Springs Station, White Sulphur Springs, West Virginia. Unidentified photographer, after 1910. P&P,LC-USZ62-91526.

IN-105. Swimming in fountain across from Union Station, Washington, D.C. Marion Post Wolcott/FSA, photographer, September 1938. P&P,LC-USF33-030043-M5.

IN-106

IN-106. Arched entry to privy stall in base of smokestack, Central of Georgia Railway, Savannah Repair Shops & Terminal Facilities, combination smokestack, water tank, & privies, bounded by West Broad, Jones, West Boundary, & Hull streets, Savannah, Chatham County, Georgia. Jack Boucher, photographer, August 1976. P&P,HAER,GA,26-SAV,55F-8.

IN-107. Detail of east wall on ground level showing recessed doors and elliptical louvered transoms, New York, New Haven & Hartford Railroad, Shell interlocking tower, New Haven milepost 16, approximately 100 feet east of New Rochelle Junction, New Rochelle, Westchester County, New York. Martin Stupich, photographer, November 1994. P&P,HAER,NY,60-NEWRO,3-7.

IN-108. "Negroes sitting on steps of the Texas & Pacific railroad station," New Roads, Louisiana. Russell Lee, photographer, November 1938. P&P,LC-USF33-011903-M2.

IN-107

IN-108

IN-109

IN-110

IN-111

IN-109. Monongahela Incline, Pittsburgh, Pennsylvania. DETR, ca. 1905. P&P,LC-D4-18660.

IN-110. Lower station front, Monongahela Incline Plane, connecting north side of Grandview Avenue at Wyoming Street with West Carson Street near Smithfield Street, Pittsburgh, Pennsylvania. David Thum, photographer, May 1993. P&P,HAER,PA,2-PITBU,66-4.

IN-111. Lower station, incline plane track, looking to upper station, Monongahela Incline Plane, connecting north side of Grandview Avenue at Wyoming Street with West Carson Street near Smithfield Street, Pittsburgh, Pennsylvania. David Thum, photographer, May 1993. P&P,HAER,PA,2-PITBU,66-10.

The upper station of the Monongahela Incline Plane dates to 1882, when freight service was added to the original passenger service. The existing lower station was built in 1904. Otis Elevator Company produced the current motor-driven cable system for the incline plane in 1935.

IN-112. The deeply recessed observation platform of he New Oriental Limited, Great Northern Railway. Unidentified photographer, 1924. P&P,LOT 7946,LC-USZ62-87661.

NOTES

1. Anne M. Lyden, *Railroad Vision: Photography, Travel, and Perception* (Los Angeles: J. Paul Getty Museum, 2003), 121.

2. Keith Wheeler, *The Railroaders* (New York: Time-Life Books, 1973), 21.

3. Previous study of the railroads, the national parks, and the park lodges—Old Faithful Inn in particular—was conducted by David Naylor in the course of writing his master's thesis, "Old Faithful Inn and Its Legacy: The Vernacular Transformed," Cornell University, 1990. A more recent study of the Inn and its history took place for its centennial: see Karen Wildung Reinhart and Jeff Henry, *Old Faithful Inn: Crown Jewel of the National Park Lodges* (Emigrant, MT: Roche Jaune Pictures, 2004).

4. A. M. Cleland, *Land of the Geysers* (St. Paul, MN: Northern Pacific Railway, 1916), 14, as quoted in Naylor, "Old Faithful Inn and Its Legacy."

5. Susan C. Scofield, *The Inn at Old Faithful* (Bozeman, MT: Crowsnest, 1975), 11, as quoted in Naylor, "Old Faithful Inn and Its Legacy."

6. Wheeler, *Railroaders*, 144.

7. Ibid.

8. Joe Walsh, with Jim Boyd and William F. Howes Jr., *The American Railroad* (Osceola, WI: MBI Publishing/Andover Junction, 1999), 10.

9. Erik Larson's *The Devil in the White City* is a work of fiction, a cleverly told murder mystery but also one based heavily on research concerning the 1893 World's Columbian Exposition and its major players, such as Daniel Burnham.

10. Kristen Schaffer, *Daniel H. Burnham: Visionary Architect and Planner* (New York: Rizzoli, 2003), 107. Schaffer's book details all of Burnham's major railroad station work, including his association with architect Charles B. Atwood (designer of the station for the Exposition). Burnham's stations are illustrated with vividly detailed photographs by Paul Rocheleau.

MID-ATLANTIC REGION I (Maryland, Delaware, West Virginia)

As the acknowledged birthplace of the American railroad, Baltimore still retains many of its original station properties, built for several different rail lines. The pioneering Baltimore & Ohio Railroad is represented not only by the Mount Clare Station buildings (now collectively the Baltimore & Ohio Railroad Museum), but also by portions of its Camden Station, which date from 1856. The station had warehouses, as high as nine stories and running 1,000 feet in length, that were famously incorporated into the Baltimore Orioles' new ballpark at Camden Yards in 1992. Other surviving properties in the city are the President Street Station (1849) built for the Philadelphia, Wilmington & Baltimore Railroad, and the Mount Royal Baltimore & Ohio Station (1896) by the B&O's in-house firm, Baldwin & Pennington, now an arts center. The relative newcomer, the Pennsylvania Station, designed by Kenneth M. Murchison (1872–1938) in 1911, is still in operation for Amtrak.

In terms of Baltimore's historic properties, the oldest extant station is outside the city limits, a dozen or so miles to the west, along the Patapsco River

1-001. Detail view of tower, Baltimore & Ohio Railroad, Point of Rocks Station, near Route 28, Point of Rocks, Frederick County, Maryland. Jack E. Boucher and William E. Barrett, photographers, 1970. P&P,HAER,MD,11-PORO,1-13.

With its spire-end resembling the prow of a ship, the Point of Rocks Station seems to bend westward toward the B&O's terminus at the Ohio River in Wheeling, West Virginia.

Valley in Ellicott City. Built in 1831, primarily of stone with a little wooden trim added later, this oldest surviving station now houses a museum for the town.

Over the last quarter of the nineteenth century the design of Maryland's railroad stations was primarily the province of E. Francis Baldwin. These B&O outposts stretch westward to Baldwin's landmark Point of Rocks Station and beyond. The B&O branch line to Point of Rocks, from Washington, D.C., includes stops like the Rockville Railroad Station, also by Baldwin.

Just over an hour to the north of Baltimore, in Wilmington, Delaware, a set of railroad properties designed by Frank Furness stands largely intact. Pennsylvania Railroad President A. J. Cassatt (brother of Impressionist painter Mary Cassatt) brought Furness down from Philadelphia to build a new station and some adjoining office buildings alongside Wilmington's Christiana River. This was a familiar neighborhood for Furness, as he had designed a station nearby for the B&O Railroad twenty years earlier.

1-002. Station and platform, looking south toward Baltimore, Baltimore & Ohio Railroad, Ellicott's Mills Station, south side of State Route 144, Ellicott City, Howard County, Maryland. P&P,HAER,MD,14-ELLCI,11-3.

Known at the time as Ellicott's Mills, this station was the last stop for the first run of railway in the United States back in 1831.

1-002

1-003. Aerial view of Mount Clare Shop complex, Baltimore & Ohio Railroad, Mount Clare Passenger Car Shop, southwest corner of Pratt & Poppleton streets, Baltimore, Independent City, Maryland. William E. Barrett, photographer, 1971. P&P,HAER,MD,4-BALT,127-1.

1-004. General view of cupola atop passenger car shop, Baltimore & Ohio Railroad, Mount Clare Passenger Car Shop, southwest corner of Pratt & Poppleton streets, Baltimore, Independent City, Maryland. William E. Barrett, photographer, 1971. P&P,HAER,MD,4-BALT,127-4

The twenty-two-sided Passenger Car Shop (built 1884, by E. Francis Baldwin) is at the heart of the eleven-acre flagship rail yard of the Baltimore & Ohio Railroad. The shop building has a diameter of 235 feet; its cupola tops out at 123 feet in height.

1-005. Passenger car shop from south level, Baltimore & Ohio Railroad, Mount Clare Passenger Car Shop, southwest corner of Pratt & Poppleton streets, Baltimore, Independent City, Maryland. Photogrammetric plate LC-HAER-GS05-1-401L. P&P,HAER,MD,4-BALT,127-18.

1-006. Front façade of Mt. Clare Station, passenger car shop in rear, Baltimore & Ohio Railroad, Mount Clare Passenger Car Shop, southwest corner of Pratt & Poppleton streets, Baltimore, Independent City, Maryland. P&P,HAER,MD,4-BALT,127-17.

1-007. Passenger car shop from west, damaged in snowstorm February 2004, Baltimore & Ohio Railroad, Mount Clare Passenger Car Shop, southwest corner of Pratt & Poppleton streets, Baltimore, Independent City, Maryland. Jet Lowe, photographer, March 2003. P&P,HAER,MD,4-BALT,127-19.

1-003

1-004

1-005

1-006

1-007

1-008

1-009

1-010

1-008. North elevation, Baltimore & Ohio Railroad, Camden Station, Camden Street, Baltimore, Independent City, Maryland. P&P,sheet no. 5.

At the time of its construction the central pavilion of Camden Station was capped by a triple-tiered lantern spire, making it the tallest building in Baltimore at 185 feet.

1-009. Detail view of center pavilion of north (front) elevation, Baltimore & Ohio Railroad, Camden Station, south side of Camden Street between Eutaw & Howard, Baltimore, Independent City, Maryland. William E. Barrett, photographer, 1970. P&P,HAER,MD,4-BALT,126-5.

1-010. Aerial view of station and yards, looking south, Baltimore & Ohio Railroad, Camden Station, south side of Camden Street between Eutaw & Howard, Baltimore, Independent City, Maryland. William E. Barrett, photographer, 1970. P&P,HAER,MD,4-BALT,126-2.

The row of warehouses to the southwest of the Camden Passenger Station now forms a backdrop for right field at the ballpark, which opened in 1992 just to the west of the station.

1-011

PASSENGER AND FREIGHT STATIONS, PRESIDENT STREET, BALTIMORE.

1-012

1-011. General view of station, Philadelphia, Wilmington & Baltimore Railroad, President Street Station, President & Fleet streets, Baltimore, Independent City, Maryland. Edgar H. Pickering, photographer, July 1936. P&P,HABS,MD,4-BALT,25-1.

1-012. General view of station (ca. 1856), Philadelphia, Wilmington & Baltimore Railroad, President Street Station, President & Fleet streets, Baltimore, Independent City, Maryland. D. C. Baxter engraver, ca. 1856. P&P,HAER,MD,4-BALT,25-1.

The President Street Station, as completed in 1850, began a century of service as a freight house in 1873 (when its passenger service was moved to Baltimore's new Union Station, the site of the current Pennsylvania Station). The original train shed ran a length of 208 feet and was covered by a series of Howe roof trusses better suited to carrying the vertical load. This shed, as updated in 1913, was destroyed by a fire that also reached part of the head house. The station began a new service as the Baltimore Civil War Museum in 1997.

1-013. Elevation and sections, Philadelphia, Wilmington & Baltimore Railroad, President Street Station, President & Fleet streets, Baltimore, Independent City, Maryland. P&P,sheet no. 3.

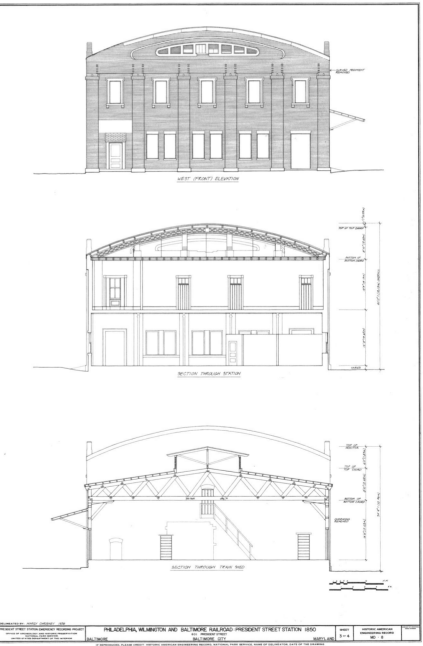

1-013

1-014

1-015

1-014. South façade, Pennsylvania Railroad, Calvert Station, Calvert & Franklin streets, Baltimore, Independent City, Maryland. E. H. Pickering, photographer, July 1936. P&P,HABS,MD,4-BALT,40-1.

1-015. North end of train shed, Pennsylvania Railroad, Calvert Station, Calvert & Franklin streets, Baltimore, Independent City, Maryland. E. H. Pickering, photographer, July 1936. P&P,HABS,MD,4-BALT,40-3.

1-016. View of train shed and station looking northeast, Baltimore & Ohio Railroad, Mount Royal Trainshed, 1400 Cathedral Street, Baltimore, Independent City, Maryland. William E. Barrett, photographer, 1971. P&P,HAER,MD,BALT-128-1.

1-017. South end of train shed, Baltimore & Ohio Railroad, Mount Royal Trainshed, 1400 Cathedral Street, Baltimore, Independent City, Maryland. Smithsonian Institution. P&P,HAER,MD,4-BALT,128-3.

Mount Royal Station was sited below grade level so it would sit even with the tracks leading from the tunnels to either side of its nearly 420-foot-long train shed. The station's campanile-style clock tower rises 143 feet high.

1-018

1-019

1-020

1-018. East (front) side, B&O Railroad, Mount Royal Station, Cathedral Street at Mount Royal Avenue, Baltimore, Independent City, Maryland. Jack E. Boucher, photographer, March 1960. P&P,HABS,MD,4-BALT,119-1.

1-019. View looking up pedestrian stairway to street, Baltimore & Ohio Railroad, Mount Royal Station, Baltimore, Independent City, Maryland. William Edmund Barrett, photographer, 1971. P&P,HAER,MD,4-BALT,1193.

1-020. Interior of station, B&O Railroad, Mount Royal Station, Cathedral Street at Mount Royal Avenue, Baltimore, Independent City, Maryland. Lanny Miyamoto, photographer, September 1958. P&P,HABS,MD,4-BALT,119-4.

The two-story waiting room filled the entire central pavilion of the former station, home since the mid-1960s to a campus of the Maryland Institute's College of Art.

1-021. Aerial view, Pennsylvania Railroad, Pennsylvania Station, Baltimore, Maryland, Northeast Railroad Corridor, Amtrak route between District of Columbia/Maryland state line & Maryland/ Delaware state line, Baltimore, Independent City, Maryland. Jack E. Boucher, photographer, April 1977. P&P,HAER,MD,4-BALT,147-23.

The design for the new Baltimore Union Station (now Pennsylvania Station) was a competition winner for architect Kenneth M. Murchison. The station rides above its train tracks, which are nearly hidden from surrounding view.

1-022. West elevation, Baltimore & Ohio Railroad, Point of Rocks Station, near State Route 28, Point of Rocks, Frederick County, Maryland. P&P,sheet no. 4.

1-023

1-025

1-024

1-023. Aerial view of station, Baltimore & Ohio Railroad, Point of Rocks Station, near State Route 28, Point of Rocks, Frederick County, Maryland. Jack E. Boucher and William E. Barrett, photographers, 1970. P&P,HAER,MD,11-PORO,1-14.

1-024. Location map, Baltimore & Ohio Railroad, Point of Rocks Station, near State Route 28, Point of Rocks, Frederick County, Maryland. P&P,sheet no. 1.

1-025. View of easterly dormer window and back of tower, Baltimore & Ohio Railroad, Point of Rocks Station, near State Route 28, Point of Rocks, Frederick County, Maryland. Jack E. Boucher and William E. Barrett, photographers, 1970. P&P,HAER,MD.11-PORO,1-3.

1-026. First floor plan, Baltimore & Ohio Railroad, Point of Rocks Station, near State Route 28, Point of Rocks, Frederick County, Maryland. P&P, sheet no. 2.

1-027. North elevation, Baltimore & Ohio Railroad, Point of Rocks Station, near State Route 28, Point of Rocks, Frederick County, Maryland. P&P, sheet no. 5.

1-028. South side of building, Baltimore & Ohio Railroad, Point of Rocks Station, near State Route 28, Point of Rocks, Frederick County, Maryland. Jack E. Boucher and William E. Barrett, photographers, 1970. P&P, HAER, MD, 11-PORO, 1-10.

Station construction occurred in two stages, in 1871 and 1875, primarily of brick and accented with granite and sandstone trim. The overall composition is slightly jumbled but undeniably picturesque.

1-029. Longitudinal section, Baltimore & Ohio Railroad, Point of Rocks Station, near State Route 28, Point of Rocks, Frederick County, Maryland. P&P, sheet no. 6.

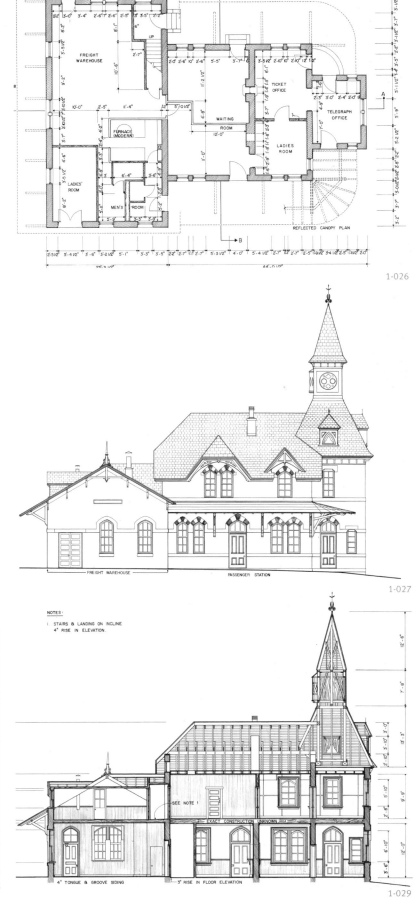

1-030

1-031

1-030. Northeast track view, Baltimore & Ohio Railroad, station & freight house, 98 Baltimore Road, Rockville, Montgomery County, Maryland. Jack Boucher, photographer, August 1978. P&P,HABS,MD,16-ROCVI,2-2.

1-031. View from northeast, Baltimore & Ohio Railroad Station, Laurel, 101 Lafayette Avenue, Laurel, Prince George's County, Maryland. Jack Boucher, photographer, March 1989. P&P,HABS,MD,17-LAUR,2-5

The station, designed by E. Francis Baldwin for Laurel, started operations in 1884, ten years after the station he designed for Rockville (1-029).

1-032

1-032. People waiting for a train at the railroad station, Silver Spring, Maryland. Ann Rosener, photographer, July 1943. P&P,LC-USW3-033279-D.

1-033. Depot, Blue Mountain House, Maryland. William Henry Jackson/DETR, photographer, ca. 1892. P&P,LC-D43-1833,LC-D43-T01-1833.

1-033

1-034

1-034. Railroad station, Hagerstown, Maryland. Arthur Rothstein/FSA, photographer, October 1937. P&P,LC-USF34-025979-C.

1-035. View of center cupola from south wing, Baltimore & Ohio Railroad, Queen City Hotel & Station, west side of Park Street, opposite Ann Street, Cumberland, Allegany County, Maryland. William E. Barrett, photographer, 1970. P&P,HAER,MD,1-CUMB,1-1.

The Queen City Hotel and Station reflect a variation on the Italianate known as the President Grant style. The buildings opened in 1872 and served as one of the B&O's premier railroad hotel stops for decades. But they were rendered obsolete and demolished in 1972, an infamous 100th birthday present.

1-036. View of wooden spiral staircase leading to cupola, Baltimore & Ohio Railroad, Queen City Hotel & Station, west side of Park Street, opposite Ann Street, Cumberland, Allegany County, Maryland. William E. Barrett, photographer, March 1971. P&P,HAER,MD,1-CUMB,1-5.

1-035

1-036

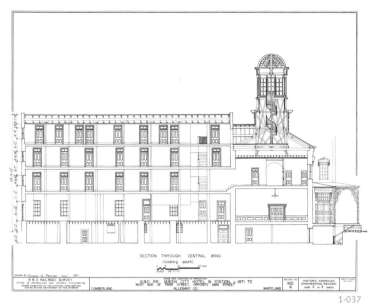

1-037

1-038

1-037. Section through central wing, Baltimore & Ohio Railroad, Queen City Hotel & Station, west side of Park Street, opposite Ann Street, Cumberland, Allegany County, Maryland. P&P,sheet no. 2.

1-038. View of building looking southwest from rooftop of Montgomery Ward store across tracks, Baltimore & Ohio Railroad, Queen City Hotel & Station, west side of Park Street, opposite Ann Street, Cumberland, Allegany County, Maryland. William E. Barrett, photographer, March 1971. P&P,HAER,MD,1-CUMB,1-27.

1-039. Aerial view of station and vicinity, looking east, Baltimore & Ohio Railroad, Queen City Hotel & Station, west side of Park Street, opposite Ann Street, Cumberland, Allegany County, Maryland. William E. Barrett, photographer, 1970. P&P,HAER,MD,1-CUMB,1-36.

1-039

1-040

1-040. Northbound underpass shelter, Aberdeen Station, Pennsylvania Station, Aberdeen, Maryland. Gottscho-Schleisner, Incorporated, April 1944. P&P,LC-G612-45209,LC-G612-T-45209.

1-041. Southbound station, chimney detail, Aberdeen Station, Pennsylvania Station, Aberdeen, Maryland. Gottscho-Schleisner, Incorporated, April 1944. P&P,LC-G612-45190,LC-G612-T-45190.

1-042. Ticket window from inside, Aberdeen Station, Pennsylvania Station, Aberdeen, Maryland. Gottscho-Schleisner, Incorporated, April 1944. P&P,LC-G612-45212,LC-G612-T-45212.

1-043. Northbound station, Aberdeen Station, Pennsylvania Station, Aberdeen, Maryland. Gottscho-Schleisner, Incorporated, April 1944. P&P,LC-G612-45206,LC-G612-T-45206.

This is a rare full-scale rail station from the 1940s, a cousin to the updated Virginia & Western Station in Roanoke, Virginia (see 8-013–8-020).

1-041

1-042

1-043

1-044. Wilmington Station, north side, Pennsylvania Railroad Improvements, Front & French streets, Wilmington, New Castle County, Delaware. George Rineer, photographer. P&P,HAER,DEL,2-WILM,33D-1.

Improvements to the station building in the early 1980s were substantial, including a sympathetically designed canopy wrapping around the corner between the Front Street and French Street façades. Later repairs included those undertaken for the four 70-pound clock faces of the squat but beautifully decorated clock tower.

1-045. Aerial view, Pennsylvania Railroad, Wilmington Station, Wilmington, New Castle County, Delaware. Jack E. Boucher, photographer, April 1977. P&P, HAER DEL,2-WILM,43-7.

A birds-eye view shows how the elevated tracks bisect the station. The dark cap of the clock tower is visible at the upper side of the station's right-hand façade.

1-044

1-045

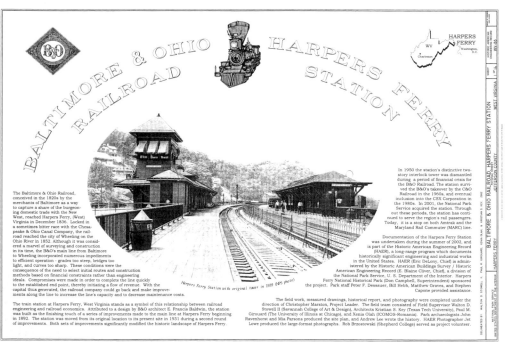

1-046. Medallion image, Baltimore & Ohio Railroad, Harper's Ferry Station, Potomac Street, Harper's Ferry, Jefferson County, West Virginia. P&P, sheet no. 1.

1-047. View from the railroad bridge of the Baltimore & Ohio Station, Harper's Ferry, West Virginia. P&P, LC-USZ62-53984.

BALTIMORE & OHIO RAILROAD HARPERS FERRY STATION

The Baltimore & Ohio Railroad, conceived in the 1820s by the merchants of Baltimore as a way to capture a share of the burgeoning domestic trade with the New West, reached Harpers Ferry, (West) Virginia in December 1836. Locked in a sometimes bitter race with the Chesapeake & Ohio Canal Company, the railroad reached the city of Wheeling on the Ohio River in 1852. Although it was considered a marvel of surveying and construction in its time, the B&O's main line from Baltimore to Wheeling incorporated numerous impediments to efficient operation - grades too steep, bridges too light, and curves too sharp. These conditions were the consequence of the need to select initial routes and construction methods based on financial constraints rather than engineering ideals. Compromises were made in order to complete the line quickly to the established end point, thereby initiating a flow of revenue. With the capital thus generated, the railroad company could go back and make improvements along the line to increase the line's capacity and to decrease maintenance costs.

The train station at Harpers Ferry, West Virginia stands as a symbol of this relationship between railroad engineering and railroad economics. Attributed to a design by B&O architect E. Francis Baldwin, the station was built as the finishing touch of a series of improvements made to the main line at Harpers Ferry beginning in 1892. The station was moved from its original location to its present site in 1931 during a second round of improvements. Both sets of improvements significantly modified the historic landscape of Harpers Ferry.

Harpers Ferry Station with original tower in 1939 (NPS photo)

In 1950 the station's distinctive two-story interlock tower was dismantled during a period of financial crisis for the B&O Railroad. The station survived the B&O's takeover by the C&O Railroad in the 1960s, and eventual inclusion into the CSX Corporation in the 1980s. In 2001, the National Park Service acquired the station. Through out these periods, the station has continued to serve the region's rail passengers. Today, it is a stop on both Amtrak and the Maryland Rail Commuter (MARC) line.

Documentation of the Harpers Ferry Station was undertaken during the summer of 2002, and is part of the Historic American Engineering Record (HAER), a long-range program which documents historically significant engineering and industrial works in the United States. HAER (Eric DeLony, Chief) is administered by the Historic American Buildings Survey / Historic American Engineering Record (E. Blaine Cliver, Chief), a division of the National Park Service, U.S. Department of the Interior. Harpers Ferry National Historical Park (Don Campbell, Superintendent) sponsored the project. Park staff Peter F. Dessauer, Bill Hebb, Matthew Graves, and Stephen Capone provided assistance.

The field work, measured drawings, historical report, and photography were completed under the direction of Christopher Marston, Project Leader. The field team consisted of Field Supervisor Walton D. Stowell II (Savannah College of Art & Design), Architects Kristian S. Key (Texas Tech University), Paul M. Girouard (The University of Illinois at Chicago), and Xenia Olah (ICOMOS-Romania). Park archaeologists John Ravenhorst and Mia Parsons produced the site plan, and Andrew Lee wrote the history. HAER Photographer Jet Lowe produced the large-format photographs. Rob Brzostowski (Shepherd College) served as project volunteer.

1-046

1-047

1-048. View of depot's north (trackside) and west elevations, with bridge at right, Chesapeake & Ohio Railroad, Thurmond Depot, northeast end of New River Bridge, Thurmond, Fayette County, West Virginia. Jet T. Lowe, photographer, November 1988. P&P,HAER,WVA,10-THUR,1A-1.

The Thurmond Depot served as a conduit for coal at the edge of the New River Gorge.

1-049. Aerial view of the "Point" at Harper's Ferry, looking east, Baltimore & Ohio Railroad, Harper's Ferry Bridge Piers, junction of Potomac & Shenandoah rivers, Sharpsburg Vic., Washington County, Maryland. William E. Barrett, photographer, 1970. P&P,HAER,MD,22-HARF,V,1-1.

This aerial view shows (left to right) the new B&O bridge completed in 1931; the 1894 bridge to the Winchester (Virginia) branch; stone piers of the former B&O Railroad; Bollman Bridge, washed out in the 1936 flood; and spanning the Shenandoah to the right, stone piers for a highway bridge. The old joke about "location, location, location" fits the storyline in Harper's Ferry, where the railroad and its station forever hug the riverfront. The location, however, has been buffeted by the Civil War and various economic upheavals. The current station, designed in 1892 by E. Francis Baldwin, was moved to its current site in 1931.

1-048

1-049

1-050

1-052

NORTH ELEVATION
(HEAD HOUSE)

1-050. Head house, front façade, Baltimore & Ohio Railroad, Wheeling Freight Station, Fourteenth & South streets, Wheeling, Ohio County, West Virginia. William E. Barrett, photographer, 1974. P&P,HABS,WVA,35-WHEEL,4-11.

1-051. Elevation and section, Baltimore & Ohio Railroad, Wheeling Freight Station, Fourteenth & South streets, Wheeling, Ohio County, West Virginia. P&P,sheet no. 5.

1-052. Head house, side view, Baltimore & Ohio Railroad, Wheeling Freight Station, Fourteenth & South streets, Wheeling, Ohio County, West Virginia. William E. Barrett, photographer, 1974. P&P,HAER,WVA,35-WHEEL,4-9.

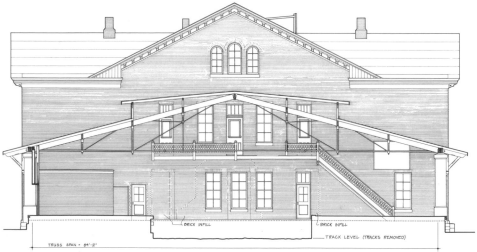

TRUSS SPAN = 84'-2"

BRICK INFILL   BRICK INFILL

TRACK LEVEL (TRACKS REMOVED)

TRANSVERSE SECTION A-A

1-051

1-053. Aerial view of Union Station, Washington, D.C. Unidentified photographer, ca. 1921. P&P,LC-F82-8107,LC-DIG-npcc-30427.

UNION STATION, WASHINGTON, D.C.

Union Station stands as a national archetype. The building functions as it was designed: to fulfill all the necessary operations of a twentieth-century railway station. More importantly, Union Station has done so with style and grace, its spaces flowing seamlessly one to the next.

All union stations were erected to unify a too-numerous batch of competing independent stations. The situation was especially dire in Washington, D. C., where lines crisscrossed along the National Mall and Pennsylvania Avenue. The McMillan Commission was appointed not only to resolve the mess, but also to apply City Beautiful principles to best effect. Accordingly, the movement's chief proponent, Daniel Burnham, was hired as the architect for the station. As his primary sculptor, Burnham chose Louis St. Gaudens, brother of the more famous Augustus (not incidentally a commission member). The younger St. Gaudens proceeded to design not only the six allegorical figures set on

1-054

pedestals atop the engaged columns of the main entrance pavilion, but also the fifty-six warriors ringing the upper reaches of the waiting room.

Overall, Burnham was the driving force at Union Station, as he had been a decade earlier at the 1893 World's Columbian Exposition in Chicago. He gave Washington the kind of national gateway that all capital-city stations aspire to be. The axial relation of the station to the U.S. Capitol Building is slightly askew, but otherwise the procession of spaces from forecourt fountain to train gate is clear and direct—and well appointed in the bargain.

The cultural significance of Union Station is similarly beyond question. U.S. Presidents from Theodore Roosevelt onward have taken its value to heart. After a horrifying stint in the 1980s with an open-pit visitors center in its main hall, Union Station was reclaimed as a thriving mixed-use venue—and functioning railroad station. In another recent note of grace, when baseball was finally slated to return to Washington at the turn of the twenty-first century, the news of the Nationals' birth was announced inside the main hall of Union Station.

1-054. Panoramic view of the construction site and equipment during the building of Union Station, Washington, D.C. Unidentified photographer, 1903. P&P,LOT 12334,LC-USZ62-136044.

1-055. Union Station under construction, Washington, D.C. Unidentified photographer, ca. 1905. P&P,LOT 12334,LC-USZ62-99164.

1-055

1-056. Construction of Union Station, particularly work on the vaulted roof, Washington, D.C. P&P,U.S. GEOG FILE,LC-USZ62-63972.

1-057. Detail, west end of main entrance pavilion, showing statuary and inscription, Union Station, 50 Massachusetts Avenue Northeast, Washington, D.C. Jack E. Boucher, photographer, 1968. P&P,HABS,DC,WASH,536-8

Thales in place, atop the innermost of the two western pedestals outside Union Station.

1-058. Union Station under construction, Washington, D.C. Harris & Ewing, photographer, ca. 1910. P&P,LC-H261-1791,LC-DIG-hec-01618.

This statue of Thales, an ancient sage of natural phenomena, weighed in at a full 25 tons.

1-059

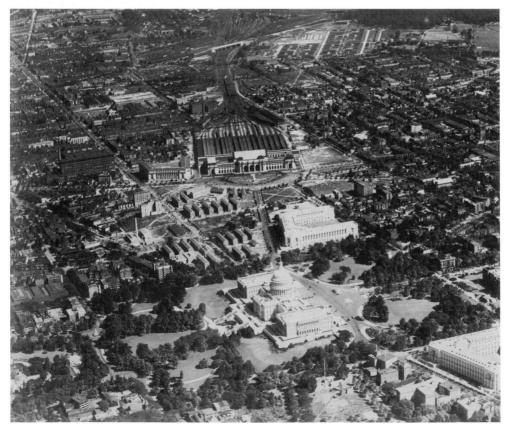

1-060

1-059. Looking down trolley tracks toward Union Station, Washington, D.C. Unidentified photographer, ca. 1910. P&P, LOT 12359-1-T, LC-USZ62-37930.

Before the Columbus Memorial and its fountain were built, the trolley ran right up to the station's front doors.

1-060. Aerial view including Capitol Hill and Union Station, Washington, D.C. Emmet F. Lanier/U.S. Army Air Service, photographer, ca. 1920. P&P, U.S. GEOG FILE, LC-USZ62-91585.

Capitol Hill was a far less cluttered place at the time of this photograph. It had fewer congressional office buildings and lacked the Supreme Court Building in the space just north of where the Library of Congress sits.

1-061. Columbus Day Memorial Celebration, 1912, Union Station, Washington, D.C. Bain News Service, 1912. P&P,LC-B2-2497-4,LC-DIG-ggbain-11299.

The statue for the new Columbus Fountain was the work of sculptor Lorado Z. Taft.

1-062. Columbus Memorial unveiling, Union Station, Washington, D.C. Harris & Ewing, photographer, 1912. P&P,LC-H261-1410,LC-DIG-hec-01183.

At the time of the memorial's unveiling in 1912, the dome of the Library of Congress was still visible (center in the distance) from the front courtyard of the Union Station.

1-063

1-064

1-063. General waiting room showing arrangement of settees, telegraph booths, and news stand; ticket lobby in the distance, Union Station, Washington, D.C. P&P,LOT 12334,LC-USZ62-92471.

1-064. Waiting room, Union Station, 50 Massachusetts Avenue Northeast, Washington, D.C. Jack E. Boucher, photographer, 1968. P&P,HABS,DC,WASH,536-21.

1-065

1-065. Concourse, Union Station, Washington, D.C. Unidentified photographer, ca. 1921. P&P,LC-F82-7991,LC-DIG-npcc-30392.

1-066. Union Station Plaza showing hotels for WACS or WAVES during World War I, Washington, D.C. Unidentified photographer, ca. 1915. P&P,U.S. GEOG FILE,LC-USZ62-93158.

These government rooming houses outlasted the war for over a decade.

1-066

MID-ATLANTIC REGION II
(Pennsylvania, Ohio)

The Pennsylvania Railroad Company established an early dominance in the state and never looked back. Its lines ran north and south from Philadelphia to New York City and to Washington, D.C., but also stretched west to Pittsburgh and on to Chicago. There were other major players in the area, notably the Reading Railroad and the Erie Railway, supplemented by smaller lines like the Lackawanna and the Lehigh Valley. Overall, Pennsylvania's trains carried a great many passengers, but in parts of the state there was a preponderance of freight trains. Around Pittsburgh these carriers brought in the raw materials to feed the furnaces of the city's steel mills.

Ohio gradually became something of a railroad crazy quilt, with lines crisscrossing the state in every direction. As far as station buildings went, most Ohio cities were quick to follow the national trend toward consolidation into union stations. Local circumstances in Cleveland and Cincinnati prompted moves in the 1920s to design two of the most ambitious unified facilities in the country. In both cases delays pushed the construction timetables on into the 1930s.

2-001. Night alley to Terminal Tower, Cleveland, Ohio. Theodor Horydczak, photographer. P&P,LC-H814-0567,LC-H814-T-0567.

The look of the Terminal Tower likely benefited from architect Howard J. White's previous tenure with the firm of McKim, Mead, & White, specifically the firm's earlier design for the New York Municipal Building.

2-002

2-003

2-004

2-002. Timetable cover illustration with view looking down four-track line, May 27, 1900, Pennsylvania Railroad. Unidentified engraver, 1900. P&P,LOT 3426,LC-USZ-75770.

2-003. Wabash Station, Pittsburgh, Pennsylvania. DETR, ca. 1905. P&P,LC-D4-18657.

Theodore C. Link (1850–1923) was the architect for the Wabash Station, which opened in 1904.

2-004. Pittsburgh & Lake Erie Railroad Station across Smithfield Street Bridge, Pittsburgh, Pennsylvania. DETR, ca. 1900. P&P,LC-D4-70747.

2-005. Pittsburgh & Lake Erie Railroad Station from Mt. Washington, Pittsburgh, Pennsylvania. DETR, ca. 1905. P&P,LC-D4-10915R.

2-006. Waiting room showing fanlight, Pittsburgh & Lake Erie Station, Smithfield & Carson streets, Pittsburgh, Allegheny County, Pennsylvania. P&P,HABS,PA,2-PITBU,55-2.

The passenger waiting room of the 1901 Pittsburgh & Lake Erie Station, was the centerpiece of the design by architect William George Burns, a recent transplant from Toronto. The space was converted into an upscale restaurant in the 1970s.

2-005

2-006

2-007

2-008

2-009

2-010

2-007. Entrance to the rotunda, Pennsylvania Railroad Station Rotunda, Liberty, Grant, & Eleventh streets, Pittsburgh, Allegheny County, Pennsylvania. Jack E. Boucher, photographer, April 1963. P&P,HABS,PA,2-PITBU,37A-3.

2-008. South view of corner pavilion, Pennsylvania Railroad Station Rotunda, Liberty, Grant, & Eleventh streets, Pittsburgh, Allegheny County, Pennsylvania. Jack E. Boucher, photographer, April 1963. P&P,HABS,PA,2-PITBU,37A-5.

2-009. Pennsylvania Station, Pittsburgh, Pennsylvania. DETR, ca. 1902. P&P,LC-D4-33486.

Daniel Burnham's design for the 1903 Pennsylvania Station featured a broad-based railroad office high-rise block, set between the welcoming carriage rotunda and the train shed directly behind.

2-010. Detail of vaulting, Pennsylvania Railroad Station Rotunda, Liberty, Grant, & Eleventh streets, Pittsburgh, Allegheny County, Pennsylvania. Jack E. Boucher, photographer, April 1963 . P&P,HABS,PA,2-PITBU,37A-6.

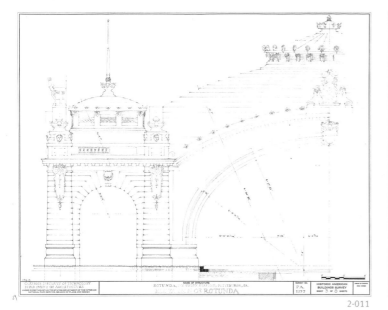

2-011

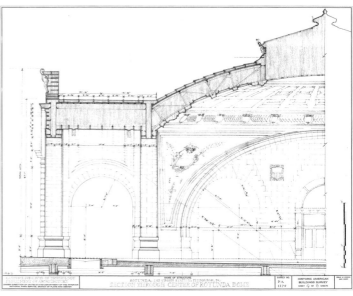

2-012

2-011. Elevation of rotunda, Pennsylvania Railroad Station Rotunda, Liberty, Grant, & Eleventh streets, Pittsburgh, Allegheny County, Pennsylvania. P&P, sheet no. 3.

2-012. Section through center of rotunda dome, Pennsylvania Railroad Station Rotunda, Liberty, Grant, & Eleventh streets, Pittsburgh, Allegheny County, Pennsylvania. P&P, sheet no. 4.

2-013. Section through pavilion and dome, Pennsylvania Railroad Station Rotunda, Liberty, Grant, & Eleventh streets, Pittsburgh, Allegheny County, Pennsylvania. P&P, sheet no. 5.

2-014. Reflected ceiling plan of rotunda, Pennsylvania Railroad Station Rotunda, Liberty, Grant, & Eleventh streets, Pittsburgh, Allegheny County, Pennsylvania. P&P, sheet no. 6.

These photographs and drawings testify to the intricacies of what might be the most elaborate cab stand ever created.

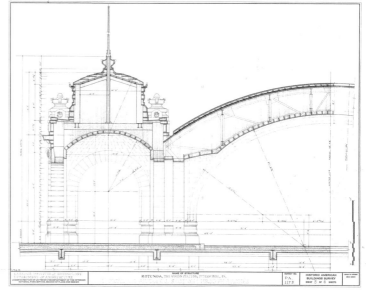

2-013

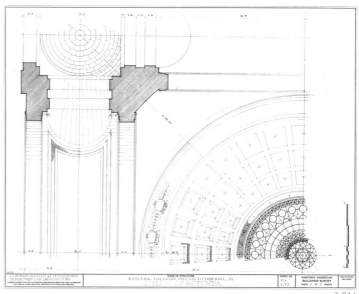

2-014

"AMERICA'S GRANDEST RAILWAY TERMINAL"
= PENNSYLVANIA RAILROAD =
NEW PASSENGER STATION, BROAD STREET, PHILADELPHIA, U.S.A.

2-015. "America's Grandest Railway Terminal," Pennsylvania Railroad, new passenger station, Broad Street, Philadelphia, Pennsylvania. Miller & More, publishers, 1893. P&P,POS-ADV 19th c. C45,no. 1 (C size),LC-USZ62-34681.

With its elaborate head house and huge train shed, Broad Street Station had a great deal in common with its British cousins, such as St. Pancras Station in London.

2-016. Train shed, Pennsylvania Railroad Station, Broad Street Station, Broad & Market streets, Philadelphia, Philadelphia County, Pennsylvania. Unidentified photographer, 1903. P&P,HABS,PA,51-PHILA,341-3.

2-017. Train shed under construction, Pennsylvania Railroad Station, Broad Street Station, Broad & Market streets, Philadelphia, Philadelphia County, Pennsylvania. Unidentified photographer, ca. 1893. P&P,HABS,PA,51-PHILA,341-2.

2-018. Train shed, Pennsylvania, Railroad Station, Broad Street Station, Broad & Market streets, Philadelphia, Philadelphia County, Pennsylvania. Unidentified photographer, ca. 1893. Philadelphia City Archives. P&P,HABS,PA,51-PHILA,521-9.

2-019. Broad Street Station of the
Pennsylvania Railroad, Philadelphia,
Pennsylvania. DETR, ca. 1900.
P&P,LC-D4-12941.

2-020. Aerial view of north and west
sides, Pennsylvania Railroad Station,
Broad Street Station, Broad & Market
streets, Philadelphia, Philadelphia County,
Pennsylvania. Unidentified photographer,
ca. 1940. P&P,HABS,PA,51-PHILA,341-6.

2-021

2-021. North (front) elevation, Baltimore & Ohio Railroad Station, Twenty-fourth & Chestnut streets, Philadelphia, Philadelphia County, Pennsylvania. P&P, sheet no. 3.

2-022. Perspective view of north and east façades, Baltimore & Ohio Railroad Station, Twenty-fourth & Chestnut streets, Philadelphia, Philadelphia County, Pennsylvania. P&P, HABS, PA, 51-PHILA, 405-7.

2-022

2-023. Plan of second (main) floor, Baltimore & Ohio Railroad
Station, Twenty-fourth & Chestnut streets, Philadelphia,
Philadelphia County, Pennsylvania. P&P,sheet no. 2.

Architect Frank Furness provided a mix of different waiting
rooms on different levels for Philadelphia's B&O Station. He
also placed a good number of staircases around the building,
which were critical for a station where the tracks were one
level down from street level.

2-024. Upper level, women's waiting room, Baltimore
& Ohio Railroad Station, Twenty-fourth and Chestnut
streets, Philadelphia, Philadelphia County, Pennsylvania.
P&P,HABS,PA,51-PHILA,405-17.

2-025. Main (upper-level) waiting room, Baltimore &
Ohio Railroad Station, Twenty-fourth & Chestnut streets,
Philadelphia, Philadelphia County, Pennsylvania.
P&P,HABS,PA,51-PHILA,405-16.

2-026. Upper waiting room, fireplace detail, Baltimore &
Ohio Railroad Station, Twenty-fourth & Chestnut streets,
Philadelphia, Philadelphia County, Pennsylvania. Cervin
Robinson, photographer, October 1959. P&P,HABS,PA,51-
PHILA,405-5.

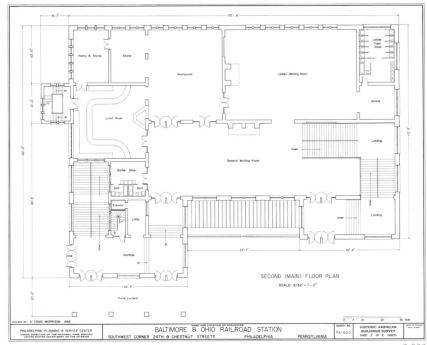

2-023

2-024

2-025

2-026

2-027

2-028

2-027. Stairway to lower-level waiting room, Baltimore & Ohio Railroad Station, Twenty-fourth & Chestnut streets, Philadelphia, Philadelphia County, Pennsylvania. P&P,HABS,PA,51-PHILA,405-14.

2-028. North (Chestnut Street) porch being demolished, Baltimore & Ohio Railroad Station, Twenty-fourth & Chestnut streets, Philadelphia, Philadelphia County, Pennsylvania. Unidentified photographer, ca. 1940. P&P,HABS,PA,51-PHILA, 405-13.

2-029. Northeast front and southeast side, Philadelphia & Reading Railroad, Terminal Station, 1115–1141 Market Street, Philadelphia, Philadelphia County, Pennsylvania. Unidentified photographer, ca. 1937. P&P,HABS PA,51-PHILA,521-2.

2-030. Northeast corner, detail of President's office, Philadelphia & Reading Railroad, Terminal Station, 1115–1141 Market Street, Philadelphia, Philadelphia County, Pennsylvania. Jack E. Boucher, photographer, 1974. P&P,HABS,PA,51-PHILA,521-4.

2-031. Construction photograph, Philadelphia & Reading Railroad, Terminal Station, 1115–1141 Market Street, Philadelphia, Philadelphia County, Pennsylvania. Unidentified photographer, ca. 1892. Reading Company Archives. P&P,HABS,PA,51-PHILA,521-8.

The train shed spanned 256 feet, a record in its day. The tracks entered at the second level of the building.

2-029

2-030

2-031

2-032

2-033

2-032. Interior, 30th Street Station, Philadelphia, Pennsylvania. Gottscho-Schleisner, Incorporated, December 1945. P&P,LC-G612-48296,LC-G612-T-48296.

The 30th Street Station is credited to Alfred Shaw, with the firm of Graham, Anderson, Probst, & White (successors to Daniel H. Burnham & Company), but designer Raymond Loewy may have had a hand in the design as well.

2-033. Aerial view, Pennsylvania Railroad, 30th Street Station, Northeast Railroad Corridor, Amtrak route between Delaware–Pennsylvania & Pennsylvania–New Jersey state lines, Philadelphia, Philadelphia County, Pennsylvania. Jack E. Boucher, photographer, April 1977. P&P,HAER,PA,51-PHILA,694-13.

The ceremonial approach to 30th Street Station is by twin roadways across the Schuylkill River. The railroad bridge to the north has mostly served the suburban Main Line over the years, with the Pennsylvania Railroad lines running parallel to the river.

2-034. The station in Harrisburg, Pennsylvania in the 1860's. Pennsylvania Railroad. P&P,LOT 2365,LC-USZ62-54366.

Trains at the station represent those from four companies: the Pennsylvania Railroad, the Northern Central, the Cumberland Valley, and the Philadelphia & Reading.

2-034

2-035

2-036

2-035. Serving bar, Harrisburg U.S.O., Pennsylvania Station, Harrisburg, Pennsylvania. Gottscho-Schleisner, Incorporated, September 1943. P&P,LC-G612-43964,LC-G612-T-43964.

2-036. Interior from entrance, Harrisburg U.S.O., Pennsylvania Station, Harrisburg, Pennsylvania, Gottscho-Schleisner, Incorporated, September 1943. P&P,LC-G612-43962,LC-G612-T-43962.

2-037. Fireplace and column elevations, main lobby details, Harrisburg Passenger Station, Pennsylvania. P&P,HAER,PA,22-HARBU,23-, sheet no. 13.

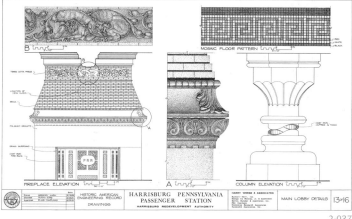

2-037

2-038

2-039

2-040

2-038. General view, Central Railroad of New Jersey, Bethlehem Station, south side of Lehigh Street, east of Main Street, Bethlehem, Lehigh County, Pennsylvania. Jack E. Boucher, photographer, February 1969. P&P,HAER,PA,39-BETH,1-1.

2-039. Looking northeast, Central Railroad of New Jersey, Bethlehem Station, south side of Lehigh Street, east of Main Street, Bethlehem, Lehigh County, Pennsylvania. Jack E. Boucher, photographer, February 1969. P&P,HAER,PA,39-BETH,1-2.

2-040. Detail of south (trackside) façade, Central Railroad of New Jersey, Bethlehem Station, south side of Lehigh Street, east of Main Street, Bethlehem, Lehigh County, Pennsylvania. Jack E. Boucher, photographer, February 1969. P&P,HAER,PA,39-BETH,1-4.

2-041

2-041. Train side front (north) ca. 1870 transportation building, Pennsylvania Railroad Bryn Mawr Station, 17th Street and Pennsylvania avenue, Bryn Mawr, Montgomery County, Pennsylvania. Pennsylvania Railroad General Library. P&P,HABS,PA,46-BRYN,1-1.

2-042. Tracks and station, Wynnewood Railroad Station, Wynnewood & Penn roads, Wynnewood, Montgomery County, Pennsylvania. P&P,HABS,PA,46-WYNN,2-1.

2-043. Front view, Wynnewood Railroad Station, Wynnewood & Penn roads, Wynnewood, Montgomery County, Pennsylvania. P&P,HABS,PA,46-WYNN,2-4.

2-042

2-043

2-044

2-045

2-046

2-044. North front ca. 1930, Pennsylvania Railroad Station, Market Street, West Chester Borough, Chester County, Pennsylvania. Unidentified photographer, ca. 1930. P&P,HABS,PA,15-WCHES,8-5.

2-045. West side ca. 1930, Pennsylvania Railroad Station, Market Street, West Chester Borough, Chester County, Pennsylvania. Unidentified photographer, ca. 1930. P&P,HABS,PA,15-WCHES,8-6.

Opened around 1875 by the Pennsylvania Railroad, the West Chester Station was demolished in 1968.

2-046. Cornice detail, Pennsylvania Railroad Station, Market Street, West Chester Borough, Chester County, Pennsylvania. Ned Goode, photographer, July 1962. P&P,HABS,PA,15-WCHES,8-3.

2-047

2-047. South and east façades, looking northwest, showing porte cochere, Greensburg Railroad Station, Harrison Avenue, Greensburg, Westmoreland County, Pennsylvania. Jet Lowe, photographer, April 1990. P&P,HAER,PA,65-GREEB,2-1.

2-048. Detail of porte cochere along south façade, Greensburg Railroad Station, Harrison Avenue, Greensburg, Westmoreland County, Pennsylvania. Jet Lowe, photographer, April 1990. P&P,HAER,PA,65-GREEB,2-2.

2-048

2-049

2-050

2-051

2-049. Interior east and north walls, Pennsylvania Railroad Station, 47 Walnut Street, Johnstown, Cambria County, Pennsylvania. Jet Lowe, photographer, September 1988. P&P,HABS,PA,11-JOTO,13-4.

2-050. West Street front and north side, Pennsylvania Railroad Station, 47 Walnut Street, Johnstown, Cambria County, Pennsylvania. Jet Lowe, photographer, September 1988. P&P,HABS,PA,11-JOTO,13-2.

Johnstown's Pennsylvania Station was completed in 1916 to the designs of Kenneth M. Murchison, who trained in the Beaux-Arts tradition.

2-051. Hamilton Street façade, Central Railroad of New Jersey, Allentown Station, Race & Hamilton streets, Allentown, Lehigh County, Pennsylvania. Jet Lowe, photographer, 1979. P&P,HAER,PA,39-ALLEN,4-1.

2-052

2-053

2-052. West side with stairs, Strafford Railroad Station, east side of Old Eagle School Road between Strafford Avenue & Penn Central Railroad tracks (Tredyffrin Township), Strafford, Chester County, Pennsylvania. P&P,HABS,PA,15-STRAFO,2-3.

2-053. North front, Strafford Railroad Station, east side of Old Eagle School Road, between Strafford Avenue & Penn Central Railroad tracks (Tredyffrin Township), Strafford, Chester County, Pennsylvania. Ned Goode, photographer, August 1958. P&P,HABS,PA,15-STRAFO,2-1.

2-054. Stairs to trackside from south, Strafford Railroad Station, east side of Old Eagle School Road between Strafford Avenue & Penn Central Railroad tracks (Tredyffrin Township), Strafford, Chester County, Pennsylvania. P&P,HABS,PA,15-STRAFO, 2-7.

The Stick Style station at Strafford was a reclamation project by the Pennsylvania Railroad Company. The structure was originally built as the Centennial Catalogue Building at the 1876 Centennial Exhibition in Philadelphia. Purchased at auction, the building served the railroad first at Wayne, Pennsylvania, in 1885 and then moved onto a new base (a street-level floor) in Strafford in 1887.

2-054

2-055

2-056

2-055. General view looking from the north, Erie Railway, Susquehanna Station & Hotel, west of intersection of Front & Main streets, north side, Susquehanna, Susquehanna County, Pennsylvania. Jack E. Boucher, photographer, July 1971. P&P,HAER,PA,58-SUSQ,3-1.

The combined building, made up by the Susquehanna Station and the Starrucca Hotel, was as long as a football field and 40 feet deep from the tracks. The hotel dining hall alone was one-third that length and reflected in the same American Gothic as the exterior.

2-056. Detail view of dormer and cornice, Erie Railway, Susquehanna Station & Hotel, west of intersection of Front & Main streets, north side, Susquehanna, Susquehanna County, Pennsylvania. Jack E. Boucher, photographer, July 1971. P&P,HAER,PA,58-SUSQ,3-4.

The arcaded patterning in brick below the cornice finds echoes in the American Gothic of the dormer windows lining the roof.

2-057. View from northwest showing building and immediate surrounding area, Erie Railway, Susquehanna Station & Hotel, west of intersection of Front & Main streets, north side, Susquehanna, Susquehanna County, Pennsylvania. Jack E. Boucher, photographer, April 1971. P&P,HAER,PA,58-SUSQ, 3-9.

2-058. Aerial view Reconnaissance I, Erie Railway Survey, Erie Railway, Susquehanna Station & Hotel, west of intersection of Front & Main streets, north side, Susquehanna, Susquehanna County, Pennsylvania. Jack E. Boucher, photographer, April 1971. P&P,HAER,PA,58-SUSQ,3-10.

2-059

2-059. East façade, Erie Railway, Susquehanna Station & Hotel, west of intersection of Front & Main streets, north side, Susquehanna, Susquehanna County, Pennsylvania. Jack E. Boucher, photographer, July 1971, P&P,HAER,PA,58-SUSQ,3-11.

2-060. North elevation and roof plan, Erie Railway, Susquehanna Station & Hotel, west of intersection of Front & Main streets, north side, Susquehanna, Susquehanna County, Pennsylvania. P&P,sheet no. 1.

2-061. Partial north (track) elevation, Erie Railway, Susquehanna Station & Hotel, west of intersection of Front & Main streets, North side, Susquehanna, Susquehanna County, Pennsylvania. P&P,sheet no. 5.

2-062. Section looking east, Erie Railway, Susquehanna Station & Hotel, west of intersection of Front & Main streets, north side, Susquehanna, Susquehanna County, Pennsylvania. P&P,sheet no. 4.

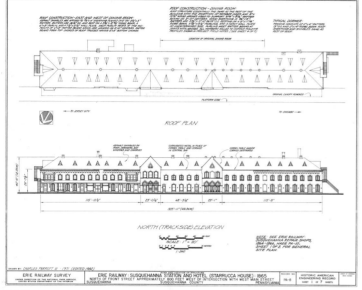
2-060

2-061

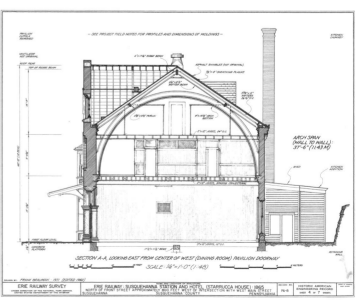
2-062

2-063

2-063. General view, Central Railroad of New Jersey, Jim Thorpe Station, Carbon County, Pennsylvania. Jet Lowe, photographer, 1979. P&P,HAER,PA,13-JIMTH,1-1.

2-064. North front and west side, Cedar Hollow Railroad Station, Cedar Hollow Road (Tredyffrin Township), Paoli Vic., Chester County, Pennsylvania. Ned Goode, photographer, August 1958. P&P,HABS,PA,15-PAOL.V,4-1.

2-064

2-065

2-065. Railroad depot, Connellsville, Pennsylvania. John Vachon/FSA, photographer, July 1940. P&P,LC-USF33-016009-M3.

2-066. Lackawanna Railway Station, Mt. Pocono, Pennsylvania. DETR, ca. 1905. P&P,LC-D4-18725.

2-066

2-067. Black Diamond Express, Lehigh Valley Railroad, at railroad station, Sayre, Pennsylvania. Unidentified photographer, ca. 1900. P&P,LC-USZ62-97412.

2-068. Reading Station, East Falls, Philadelphia, Pennsylvania. P&P,U.S. GEOG FILE,LC-USZ62-98732.

2-069. Reynoldsville, Pennsylvania. Unidentified photographer, ca. 1909. P&P,U.S. GEOG FILE,LC-USZ62-95806.

2-067

2-068

2-069

2-070

2-071

2-072

2-070. Easton, Pennsylvania, panorama from Picadilly Hill. William Herman Rau, photographer, ca. 1896. P&P,PAN US GEOG-Pennsylvania no. 76 (E size).

2-071. Panoramic photo of Erie, Pennsylvania (station at far left). Haines Photo Company, ca. 1912. P&P,PAN US GEOG-Pennsylvania no. 6 (F size).

2-072. Central Union Station, Cincinnati, Ohio. DETR, ca. 1910. P&P,LC-D4-71318.

This station was one of the five that became obsolete in 1933 with the opening of the Cincinnati Union Terminal.

2-073. Union Station, Dayton, Ohio. DETR, ca. 1904. P&P,LC-D4-17986.

2-074. Union Station, Toledo, Ohio. DETR, ca. 1910. P&P,LC-D4-72778.

2-075. Union Station, Columbus, Ohio. Unidentified photographer, 1919. P&P,LC-USZ62-61260.

The Columbus Union Station (1897, razed 1977) boasts a richly decorated arcade designed by architect Daniel Burnham as a precursor to his Union Station in Washington, D.C. Still, his Columbus design was not nearly as exotic as that of the Toledo & Ohio Central Station (1895) across town. Its busy roofline and tower all had broad eaves, with the look fitting somewhere between that of a Dutch windmill and a pagoda.

2-073

2-074

2-075

2-076

CLEVELAND UNION TERMINAL AND CINCINNATI UNION TERMINAL

Two of the largest unified station projects ever conceived, each replacing several out-of-date facilities (including a Civil War–vintage depot in Cleveland), these were also two of the last major railroad stations built in America. Located at opposite corners of Ohio, the two terminals have rarely had cause to operate at full capacity, aside from the years around World War II. For both terminals at least the artistry came at full throttle.

The Terminal Tower and its six consorts aimed to prove that Cleveland was still the world-class city it had been late in the nineteenth century. The site for the complex was chosen in late 1919, followed by a full decade of construction. Train operations began in June 1930.

The Cleveland Union Terminal is the subterranean podium for the fifty-two-story Terminal Tower. The lantern-topped skyscraper was sited to front directly onto the city's Public Square and to be flanked by the pre-existing Hotel Cleveland and the new Higbee's Department Store. The architectural pedigree of the complex came with the choice of the firm. Graham, Anderson, Probst, & White had inherited Daniel Burnham's practice and included partner Howard J. White (1870–1956), who had previously worked for his uncle Stanford's firm, McKim, Mead, & White.

Fellheimer & Wagner, principal architects for the Cincinnati Union Terminal, had a prior track record that included the Buffalo Central Terminal, completed in 1930 in

2-077. South view in context from across the Cuyahoga River, Terminal Tower Building, Cleveland Union Terminal, 50 Public Square, Cleveland, Cuyahoga County, Ohio. Jonnie Jones, photographer, 1987. P&P,HABS,OHIO,18-CLEV,45-2.

upstate New York. The firm's genius in Ohio is most evident in the circulation system, with ramps everywhere—for passengers, cars, taxis, and even provisions out front for airplane landings. The architects took an axial cue for their design from the relation of their site to the city's beloved, half-century-old Cincinnati Music Hall. The line from the theater building cuts the station site in neat halves, running through the center of the entry hall and down the concourse, bisecting the platform area. The layout was as grand as the scale.

Seeking additional architectural flair, the board of the Cincinnati Union Terminal Company brought in Paul Philippe Cret (1876–1945), best known as designer of the Folger Shakespeare Library in Washington, D.C. Cret meshed his Beaux-Arts background with the new Art Deco sensibility of the day. He gave the whole a bright color palette, with assists from mosaic artist Winold Reiss, woodworker Jean Boudelle, and sculptor Maxfield Keck. This international collaboration produced a masterpiece in artistic terms as well as functional. The complex has ultimately proved adaptable in its function, being home since 1990 to the Cincinnati Museum Center, even as Amtrak has resumed service at the terminal.

2-078. Steam concourse roof, Terminal Tower Building, Cleveland Union Terminal, 50 Public Square, Cleveland, Cuyahoga County, Ohio. Jonnie Jones, photographer, 1987. P&P,HABS,OHIO,18-CLEV,45-5.

The roof provides light and ventilation for six of the passenger tracks in the station below.

2-079. Public Square entrance, Terminal Tower Building, Cleveland Union Terminal, 50 Public Square, Cleveland, Cuyahoga County, Ohio, Jonnie Jones, photographer, 1987. P&P,HABS,OHIO,18-CLEV,45-6.

2-080. Detail, Public Square entrance, entablature with clock, Terminal Tower Building, Cleveland Union Terminal, 50 Public Square, Cleveland, Cuyahoga County, Ohio. Jonnie Jones, photographer, 1987. P&P,HABS,OHIO,18-CLEV,45-11.

The tower and the terminal shared the grand entrance off the city's Public Square.

2-081. Terminal Tower under construction, Public Square façade, Terminal Tower Building, Cleveland Union Terminal, 50 Public Square, Cleveland, Cuyahoga County, Ohio. Louis Rosenberg, etching/Tower City Development Office/Edgarton Studios, Incorporated, 1987. P&P,HABS,OHIO,18-CLEV, 45-153.

2-082

2-084

2-083

2-082. Detail, English Oak Room, column millwork, paneling, grate, Terminal Tower Building, Cleveland Union Terminal, 50 Public Square, Cleveland, Cuyahoga County, Ohio. Jonnie Jones, photographer, 1987. P&P,HABS,OHIO,18-CLEV,45-108.

2-083. English Oak Room, typical column capital, plaster ceiling pattern, Terminal Tower Building, Cleveland Union Terminal, 50 Public Square, Cleveland, Cuyahoga County, Ohio. Jonnie Jones, photographer, 1987. P&P,HABS,OHIO,18-CLEV,45-110.

2-084. Portico, level 85, north wall, Terminal Tower Building, Cleveland Union Terminal, 50 Public Square, Cleveland, Cuyahoga County, Ohio. Jonnie Jones, photographer, 1987. P&P,HABS,OHIO,18-CLEV,45-23.

2-085. Center concourse, Terminal Tower Building, Cleveland Union Terminal, 50 Public Square, Cleveland, Cuyahoga County, Ohio. Jonnie Jones, photographer, 1987. P&P,HABS,OHIO,18-CLEV,45-72.

The traditional décor of the street-level entry yielded to a more streamlined appearance in the areas below ground.

2-085

2-086

2-088

2-086. Excavation of track area, construction of arcade, view east to west, Terminal Tower Building, Cleveland Union Terminal, 50 Public Square, Cleveland, Cuyahoga County, Ohio. Tower City Archives/Edgarton Studios, Incorporated, 1987. P&P,HABS,OHIO,18-CLEV,45-144.

2-087. The station area under construction, temporary bridges, view west to east, Terminal Tower Building, Cleveland Union Terminal, 50 Public Square, Cuyahoga County, Ohio. Louis Rosenberg, etching/Tower City Development Office/Edgarton Studios, Incorporated, 1987. P&P,HABS,OHIO,18-CLEV,45-154.

2-088. The site under construction with conceptual image of the Ress Building, view north to south, Terminal Tower Building, Cleveland Union Terminal, 50 Public Square, Cleveland, Cuyahoga County, Ohio. Tower City Archives/Edgarton Studios, Incorporated, 1987. P&P,HABS,OHIO,18-CLEV,45-150.

2-087

2-089. Aerial view, looking west, Cincinnati Union Terminal, 1301 Western Avenue, Cincinnati, Hamilton County, Ohio. Unidentified photographer, 1947. P&P,HABS,OHIO,31-CINT,29-16.

2-090. Distant view, looking west, Cincinnati Union Terminal, 1301 Western Avenue, Cincinnati, Hamilton County, Ohio. P&P,HABS,OHIO,31-CINT,29-17.

The broad façade of the Cincinnati Union Terminal became fondly linked in the popular imagination with the face of a 1930s-vintage radio (the clock face being the dial).

2-091

2-091. Fountain and cascade, looking east from third level of terminal, Cincinnati Union Terminal, 1301 Western Avenue, Cincinnati, Hamilton County, Ohio. P&P,HABS,OHIO,31-CINT,29-18.

2-092. Close view of cascade, looking west, Cincinnati Union Terminal, 1301 Western Avenue, Cincinnati, Hamilton County, Ohio. Caleb Faux, photographer, July 1981. P&P,HABS,OHIO,31-CINT,29-3.

The cascading fountain, outlined by a terrazzo walkway, splits the axis of the overall design to divert traffic around the curve of the driveway.

2-093. Fountain and cascade detail, looking north, Cincinnati Union Terminal, 1301 Western Avenue, Cincinnati, Hamilton County, Ohio. Caleb Faux, photographer, July 1981. P&P,HABS,OHIO,31-CINT,29-4.

2-092

2-093

2-094. Lighting pylons, looking north, Cincinnati Union Terminal, 1301 Western Avenue, Cincinnati, Hamilton County, Ohio. Caleb Faux, photographer, July 1981. P&P,HABS,OHIO,31-CINT,29-5.

Each pylon rises 14 feet to support its cylindrical lighting fixture.

2-095. South bas-relief on front, looking west. Cincinnati Union Terminal, 1301 Western Avenue, Cincinnati, Hamilton County, Ohio. Caleb Faux, photographer, July 1981. P&P,HABS,OHIO,31-CINT,29-7.

The limestone figure to the north of the entry represents Mercury; to the south, Progress. Maxfield Keck originated the designs and supervised the work.

2-096. North bas-relief on front, looking west, Cincinnati Union Terminal, 1301 Western Avenue, Cincinnati, Hamilton County, Ohio. Caleb Faux, photographer, July 1981. P&P,HABS,OHIO,31-CINT,29-6.

2-094

2-095

2-096

2-097

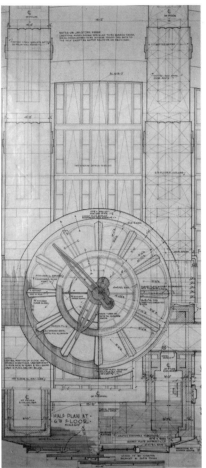

2-098

2-097. Clock on east front, Cincinnati Union Terminal, 1301 Western Avenue, Cincinnati, Hamilton County, Ohio. P&P,HABS,OHIO,31-CINT,29-20.

2-098. Part plan of clock and pylon, Cincinnati Union Terminal, 1301 Western Avenue, Cincinnati, Hamilton County, Ohio. Original architect's drawings. P&P,HABS,OHIO,31-CINT,29-45.

The 18-foot-diameter electric clock has hands made of neon tubes, held by satin-finish aluminum bands, circling around a face of diffused amber glass.

2-099. Concourse, looking east, Cincinnati Union Terminal, 1301 Western Avenue, Cincinnati, Hamilton County, Ohio. P&P,HABS,OHIO,31-CINT,29-23.

Architects Alfred Fellheimer (1875–1959) and Steward Wagner (1886–1958) had already tried out a version of the great front window in Cincinnati at their Buffalo Central Terminal.

2-099

2-100. Taxi entrance (north) ramp, Cincinnati Union Terminal, 1301 Western Avenue, Cincinnati, Hamilton County, Ohio. P&P,HABS,OHIO,31-CINT,29-21.

2-101. Taxi exit (south) ramp, Cincinnati Union Terminal, 1301 Western Avenue, Cincinnati, Hamilton County, Ohio. P&P,HABS,OHIO,31-CINT,29-22.

2-102

2-102. Concourse, looking west from second-level balcony, clock and newsstand in center, train concourse–waiting room in distance, Cincinnati Union Terminal, 1301 Western Avenue, Cincinnati, Hamilton County, Ohio. P&P,HABS,OHIO,31-CINT,29-24.

The 450-foot-long train concourse, leading off to the main waiting room in the far distance, was demolished in 1974. The fourteen mosaics lining its walls were carefully relocated to the Greater Cincinnati/Northern Kentucky International Airport. German-born Winold Reiss created the designs for all the murals inside the Cincinnati Union Terminal. Within the rotunda the mural on the northwest wall was an homage to the city's riverfront history. The southwest wall showed scenes charting the history of America. Each mural measured 25 feet high and 105 feet long.

2-103. Mural and ticket wickets, northwest quadrant of concourse, Cincinnati Union Terminal, 1301 Western Avenue, Cincinnati, Hamilton County, Ohio. Caleb Faux, photographer, July 1981. P&P,HABS,OHIO,31-CINT,29-26.

2-103

2-104

2-106

2-105

2-104. Linoleum sculpture, entrance to women's room off restaurant, Cincinnati Union Terminal, 1301 Western Avenue, Cincinnati, Hamilton County, Ohio. P&P,HABS,OHIO,31-CINT,29-37.

Pierre Boudelle designed the carved linoleum panels found in lounges and restaurant spaces around the terminal interior.

2-105. Board chairman's office, looking southeast, Cincinnati Union Terminal, 1301 Western Avenue, Cincinnati, Hamilton County, Ohio. P&P,HABS,OHIO,31-CINT,29-34.

2-106. Board chairman's office, looking northeast, Cincinnati Union Terminal, 1301 Western Avenue, Cincinnati, Hamilton County, Ohio. P&P,HABS,OHIO,31-CINT,29-33.

2-107. Board chairman's office, looking south, Cincinnati Union Terminal, 1301 Western Avenue, Cincinnati, Hamilton County, Ohio. P&P,HABS,OHIO,31-CINT,29-35.

Walls of inlaid wood and patterned cork flooring decorated the office of the Chairman of the Board for the Cincinnati Union Terminal Company. The representation of the station front, placed above the entry doors, was a clock. The map of the United States above the fireplace was made of woods indigenous to each of the states represented. Pierre Boudelle is credited with the designs.

2-107

2-108

2-109

2-108. Structural framing of dome, looking southwest during construction, Cincinnati Union Terminal, 1301 Western Avenue, Cincinnati, Hamilton County, Ohio. Unidentified photographer, ca. 1931. P&P,HABS,OHIO,31-CINT,29-15.

Steel framing for the half-dome enabled it to span 180 feet, with a height of 106 feet.

2-109. Distant view looking north during construction, Cincinnati Union Terminal, 1301 Western Avenue, Hamilton County, Ohio. Unidentified photographer, March 1932. P&P,HABS,OHIO,31-CINT,29,19.

The sheds for Cincinnati Union Terminal's eight station platforms, each 1,600 feet long (roughly one-third of a mile), were demolished in 1974.

2-110. Plot plan, Cincinnati Union Terminal, 1301 Western Avenue, Cincinnati, Hamilton County, Ohio. Original architect's drawings, June 1931. P&P,HABS,OHIO,31-CINT,29-39.

The plot plan shows the slight axial shift allowed for the train platforms from the strong east-west orientation of the terminal plan overall.

2-111. Cross-section on north and south axis looking west, Cincinnati Union Terminal, 1301 Western Avenue, Cincinnati, Hamilton County, Ohio. Original architect's drawing, June 1931. P&P,HABS,OHIO,31-CINT,29-42.

At the center of the cross-section sits the opening to the long concourse down to the arrival and departure lobby. The deep underpinnings of the station are clearly visible.

2-112. Longitudinal section looking south, Cincinnati Union Terminal, 1301 Western Avenue, Cincinnati, Hamilton County, Ohio. Original architect's drawing, June 1931. P&P,HABS,OHIO,31-CINT,29-43.

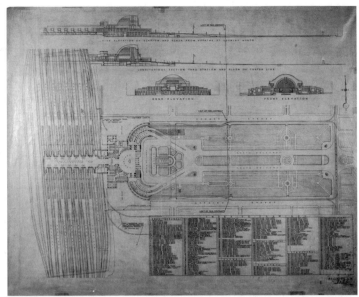

2-110

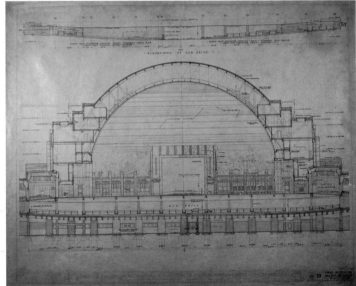

2-111

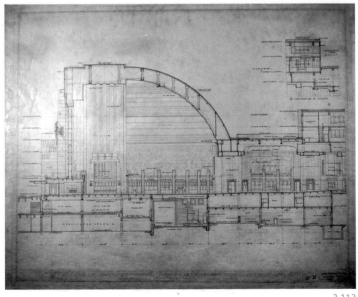

2-112

MID-ATLANTIC REGION III (New Jersey, New York)

The trains in New Jersey ran principally in two directions. Either they were headed through the state between Philadelphia and New York City, or they were bound for the Jersey shore. The tracks were more scattered in New York State, stretching not only out to the eastern end of Long Island but also up the Hudson River and fanning out from there all across the upstate area. The key to the whole operation has always been getting the trains in and out of New York City. The surrounding rivers of Manhattan Island made the entire situation problematic until a few years into the twentieth century.

Until that time trains coming from the south through New Jersey essentially reached a dead end at the Hudson River. Along the riverside of Hoboken, New Jersey, and a handful of other sites, combination train-and-ferry terminals were built to handle the heavy traffic. Passengers and freight traveled the last few miles to Manhattan by boat. Remarkably, now a century after tunnels under the Hudson River allowed through trains to reach New York's Pennsylvania Station in 1910, the Hoboken ferry terminal is back in business offering passenger service to Manhattan.

3-001. Waiting room, Newark passenger station, Pennsylvania Railroad, Newark, New Jersey. Gottscho-Schleisner, Incorporated, June 1935. P&P,LC-G612-24242,LC-G612-T-24242.

The Newark Pennsylvania Railroad Station, which opened in 1935, was a block of limestone and granite carved in an Art Moderne fashion that might have had the original partners of McKim, Mead, & White (now all deceased but credited with the design) turning in their graves. The new station and the tracks leading to it required substantial remodeling of its Newark neighborhood.

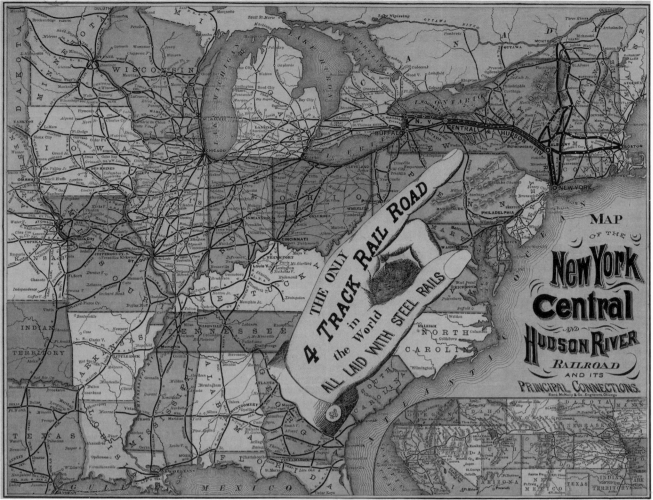

3-002

3-003

3-002. Map of the New York Central & Hudson River Railroad and its principal connections. Rand McNally & Company, 1876. LC-Railroad maps,486.

The hand indicator notes, "The only 4 track rail road in the world all laid with steel rails."

3-003. Ferry building and Lackawanna Railroad Station, Hoboken, New Jersey. P&P,U.S. GEOG FILE,LC-USZ62-95818.

Architect Kenneth M. Murchison was reportedly able to use copper plate left over from construction of the Statue of Liberty (a short distance away in New York Harbor) to build the lightweight façade of the main terminal building in Hoboken. The great clock tower, twenty-two stories tall, was electric-powered and visible far up and down the river.

3-004. Aerial view looking west, Erie-Lackawanna Railroad & Ferry Terminal, ferry slips and bridges, bounded by Observer Highway, Newark & River streets, and the Hudson River, Hoboken, Hudson County, New Jersey. Celia Orgel, photographer, August 1983. P&P,HAER,NJ,9-HOBO,2-1.

The ferryboats that carried train passengers from the slips in Hoboken to Manhattan Island also brought new immigrants over from Ellis Island for their first landing on the American mainland. The combination station, which opened in 1907, handled roughly 100,000 passengers each day in its busiest years.

3-005. Detail view of east façade, ferry shed entrance and ferry bridge, Erie-Lackawanna Railroad & Ferry Terminal, ferry slips and bridges, bounded by Observer Highway, Newark & River streets, and the Hudson River, Hoboken, Hudson County, New Jersey. Celia Orgel, photographer, August 1983. P&P,HAER,NJ,9-HOBO,2-7.

3-006

3-006. Courtyard façade, view showing loading docks for New York ferries, Erie-Lackawanna Railroad Ferry Terminal & Warehouse, Hudson Place, Hoboken, Hudson County, New Jersey. George Eisenman, photographer, 1967. P&P,HABS,NJ,9-HOBO,4-4.

3-007. Main waiting room, ceiling, Erie-Lackawanna Railroad Ferry Terminal & Warehouse, Hudson Place, Hoboken, Hudson County, New Jersey. George Eisenman, photographer, 1967. P&P,HABS,NJ,9-HOBO,4-7.

The 50-foot-high ceiling featured glassworks by the Tiffany Company.

3-007

3-008

3-009

3-008. West end of train sheds, roof of terminal visible at right, Central Railroad of New Jersey, Jersey City Ferry Terminal, Johnson Avenue at the Hudson River, Jersey City, Hudson County, New Jersey. Michael Spozorsky, photographer, January 1981. P&P,HAER,NJ,9-JERCI,4-1.

3-009. Entrance to train sheds, Central Railroad of New Jersey, Jersey City Ferry Terminal, Johnson Avenue at the Hudson River, Jersey City, Hudson County, New Jersey. Michael Spozorsky, photographer, January 1981. P&P,HAER,NJ,9-JERCI,4-2.

The train sheds, as well as the ferry slips, were the work of the railroad engineers. The Bush sheds were part of an enlargement carried out in 1914.

3-010. Roof of terminal building, Central Railroad of New Jersey, Jersey City Ferry Terminal, Johnson Avenue at the Hudson River, Jersey City, Hudson County, New Jersey. Michael Spozorsky, photographer, January 1981. P&P,HAER,NJ,9-JERCI,4-3.

3-011. View, looking west, of waterfront (east) façade of ferry sheds, Central Railroad of New Jersey, Jersey City Ferry Terminal, Johnson Avenue at the Hudson River, Jersey City, Hudson County, New Jersey. Michael Spozorsky, photographer, January 1981. P&P,HAER,NJ,9-JERCI,4-16.

3-010

3-011

3-012

3-012. Terminal lobby, Central Railroad of New Jersey, Jersey City Ferry Terminal, Johnson Avenue at the Hudson River, Jersey City, Hudson County, New Jersey. Michael Spozorsky, photographer, January 1981. P&P,HAER,NJ,9-JERCI,4-6.

The main station house, built in 1889 in Jersey City, was the work of the firm of Peabody & Stearns. The 1914 modifications left it largely unchanged.

3-013. Entrance to Platform 14, east end of train sheds, Central Railroad of New Jersey, Jersey City Ferry Terminal, Johnson Avenue at Hudson River, Jersey City, Hudson County, New Jersey. Michael Spozorsky, photographer, January 1981. P&P,HAER,NJ,9-JERCI,4-4.

3-014. Manhattan from ferry gate, suspended gangways upper left and upper right, Central Railroad of New Jersey, Jersey City Ferry Terminal, Johnson Avenue at the Hudson River, Jersey City, Hudson County, New Jersey. Michael Spozorsky, photographer, January 1981. P&P,HAER,NJ,9-JERCI,4-15.

3-013

3-014

3-015. General view of station, Erie Railway, Clifton Station, Clifton, Passaic County, New Jersey. Erie Railroad Company, ca. 1910. P&P,HAER,NJ,16-CLIF,6-1.

3-016. Train and yards at Beaver Lake Railroad Station, Beaver Lake, New Jersey. P&P,LC-USZ62-73849.

3-015

3-016

3-017

3-018

3-017. Street façade, Atlantic City
Union Station, 2121 2125 Artic Avenue,
Atlantic City, Atlantic County, New Jersey.
P&P,HABS,NJ,1-ATCI,22-6.

3-018. Erie Railroad station, New Milford,
New Jersey. P&P,LC-USZ62-107560.

3-019. Elizabeth Station, Elizabeth,
New Jersey. William Henry Jackson,
photographer, 1892. P&P,LC-D43-1896,LC-
D4-T01-1896.

The clock tower of the 1892 Central Railroad
of New Jersey station in Elizabeth rises 75
feet above the track level.

3-019

3-020

3-021

3-020. Main façade, Newark passenger station, Pennsylvania Railroad, Newark, New Jersey. Gottscho-Schleisner, Incorporated, June 1935. P&P,LC-G612-24250-1/2,LC-G612-T01-24250-1/2.

3-021. Platform bridge over Market Street, Newark passenger station, Pennsylvania Railroad, Newark, New Jersey. Gottscho-Schleisner, Incorporated, June 1935. P&P,LC-G612-24245,LC-G612-T-24245.

3-022. Market Street entrance, Newark passenger station, Pennsylvania Railroad, Newark, New Jersey. Gottscho-Schleisner, Incorporated, June 1935. P&P,LC-G612-24247,LC-G6112-T-24247.

3-022

3-023

3-024

3-025

3-026. Long Island Railroad Station, Port Jefferson, Long Island, New York. Arthur Smedley Greene, photographer, June 1906. P&P,U.S. GEOG FILE,LC-USZ62-99027.

3-027. View from southwest of main station building, Bronxville Railroad Station, Parkway Road at Pondfield Road, Bronxville, Westchester County, New York. Stephen L. Senigo, photographer, May 1988. P&P,HABS,NY,60-BROV,1-2.

3-028. View of main station entrance, Bronxville Railroad Station, Parkway Road at Pondfield Road, Bronxville, Westchester County, New York. Stephen L. Senigo, photographer, May 1988. P&P,HABS,NY,60-BROV,1-4.

The Bronxville Station of the New York Central, which opened in 1917, was designed by A. F. Haldeman, reportedly a staff architect for the line. He chose a Mission Revival style in keeping with the look of the town's best-known hotel, the Gramatan.

3-029

3-029. View of inbound station, north wing, east façade, Hartsdale Railroad Station, East Hartsdale Avenue, Hartsdale, Westchester County, New York. Stephen L. Senigo, photographer, May 1988. P&P,HABS,NY,60-HART,1-6.

3-030. Interior view toward street entrance, Hartsdale Railroad Station, East Hartsdale Avenue, Hartsdale, Westchester County, New York. Stephen L. Senigo, photographer, May 1988. P&P,HABS,NY,60-HART,1-9.

The "mock Tudor" Hartsdale Railroad Station of 1912 was the Westchester County follow-up to Manhattan's Grand Central Terminal (designed by the firm of Warren & Wetmore).

3-030

3-031. View of inbound station from the southwest, Scarsdale Railroad Station, East Parkway, Scarsdale, Westchester County, New York. Stephen L. Senigo, photographer, May 1988. P&P,HABS,NY,60-SCARD,3-12.

Reed & Stem, the original designers of the current Grand Central Terminal, designed this station for the New York Central line in 1908.

3-032. Quaker Ridge Station, New York, West Shore & Buffalo Railroad, New Rochelle, New York. Irving Underhill, photographer, ca. 1913. P&P,LOT 12454,LC-USZ-94026.

The station building sits raised between the tracks and is reachable only by tunnel or train.

3-033. General view of station, Erie Railway, Sparkill Station, Sparkill, Rockland County, New York. Erie Railway Company, ca. 1910. P&P,HAER,NY,44-SPARK,1-1.

3-031

3-032

3-033

3-034

3-035

3-034. General view of station from south, Erie Railway, Middletown Station, James Street, Middletown, Orange County, New York. Jack Boucher, photographer, July 1971. P&P,HAER,NY,36-MID,1-1.

3-035. View of southwest end and entrance, Erie Railway, Middletown Station, James Street, Middletown, Orange County, New York. Jack Boucher, photographer, July 1971. P&P,HAER,NY,36-MID,1-3.

3-036. View of railroad station looking north, U.S. Military Academy, West Shore Railroad Station, West Point, Orange County, New York. Jet Lowe Jr., photographer, April–June 1982. P&P,HABS,NY,36-WEPO,1/29-1.

3-037. Interior view looking south, U.S. Military Academy, West Shore Railroad Station, West Point, Orange County, New York. Jet Lowe Jr., photographer, April–June 1982. P&P,HABS,NY,36-WEPO,1/29-4.

3-038. West Shore station, West Point, New York. DETR, ca. 1900. P&P,LC-D418-30740.

The neo-Gothic masonry West Shore Railroad Station of 1926 replaced an earlier wooden station that had stood nearby.

3-039. General view of station, Erie Railway, Port Jervis Station, Jersey Avenue, Port Jervis, Orange County, New York. Jack Boucher, photographer, 1971. P&P,HAER,NY,38-POJE,1-4.

3-040. Detail of millwork and sign on the driveway side of the station, Erie Railway, Port Jervis Station, Jersey Avenue, Orange County, New York. Jack Boucher, photographer, 1971. P&P,HAER,NY,38-POJE,1-9.

This is one of the finer signs to survive anywhere along the railroad lines.

WEST SHORE STATION
HIGHLAND, N.Y.

3-041. West Shore Station, Highland, New York. C. E. Browne, photographer. P&P,LC-USZ62-68456.

While not strictly a maritime station, this West Shore facility does seem to have its own dock on the Hudson River.

3-042. New York Central Railroad Station, Albany, New York. DETR, ca. 1900. P&P,LC-D4-34797.

The firm of Shepley, Rutan, & Coolidge gets credit for this 1900-vintage capital station.

3-043

3-044

3-043. Union Station, Troy, New York. DETR, ca. 1905. P&P,LC-D4-18818.

3-044. Delaware & Hudson Railroad Station, Saratoga Springs, New York. DETR, ca. 1900. P&P,LC-D4-71552.

3-045. Delaware & Hudson Railroad Station, Plattsburgh, New York. DETR, ca. 1904. P&P,LC-D4-10830.

An upper portion of the station building served as a reading room for local representatives of the Delaware & Hudson Company.

3-045

3-046. Delaware & Hudson Railroad Station, Hotel Champlain, New York. DETR, ca. 1906. P&P,LC-D4-19782.

3-047. Crowd at railroad station, Sylvan Beach, New York. P&P,LC-USZ62-116331.

Summer camps and beaches were well served by the railroads in the era when Chautauquas were popular retreats.

3-048. Train at station, with hotel in background, Fulton, New York. P&P,LC-USZ62-117085.

3-046

3-047

3-048

3-049

3-049. Catskill Mountain railway station, Haines Corners, Catskill Mountains, New York. DETR, ca. 1902. P&P,LC-D4-14510.

3-050. Central station, Saranac Lake, Adirondack Mountains, New York. DETR, ca. 1909. P&P,LC-D4-71219.

3-051. New York Central Station, Garrison, New York. P&P,LC-USZ62-91527.

3-050

3-051

3-052. New York Central Railroad depot, Syracuse, New York. DETR. P&P,LC-D4-39361.

3-053. General view from north, Erie Railway, Jamestown Station, East Second & Lafayette streets, Jamestown, Chautauqua County, New York. Jack Boucher, photographer, October 1972. P&P,HAER,NY,7-JAMTO,1A-1.

3-054. New York Central Railroad station, Rochester, New York. DETR. P&P,LC-D4-36769.

A pair of Richardsonian Romanesque stations in Syracuse and Rochester are long departed, while the shaved-down Art Moderne station in Jamestown survives.

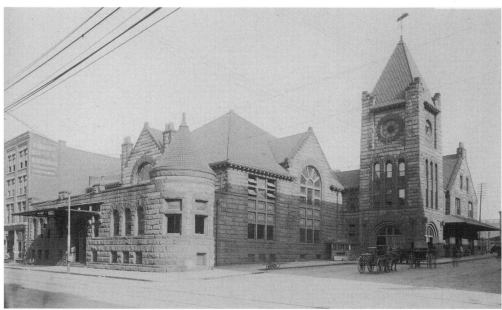

3-052

3-053

3-054

3-055

3-056

3-057

3-055. Station under construction, Erie Railway, Wellsville Station, Pearl & Depot streets, Wellsville, Allegany County, New York. Erie Railway Company, ca. 1910. P&P,HAER,NY,2-WELV,1-5.

3-056. Station in completed stage, Erie Railway, Wellsville Station, Pearl & Depot streets, Wellsville, Allegany County, New York. Erie Railway Company, November 1911. P&P,HAER,NY,2-WELV,1-7.

3-057. Station from northwest, Delaware, Lackawanna & Western Railroad, Vestal Passenger & Freight Station, North Main Street, Vestal, Broome County, New York. Jack Boucher, photographer, July 1971. P&P,HAER,NY,4-VES,1-1.

For all the great Carpenter Gothic houses in upstate New York, the modest Vestal station was a rare example in railroad building—something of a lost cousin, or dowager aunt, to San Francisco's painted lady Victorians.

3-058. West side and south front showing tower, Delaware, Lackawanna & Western Railroad Station, Lewis & Chenango streets, Binghamton, Broome County, New York. Jack Boucher, photographer, 1966. P&P,HABS,NY,4-BING,26-1.

3-059. North side (track side), Delaware, Lackawanna & Western Railroad Station, Lewis & Chenango streets, Binghamton, Broome County, New York. Jack Boucher, photographer, 1966. P&P,HABS,NY,4-BING,26-4.

3-060. South front showing tower, Delaware, Lackawanna & Western Railroad Station, Lewis & Chenango streets, Binghamton, Broome County, New York. Unidentified photographer, ca. 1910. P&P,HABS,NY,4-BING,26-6.

The Delaware, Lackawanna & Western brought in Philadelphia architect Samuel W. Huckel Jr. (1858–1917) to design the new station for Binghamton. Earlier Huckel had performed substantial work to remodel the old Grand Central Station in New York City.

3-058

3-059

3-060

3-061

3-062

3-063

3-061. General view of station before remodeling, Erie Railway, Corning Station, Erie Avenue & Pine Street, Corning, Steuben County, New York. Erie Railroad Company. P&P,HAER,NY,51-CORN,1-1.

3-062. Remodeling of station Erie Railway, Corning Station, Erie Avenue & Pine Street, Corning, Steuben County, New York. Erie Railroad Company. P&P,HAER,NY,51-CORN,1-3.

3-063. Main building, old waiting room (now formal dining hall), Lehigh Valley Railroad Station, West Buffalo Street & Taughannock Boulevard, Ithaca, Tompkins County, New York. C. Hadley Smith, photographer, July 1975. P&P,HABS,NY,55-ITH,6-5.

3-064. Trackside exterior, Erie Railway, Suspension Bridge Station, Suspension Bridge, Erie County, New York. Erie Railroad Company, June 1913. P&P,HAER,NY,15-SUSBR,1-1.

The station sat near the old Niagara Suspension Bridge, just north of Buffalo.

3-064

3-065

3-066

3-065. General view, Erie Railway, Niagara Falls Station, Niagara Falls, Niagara County, New York. Erie Railroad Company, June 1913. P&P,HAER,NY,32-NIAF,4-1.

3-066. View of station, built 1887, Erie Railway, Kensington Avenue Station, Kensington Avenue, Buffalo, Erie County, New York. Erie Railroad Company, 1913. P&P,HAER,NY,15-BUF,18-1.

With comparable rooflines, the various Buffalo-Niagara area stations all seem likely to have been designed by the staff of the Erie Railway.

3-067. View of Delaware, Lackawanna & Western complex from across Buffalo River, Delaware, Lackawanna & Western Railroad, Lackawanna Terminal, Main Street & Buffalo River, Buffalo, Erie County, New York. Jack Boucher, photographer, 1971. P&P,HAER,NY,15-BUF,22-8.

Two passenger buildings are located at the center, with a train shed extending toward right.

3-067

3-068. Interior of larger Delaware, Lackawanna & Western passenger building showing main concourse on upper level, with stairway from street level at right of photo and passage to trains at left, Delaware, Lackawanna & Western Railroad, Lackawanna Terminal, Main Street & Buffalo River, Buffalo, Erie County, New York. Jack Boucher, photographer, 1971. P&P,HAER,NY,15-BUF,22-11.

A stairway from street level is at the right of photo, with passage to trains at left.

While the riverfront exterior of the passenger building remains largely intact, the décor of the raised main concourse has been peeling off its steel frame for some time. Architect Kenneth Murchison, trained in the Beaux-Arts style, was responsible for the design of the station complex. It was finished in 1917 with the help of Lackawanna's chief engineer, Lincoln Bush.

3-068

3-069

Great volumes lit from above constitute the dominant feature of the stations' main halls.

NEW YORK CITY STATIONS

For the past century or so, any story of rail travel into and out of Manhattan would revolve around two principal entities: Pennsylvania Station and the Grand Central Terminal. For the moment at least, the glamour that was Penn Station is just a ghostly presence, its remnants buried beneath Madison Square Garden since the mid-1960s. The well-known upside of the travesty of the station building's demolition was the resultant rise of New York City's landmarks commission, which in turn helped spawn the national preservation movement. Not incidentally, Pennsy's crosstown rival, Grand Central, was saved in the bargain.

3-070. Title page of *King's Views, New York*, skyward trend of thought in New York, Municipal Office Building and railroad terminal near the city hall, New York, New York. Moses King, artist, ca. 1905. P&P,LOT 5199,LC-USZ62-67473.

By 1906, the date of this collection of views, both Pennsylvania Station and Grand Central Terminal were well under way a couple miles north of the City Hall district.

3-071. New York City views, Pennsylvania Station, New York, New York. Samuel H. Gottscho, photographer, ca. 1910. P&P,LC-G623-81603,LC-G623-T01-81603.

3-070

3-071

The major problem with Grand Central, in its various guises, is that it has never been large enough. The original Grand Central Depot of 1871 had to be revamped repeatedly and finally enlarged overall in 1898. The current building opened in 1913, made possible only by burying the tracks north of the terminal beneath Park Avenue and then wrapping the avenue itself around the building on an elevated roadway.

Penn Station, by contrast, may have simply been too big. The building—the word seems an inadequate descriptor—had a magnificent greenhouse cage for a concourse, fronted by Charles McKim's (1847–1909) waiting hall modeled after the frigidarium of the Baths of Caracalla in Rome. Perhaps the thought that first-time visitors would pass

3-072

3-072. Grand Central Depot, New York City, New York. A. P. Yates, photographer, ca. 1895. P&P,U.S. GEOG FILE,LC-USZ62-74617.

The design for the original Grand Central Depot of 1871 had a strong French flavor.

through these immense spaces was seen as providing a cautionary tale about just how large a role anyone could expect to find in the great urban drama waiting outside.

Railroad historian Herbert H. Harwood Jr. provided some perspective on the two stations and their relationship: "Grand Central Terminal . . . had a warmth and humanity about it that its imperial peer on 7th Avenue and 33rd Street sorely lacked." In the end, it remains a sad tale that we had to sacrifice one world-class station in order to save the second.

3-073. 42nd Street Grand Central Station, New York City—1890, New York, New York. Unidentified photographer, 1890. P&P,LOT 7357,LC-USZ62-55554.

A view of the updated exterior of the Grand Central Station.

3-074. Primrose & West's Big Minstrels all white performers, departing from the Grand Central Depot, New York, New York. Strobridge & Company, lithographers, ca. 1897. P&P,POS-MIN-.P759,no.18 (D size),LC-USZ62-21473A.

For the moment the minstrels in their white coats seemed unconcerned about the sooty conditions inside the old Grand Central's train shed.

3-075. Interior of Grand Central Depot, New York, New York. P&P,LOT 13650,no. 9,LC-DIG-stereo-1s01729.

3-076. Elevation rendering, Grand Central Terminal, New York, New York. Barry A. Birrie, artist, April 1910. P&P,LC-USZ62-125747.

This principal elevation shows the clock and a suggestion of the sculptural group above.

3-073

3-074

3-075

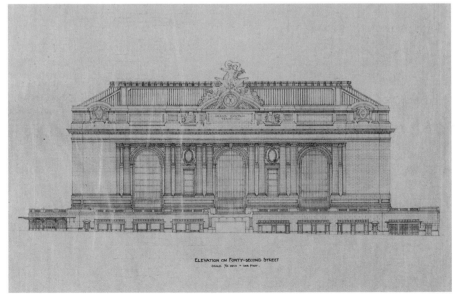

3-076

3-077

3-078

3-079

3-077. Grand Central Terminal, New York, New York. Unidentified artist, ca. 1910. P&P,LC-D4-72984.

This perspective view gives a sense of the terminal before its ever-larger neighbors to the north were built.

3-078. Excavations for N.Y. Grand Central Station (Terminal), New York, New York. DETR, ca. 1908. P&P,LC-D4-70798.

3-079. Grand Central Depot (Terminal), Park Avenue and 42nd Street, New York, New York. Irving Underhill, photographer, ca. 1914. P&P,LOT 3788,LC-USZ62-80249.

This view, likely prior to World War I, shows the south face of the station before the elevated roadway around it was connected to Park Avenue South.

3-080. Grand Central Terminal, New York, New York. P&P,U.S. GEOG FILE,LC-USZ62-85992.

Jules Coutan's sculpture of Mercury, installed above the 13-foot-diameter clock, could still stand out against the sky even with the tower of the New York Central Building (designed in 1929 by Grand Central's chief architect, Whitney Warren) looming behind. This was nothing compared with the "backdrop" later provided in 1963 by the Pan Am Building, which was fifty-nine stories high.

3-081. Grand Central Station (Terminal), Park Avenue Bridge in foreground, New York, New York. Unidentified photographer, ca. 1919. P&P,U.S. GEOG FILE,LC-USZ62-74590.

3-082. Forty-second Street looking west from Grand Central Station, New York, New York. Unidentified photographer, ca. 1919. P&P,U.S. GEOG FILE,LC-USZ62-85991.

3-080

3-081

3-082

3-083

3-084

3-083. Grand Central Terminal, New York, New York. Irving Underhill, photographer, October 1927. P&P,U.S. GEOG FILE,LC-USZ62-64525.

An oblique view gives a sense of how detached the elevated roadway is from all the sidewalk activity down below. Architects Reed & Stem called this a "circumferential plaza."

3-084. Main concourse, Grand Central Terminal, N.Y. Central Lines, New York, New York. DETR, ca. 1910. P&P,LC-D4-72981.

The great central hall of Grand Central featured a celestial ceiling of painted and illuminated constellations of the zodiac, since concealed but now restored in its original reversed order.

3-085. Main waiting room, Grand Central Terminal, N.Y.
Central Lines, New York, New York, DETR, ca. 1910.
P&P,LC-D4-72978.

This view seems an unbelievable counterpoint to the
frenetic activity inside the main hall.

3-086. Incline to suburban concourse, Grand Central
Terminal, New York, New York. DETR, ca. 1910.
P&P,LC-D4-72976.

The original plan, by architects Reed & Stem, emphasized
ramps over stairways. The vaulting permitted special
acoustic effects, such as whispers traveling clearly overhead
even as passengers streamed up and down the concourse.

3-087. Restaurant, Grand Central Terminal, N.Y.
Central Lines, New York, New York. DETR, ca. 1910.
P&P,LC-D4-72979.

This restaurant, located just beneath the main waiting
room, eventually became home to the famous Oyster
Bar, which hosted such frequent customers as Jacqueline
Kennedy Onassis.

3-088. Suburban concourse, Grand Central Terminal,
N.Y. Central Lines, New York, New York. DETR, ca. 1910.
P&P,LC-D4-72973.

3-089. Pennsylvania Railroad Station, New York, New York. Unidentified photographer, ca. 1910. P&P,U.S. GEOG FILE,LC-USZ62-68677.

This view shows Penn Station as completed in 1910, but before the hole in front was filled.

3-090. The big Pennsylvania hole (for station), New York, New York. DETR, ca. 1908. P&P,LC-D4-70693.

An estimated three million cubic yards of Manhattan Island had to be excavated to allow space for Pennsylvania Station and its tracks.

3-091. Pennsylvania Railroad Station, in construction, New York, New York. Bain News Service, October 1908. P&P,LC-B2-487-8,LC-DIG-ggbain-02324.

3-092. Pennsylvania Railroad Station, in construction, New York, New York. Bain News Service, October 1908. P&P,LC-B2-487-9,LC-DIG-ggbain-02325.

3-093. East façade, Pennsylvania Station, New York, New York. DETR, ca. 1910. P&P,LC-D4-73004.

3-094. Thirty-second Street entrance, Pennsylvania Station, New York, New York. Unidentified photographer, ca. 1915. P&P,LC-D4-500206.

3-091

3-092

3-093

3-094

3-095. Pennsylvania Railroad Station, New York, New York. Unidentified photographer, ca. 1911. P&P,U.S. GEOG FILE,LC-USZ62-68671.

The retail arcade ran for 225 feet prior to entering the main station hall.

3-096. Arcade entrance to loggia and main waiting room, Pennsylvania Station, New York, New York. Unidentified photographer, ca. 1911. P&P,LC-D4-71930.

3-097. Main waiting room, Pennsylvania Station, New York, New York. Unidentified photographer, ca. 1911. P&P,LC-D401-71928.

Measuring 277 by 103 feet, with a height of 150 feet, this space was billed at completion as the largest room in the world.

3-098. Pennsylvania Railroad Station, New York, New York. Unidentified photographer, ca. 1911. P&P,U.S. GEOG FILE,LC-USZ62-84010.

3-099. Concourse showing gates, indicators, Pennsylvania Station, New York, New York. DETR, ca. 1910. P&P,LC-D4-39796.

The glass-caged concourse at Pennsylvania Station included twenty-one platforms, with the tracks directly below (a configuration made possible, as at Grand Central, by electrified train travel).

3-100. Main concourse, track levels, stair entrance, Pennsylvania Station, New York, New York. DETR, ca. 1910. P&P,LC-D4-39797.

3-098

3-099

3-100

3-101

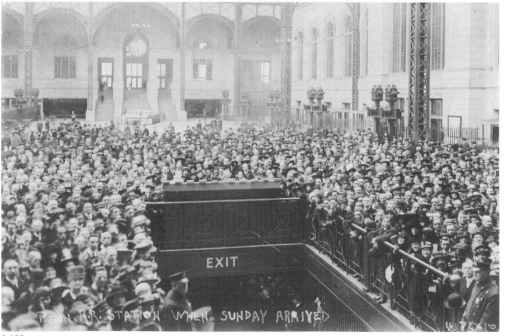

3-102

3-101. Main concourse, Pennsylvania Station, New York, New York. DETR, ca. 1911. P&P,LOT 9150-K,LC-USZ62-68678.

3-102. Crowd gathered around exit when the American evangelist, Billy Sunday (1862–1935), arrived, Pennsylvania Station, New York, New York. Bain News Service, 1917. P&P,LOT 7151,LC-USZ62-84387.

3-103. Waiting room from northwest, Pennsylvania Station, 370 Seventh Avenue, West Thirty-first–Thirty-third streets, New York, New York County, New York. Cervin Robinson, photographer, May 1962. P&P,HABS,NY,31-NEYO,78-6.

An escalator was installed in the middle of the grand staircase down from the retail arcade in the years prior to the demolition, which began late in 1963.

3-104. East (Seventh Avenue) façade, Pennsylvania Station, 370 Seventh Avenue, West Thirty-first Thirty-third streets, New York, New York County, New York. Cervin Robinson, photographer, May 1962. P&P,HABS,NY,31-NEYO,78-2.

In an infamous turn of events, the eagles fronting the top of the main entry pavilion were exiled to the wetland refuse tip in New Jersey during demolition of the station.

3-105. Concourse from southeast, Pennsylvania Station, 370 Seventh Avenue, West Thirty-first–Thirty-third streets, New York, New York County, New York. Cervin Robinson, photographer, April 1962. P&P,HABS,NY,31-NEYO,78-8.

3-103

3-104

3-105

3-106

3-107

3-106. Concourse from south, Pennsylvania Station, 370 Seventh Avenue, West Thirty-first–Thirty-third streets, New York, New York County, New York. Cervin Robinson, photographer, April 1962. P&P,HABS,NY,31-NEYO,78-9.

3-107. Concourse from southwest, Pennsylvania Station, 370 Seventh Avenue, West Thirty-first–Thirty-third streets, New York, New York County, New York. Cervin Robinson, photographer, April 1962. P&P,HABS,NY,31-NEYO,78-10.

3-108. Concourse roof detail, Pennsylvania Station, 370 Seventh Avenue, West Thirty-first—Thirty-third streets, New York, New York County, New York. Edward Popko, photographer, 1965. P&P,HABS,NY,31-NEYO,78-20.

The latticework of the concourse roof lasted until near the end of demolition, as the station fell while Madison Square Garden went up.

3-109. Track level and concourses, Pennsylvania Station, New York, New York. DETR, ca. 1910. P&P,LC-D4-71936.

An Erector Set of pillars and stairways marked the transition from the concourse to the platforms inside New York's Penn Station.

3-110. Shell interlocking tower to southwest, New York, New Haven & Hartford Railroad, shell interlocking tower, New Haven milepost 16, approximately 100 feet east of New Rochelle Junction, New Rochelle, Westchester County, New York. Martin Stupich, photographer, November 1994. P&P,HAER,NY,60-NEWRO,3-5.

The tower building, which dates to 1909, originally boasted highly innovative electrical switching equipment, now long since removed.

3-109

3-110

NEW ENGLAND

The survival of a portion of New England's railroad stations has depended for years on heavy commuter traffic into Boston and New York City, along with Amtrak service between the two cities. As a result, the nature of operations along the Connecticut shoreline and through Rhode Island has been drastically altered from its peak a century or so back. But a good many stations are still in business.

Elsewhere in the region some towns have seen their station buildings converted into restaurants or civic offices. In other cases—most notably the masonry works of H. H. Richardson—the buildings' sheer mass has kept them from being demolished. Instead they are left deserted or with minimal commuter traffic.

In the brief span of the half-dozen years prior to his death in 1886, Richardson drew up plans for nine station buildings for the Boston & Albany Railroad, along with his work for the Old Colony line. The Boston & Albany had long been the major line in the region, formed through a merger in 1867 of two previous railways. By 1900 the B&A itself was pulled into the New York Central

4-001. South Terminal Station, Boston, Massachusetts. DETR, ca. 1899. P&P,LC-D4-11327.

4-002

4-002. Grand Trunk Station, Portland, Maine. DETR, ca. 1906. P&P,LC-D4-17720.

System. In the new century the line shared space in the big cites—with the New Haven Railroad at South Station (1899) in Boston, and with the Boston & Maine Railroad in Worcester's new Union Station (1912).

In other parts of New England the larger stations are long gone. Of all the losses perhaps the most keenly felt was in Providence, Rhode Island, where the city's Union Station of 1899 was severely damaged by fire in 1987. The new station, primarily serving Amtrak, shares little with its predecessor in appearance, instead presenting a Postmodern look.

4-003. Union Station, Portland, Maine. DETR, ca. 1904. P&P,LC-D4-17719.

4-004. Union Station, Portland, Maine. DETR, ca. 1910, P&P,LC-D4-71508.

Only a few fragments of Portland's modified Union Station survive today.

4-003

4-004

4-005

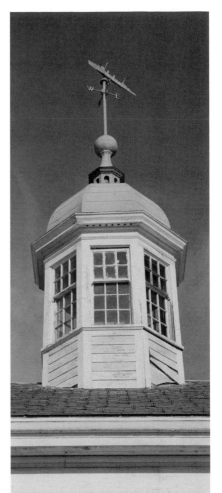

4-007

4-006

4-005. Close-up view of station, Bath Railroad Station, 15 Commercial Street, Bath, Sagadahoc County, Maine. Brian Vanden Brink. P&P,HABS,ME,12-BATH,11-2.

4-006. Northeast view showing roof detail, Bath Railroad Station, 15 Commercial Street, Bath, Sagadahoc County, Maine. Brian Vanden Brink, photographer. P&P,HABS,ME,12-BATH,11-7.

4-007. Cupola as viewed from south at track level, Bath Railroad Station, 15 Commercial Street, Bath, Sagadahoc County, Maine. Brian Vanden Brink, photographer. P&P,HABS,ME,12-BATH,11-9.

The cupola atop the station features a weathervane cut to resemble one of the destroyers that would have been built at the Bath Iron Works, right next door along the riverfront. The station was opened by the Maine Central Railroad in 1941, which cut service to the town in 1959.

4-008. Fertilizer warehouse at the Bangor & Aroostock railroad terminal, Caribou, Maine. Jack Delano, photographer, October 1940. P&P,LC-USF34-042097-D.

4-009. Railroad station in Caribou, Maine. Jack Delano, photographer, October 1940. P&P,LC-USF34-042037-D.

According to notes, this station was referred to as the "greatest potato shipping point in the world."

4-010. Railroad station, Manchester, New Hampshire. DETR, ca. 1910. P&P,LC-D4-72127.

4-011

4-012

4-011. Railway station, North Conway, New Hampshire. Marion Post Wolcott, photographer, March 1940. P&P,LC-USF34-053537-D.

4-012. Railway station, Laconia, New Hampshire. DETR, ca. 1900. P&P,LC-D4-34936.

The broad shed roof and porte cochere marked Bradford Lee Gilbert's (1853–1911) design for this 1892 station in Laconia.

4-013

4-013. The Notch and the railroad station from the window of Crawford House, White Mountains, New Hampshire. DETR, ca. 1906. P&P, LC-D4-12614.

4-014. Railroad station, Randolph, Vermont. Arthur Rothstein/FSA, photographer, September 1937. P&P, LC-USF34-025753-C.

4-014

4-015. Aerial view looking northwest, Providence Union Station, Northeast Corridor Project, Exchange Terrace, Providence, Providence County, Rhode Island. William Edmund Barrett, photographer, 1982–1983. P&P,HABS,RI,4-PROV,177-1.

The Rhode Island State Capitol Building sits on a hilltop behind the site of the original Providence Union Station. An updated rail station was underway when fire destroyed the older station (pictured here), in 1987.

4-016. Aerial view, Providence Station, Northeast Railroad Corridor, Amtrak route between Connecticut and Massachusetts state lines, Providence, Providence County, Rhode Island. Jack Boucher, photographer, April 1987. P&P,HAER,RI,4-PROV,174-16.

4-017

4-017. Main terminal building looking northeast, Providence Union Station, Northeast Corridor Project, Exchange Terrace, Providence, Providence County, Rhode Island. William Edmund Barrett, photographer, 1982–1983. P&P,HABS,RI,4-PROV,177-5.

4-018. Aerial view, Pawtucket Station, Northeast Railroad Corridor, Amtrak route between Connecticut and Massachusetts state lines, Pawtucket, Providence County, Rhode Island. Jack Boucher, photographer, April 1987. P&P,HAER,RI,4-PROV,174-32.

4-018

4-020

4-019

4-019. Close-up of steeple showing weathervane (engine and coal car), Providence & Worcester Railroad Station, 1 Depot Square, Woonsocket, Providence County, Rhode Island. Jack E. Boucher, photographer, July 1969. P&P,HABS,RI,4-WOON,6-3.

The clocks are gone, but the weathervane survives atop Woonsocket's steeple.

4-020. Street façade, Providence & Worcester Railroad Station, 1 Depot Square, Woonsocket, Providence County, Rhode Island. Jack E. Boucher, photographer, July 1969. P&P,HABS,RI,4-WOON,6-1.

4-021. South façade of station showing arcade, eaves details, and ornate parapet, facing northeast, Westerly Station, 14 Railroad Street, Westerly, Washington County, Rhode Island. Robert Brewster, photographer. P&P,HABS,RI,5-WEST,3-2.

Terra cotta ornament crests the arcaded front face of the Westerly Station.

4-021

4-022

4-022. Aerial view, New York, New Haven & Hartford Railroad, New London Station, New London, New London County, Connecticut, Northeast Railroad Corridor, Amtrak Route between New York/Connecticut and Connecticut/Rhode Island state lines, New Haven, New Haven County, Connecticut. Jack E. Boucher, photographer, April 1977. P&P,HAER,CONN,5-NEWHA,37-114.

The railroad station still has pride of place at the waterfront heart of New London.

4-023. Detail of dormer in east end of roof, south façade, New London Railroad Station, State Street Vicinity, New London, New London County, Connecticut. Jack E. Boucher, photographer, April 1973. P&P,HABS,CONN,6-NEWLO,14-10.

For this design, executed late in Richardson's life (the station opened in 1887, the year after his death), he continued to produce novel motifs such as this broad, grouped dormer.

4-024. South façade with passenger shed in foreground, New London Railroad Station, State Street Vic., New London, New London County, Connecticut. Jack E. Boucher, photographer, April 1973. P&P,HABS,CONN,6-NEWLO,14-11.

The thin slits in the otherwise blank brick pediment face recall Richardson's work in stone for such works as the Allegheny County Jail in Pittsburgh. The windows of the lower stories, all trimmed with stone, stretch taller in accordance with the slits above.

4-023

4-024

4-025

4-025. South side, Hartford & New Haven Railroad, Depot, 35 Central Street, Windsor, Hartford County, Connecticut. Leonard Lang, photographer, October 1985. P&P,HAER,CONN,2-WIND,7-A-2.

4-026. Detail of north side, dormer window and roof ventilator, Hartford & New Haven Railroad, Depot, 35 Central Street, Windsor, Hartford County, Connecticut. Leonard Lang, photographer, October 1985. P&P,HAER,CONN,2-WIND,7-A-5.

4-027. Detail of attic, north chimney, Hartford & New Haven Railroad, Depot, 35 Central Street, Windsor, Hartford County, Connecticut. Leonard Lang, photographer, October 1985. P&P,HAER,CONN,2-WIND,7-A-13.

4-026

4-027

4-028. General view, New York, New Haven & Hartford Railroad Station, Railroad Place, Southport, Fairfield County, Connecticut. Jack E. Boucher, photographer, September 1966. P&P,HABS,CONN,1-SOUPO,41-1.

The open woodwork of the Carpenter Gothic vergeboards—elaborately carved overhangs—accentuates the gable ends of the central station building.

4-029. Exterior view, New York, New Haven & Hartford Railroad Station, Stamford, Connecticut. P&P,HABS,CONN,1-NOWA,16-7.

4-030. Detail view from trackside of former pedimented entrance of eastbound station, New York, New Haven & Hartford Railroad, Stamford Station, 44 Station Place, Stamford, Fairfield County, Connecticut. William Edmund Barrett, photographer, 1983. P&P,HAER,CONN,1-STAMF,1-8.

4-031. Three-quarter view of south (street) façade of westbound station, New York, New Haven & Hartford Railroad, Stamford Station, 44 Station Place, Stamford, Fairfield County, Connecticut. William Edmund Barrett, photographer, 1983. P&P,HAER,CONN,1-STAMF,1-13.

4-028

4-029

4-030

4-031

4-032

4-032. South Station and elevated railroad line, Boston, Massachusetts. P&P,LC-USZ62-50045.

First the Atlantic Avenue elevated railway and then the raised interstate highway obscured the curved corner of South Station. Following completion of the "Big Dig" underground highway, the view of the station is once again unmarred.

4-033. Aerial view, South Station, Boston, Northeast Railroad Corridor, Amtrak Route between Rhode Island/Massachusetts state line and South Station, Boston, Suffolk County, Massachusetts. Jack E. Boucher, photographer, April 1973. P&P,HAER,MASS,13-BOST,83-30.

The unusual, curved head house of South Station was designed by the hometown firm of Shepley, Rutan, & Coolidge, inheritors of H. H. Richardson's practice.

4-033

4-034

4-034. North Station, Boston,
Massachusetts. DETR, ca. 1905.
P&P,LC-D4-34097.

4-035. West front, Back Bay Station,
145 Dartmouth Street, Boston, Suffolk
County, Massachusetts. Richard
Cheek, photographer, October 1979.
P&P,HABS,MASS,13-BOST,96-1.

Back Bay Station (1929) marks the point
where the Boston & Providence and the
Boston & Albany lines crossed on their way
into central Boston.

4-035

4-036

4-036. South (street) façade, Boston & Albany Railroad Station, Waverly Street, Framingham, Middlesex County, Massachusetts. Cervin Robinson, photographer, June 1959. P&P,HABS,MASS,9-FRAM,10-1.

Long and low, the Framingham station was the largest one designed by Henry Hobson Richardson for the Boston & Albany Railroad. The architect used arched dormers to serve as clerestory lights to brighten the station interior.

4-037. North (trackside) façade, Boston & Albany Railroad Station, Waverly Street, Framingham, Middlesex County, Massachusetts. Cervin Robinson, photographer, June 1959. P&P,HABS,MASS,9-FRAM,10-2.

4-038. East interior view, Boston & Albany Railroad Station, Waverly Street, Framingham, Middlesex County, Massachusetts. Cervin Robinson, photographer, June 1959. P&P,HABS,MASS,9-FRAM,10-4.

4-039. Fireplace on south interior wall, Boston & Albany Railroad Station, Waverly Street, Framingham, Middlesex County, Massachusetts. Cervin Robinson, photographer, June 1959. P&P,HABS,MASS,9-FRAM,10-5.

4-037

4-038

4-039

4-040

4-041

4-040. Ticket booth and waiting room, Boston & Albany Railroad Station, Palmer, Hampden County, Massachusetts. Cervin Robinson, photographer, June 1959. P&P,HABS,MASS,7-PALM,1-2.

The arched entry portals play off the curvature of the ticket booth to enliven the space inside this boxy waiting room.

4-041. Ticket booth, Boston & Albany Railroad Station, Palmer, Hampden County, Massachusetts. Cervin Robinson, photographer, June 1959. P&P,HABS,MASS,7-PALM,1-4.

4-042. North (trackside) façade, Boston & Albany Railroad Station, Wellesley, Norfolk County, Massachusetts. Cervin Robinson, photographer, June 1959. P&P,HABS,MASS,11-WEL,3-1.

The exterior of Wellesley's Boston & Albany Station made a cameo appearance near the start of the feature film, *Mona Lisa Smiles*.

4-043. Waiting room, Boston & Albany Railroad Station, Wellesley, Norfolk County, Massachusetts. Cervin Robinson, photographer, June 1959. P&P,HABS,MASS,11-WEL,3-2.

4-042

4-043

4-044

4-045

4-044. Boston & Maine Railroad Depot, Riley Plaza, Salem, Massachusetts. DETR, ca. 1910. P&P,LC-D4-39498.

4-045. East waiting room looking toward the ticket office, Auburndale, Massachusetts. Cervin Robinson, photographer, June 1959. P&P,HABS,MASS,9-AUB,1-3.

4-046. Southwest (trackside) façade, Boston & Albany Railroad Station, 1897 Washington Street, Newton, Middlesex County, Massachusetts. Cervin Robinson, photographer, June 1959. P&P,HABS,MASS,9-NEWT,13-2.

4-047. Detail view showing where tracks entered the depot, Lexington & West Cambridge Railroad, Lexington Depot, Depot Square, Lexington, Middlesex County, Massachusetts. Peter Stott, photographer. P&P,HAER,MASS,9-LEX,16-1.

4-048. General exterior view showing side of depot where horses, carriages, pedestrians, etc. arrived, Lexington & West Cambridge Railroad, Lexington Depot, Depot Square, Lexington, Middlesex County, Massachusetts. Peter Stott, photographer. P&P,HAER,MASS,9-LEX,16-3.

The station was one of New England's first, an outpost of the Lexington & West Cambridge Railroad that was chartered in 1845. The station was completed the following year, with full provision to cover the entire train under its shed roof. A fire in 1918 damaged the building but did not affect its configuration. However, the pseudo-colonial decorations were added at that time as part of the repair work.

4-046

4-047

4-048

4-049. Boston & Maine
Railroad Station, Lowell,
Massachusetts. DETR, ca. 1908.
P&P,LC-D401-70429.

4-050. Union Station, Springfield,
Massachusetts. DETR, ca. 1905.
P&P,LC-D4-18055.

4-051

4-051. View from northeast showing clock tower and carriage porch, Boston & Providence Railroad, Stoughton Station, 53 Wyman Street, Stoughton, Norfolk County, Massachusetts. Jet Lowe, photographer, 1982. P&P,HAER,MASS,11-STOU,3-1.

The Stoughton Station, designed by Charles Brigham (1841–1925), dates to 1888.

4-052. West side view, New Haven Railroad Station, Wyman Street, Stoughton, Norfolk County, Massachusetts. George M. Cushing, photographer, May 1969. P&P,HABS,MASS,11-STOU,5-3.

4-053. View of the station which preceded the present station on the same site, Williamstown Railroad Station, North Hoosac Road & Cole Avenue, Williamstown, Berkshire County, Massachusetts. Picturesque Publishing Company, ca. 1893. P&P,HABS,MASS,2-WILL,6-8.

4-054. Railroad station at North Adams, Massachusetts. P&P,LC-USZ62-52624.

4-053

4-054

THE SOUTH

Given its defeat in the Civil War, the South essentially had to start from scratch

afterward to rebuild its railroad infrastructure. As a consequence many of the

major city stations, such as the two home bases for the Louisville & Nashville

line, had a certain gravitas. There was the unmistakable sense that these

buildings were meant to last. Small-town stations, designed mainly to handle

freight as well as crops like cotton and tobacco, were far simpler by comparison.

As a whole the region featured some of the most fanciful stations in the

country. Both the Union Depot (1907) in Mobile, Alabama, and Terminal Station

(1905, demolished) in Atlanta, Georgia, were the work of P. Thornton Mayre

(1872–1935). Twenty years later his firm was engaged in designing the foremost

movie palace in the South, the Atlanta Fox (colorfully nicknamed Mecca on

Peachtree Street). Both Savannah, Georgia, and Charleston, South Carolina, had

festive stations of their own, but neither remains standing.

The most ornate survivor in the southern states is Richmond's Main Street

Station (1901). Its exterior encrusted with decorative flourishes, the station

5-001. High Bridge Station, High Bridge, Kentucky. Photographer unknown/DETR, ca. 1907. P&P, LC-D4-19980.

5-002

reaches a crescendo at its roofline. Its steep pitch has rows of dormers and is anchored at its southwest corner by a tower with four illuminated clock faces.

Only slightly less elaborate is the Seaboard Airline Railway Station (1925) in West Palm Beach, Florida. Architect L. Phillips Clarke (1866–1957) gave the building a Spanish Baroque treatment, considered suitable for Florida's Mediterranean climate. An over-scaled fireplace (echoed in Orson Welles' film, *Citizen Kane*) fills a wall inside what was originally a "whites only" waiting room. The fireplace might have fit equally well in the living room of one of the railway stockholders, whose winter homes were located not far from the station.

5-003. View from north, Main Street Station, 1520 East Main Street, Richmond, Independent City, Virginia. P&P,HABS,VA,44-RICH,97-1.

5-004. View of street front from southwest, Main Street Station, 1520 East Main Street, Richmond, Independent City, Virginia. Jack E. Boucher, photographer, April 1971. P&P,HABS,VA,44-RICH,97-10.

The Seaboard Airline Railroad combined with the Chesapeake & Ohio Railroad to open this station in 1901, to the glorious designs of the Philadelphia firm of Wilson, Harris, & Richards. The station still has limited train service, though it has been crowded a bit for decades from an elevated portion of Interstate 95. From the highway's northbound lanes the nearest of the clock tower's four 6-foot-diameter clock faces seems almost within reach.

5-005

5-006

5-007

5-008

5-005. Main Street Station, Richmond, Virginia. DETR, ca. 1910. P&P,LC-D4-36645.

An early view of the station shows elevated tracks along its eastern flank where the interstate now runs. (In all cases the elevation of routes was a precautionary measure in light of periodic flooding of the James River nearby.)

5-006. Eastern trackside façade, Main Street Station, 1520 East Main Street, Richmond, Independent City, Virginia. P&P,HABS,VA,44-RICH,97-3.

5-007. Bales of cotton on railroad station platform, Aiken, South Carolina. P&P,LC-USZ62-48540.

5-008. Railroad station and wharf in City Point, now Hopewell, Virginia. Andrew J. Russell, photographer, ca. 1861. P&P,LOT 11486-B,no. 9,LC-DIG-ppmsca-08248.

5-009

5-009. Railroad station
with clock tower, Newport
News, Virginia. Unidentified
photographer, ca. 1910.
P&P,LC-USZ62-113355.

5-010. Chesapeake & Ohio
Railway Company station
and terminal, Newport News,
Virginia. DETR, ca. 1910.
P&P,LC-D4-33813.

5-010

5-011

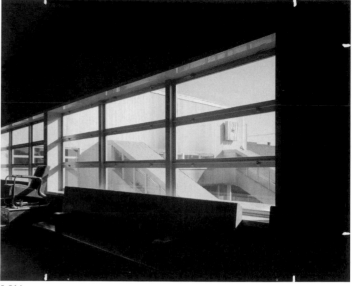

5-014

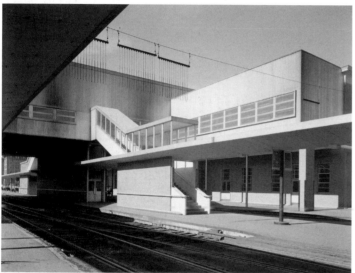

5-012

5-013

5-011. Portico, Roanoke station of the Virginia & Western Railroad, Roanoke, Virginia. Gottscho-Schleisner, Incorporated, February 1950. P&P,LC-G613-56518,LC-G613-T-56518.

The modernistic look of the station in Roanoke was the product of an updating of a 1905 structure carried out between 1947 and 1949 by the firm of Raymond Loewy Associates. The Western Virginia Foundation for the Arts and Sciences purchased the building in 2000 as a museum venue.

5-012. Stairway II, Roanoke station of the Virginia & Western Railroad, Roanoke, Virginia. Gottscho-Schleisner, Incorporated, February 1950. P&P, LC-G613-56520,LC-G613-T-56520.

5-013. East façade and tracks, Roanoke station of the Virginia & Western Railroad, Roanoke, Virginia. Gottscho-Schleisner, Incorporated, February 1950. P&P,LC-G613-56514,LC-G613-T-56514.

5-014. Window to tracks, Roanoke station of the Virginia & Western Railroad, Roanoke, Virginia. Gottscho-Schleisner, Incorporated, February 1950. P&P, LC-G613-56526,LC-G613-T-56526.

5-015

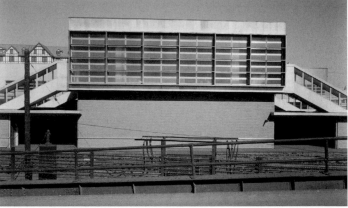

5-016

5-015. West side of concourse, Roanoke station of the Virginia & Western Railroad, Roanoke, Virginia. Gottscho-Schleisner, Incorporated, February 1950. P&P,LC-G613-56534,LC-G613-T-56534.

5-016. Waiting room view to tracks, Roanoke station of the Virginia & Western Railroad, Roanoke, Virginia. Gottscho-Schleisner, Incorporated, February 1950, P&P,LC-G613-56538,LC-G613-T-56538.

5-017. General view, Roanoke station of the Virginia & Western Railroad, Roanoke, Virginia. Gottscho-Schleisner, Incorporated, February 1950. P&P,LC-G613-56517,LC-G613-T-56517.

5-017

5-018. Map and ticket counter, Roanoke station of the Virginia & Western Railroad, Roanoke, Virginia. Gottscho-Schleisner, Incorporated, February 1950. P&P,LC-G613-56532,LC-G613-T-56532.

5-018

5-019

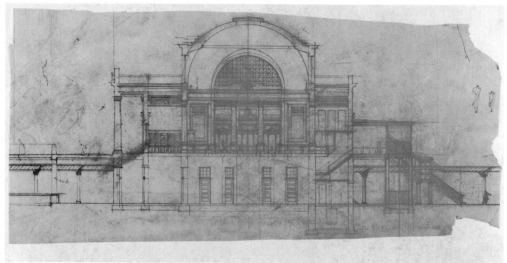

5-020

5-022

5-019. Railroad station, Charlottesville, Virginia. Waddy B. Wood, photographer, ca. 1916. P&P,PAN US GEOG-Virginia no. 47 (E size),LC-USZ62-125528.

5-020. Section, Southern Railway Building, University Street, Charlottesville, Virginia. Waddy B. Wood, artist, 1916. P&P,ADE-UNIT 1111,no. 29 (A size),LC-USZ62-113960.

The main floor of the station building housed a ticket booth and segregated waiting rooms.

5-021. Union Depot, Norfolk, Virginia. DETR, ca. 1910. P&P,LC-D4-73113.

5-022. Passenger depot, Southern Railway Company, Chatham, Virginia. P&P,LC-USZ62-65320.

5-023

5-023. Southern Railway Station, Asheville, North Carolina. P&P,LC-USZ62-56937.

5-024. Union Station, Newton, North Carolina. P&P,LC-USZ62-65316.

5-025. Union Station, Charleston, South Carolina. Irving Underhill, photographer, ca. 1910. P&P,U.S. GEOG FILE,LC-USZ62-61271.

5-026. Southern Railway Station, Greenville, South Carolina. P&P,LC-USZ62-61263.

5-024

5-025

5-026

5-027

5-028

5-027. North and west sides, East Bay–Seaboard Airline, Railway Freight Station, 55 East Bay Street, Charleston, Charleston County, South Carolina. Charles N. Bayless, photographer. P&P,HABS,SC,10-CHAR,331A-4.

5-028. General view, East Bay–Seaboard Airline, Railroad Freight Station, 55 East Bay Street, Charleston, Charleston County, South Carolina. P&P,HABS,SC,10-CHAR,331A-1.

5-029. General view, South Carolina Railroad–Southern Railway Company, Camden Depot, Anne Street, Charleston, Charleston County, South Carolina. Charles N. Bayless, photographer. P&P,HABS,SC,10-CHAR,330A-2.

5-030. Northeast entry pier, South Carolina Railroad–Southern Railway Company, Camden Depot, Anne Street, Charleston, Charleston County, South Carolina. Charles N. Bayless, photographer. P&P,HABS,SC,10-CHAR,330A-4.

5-029

5-030

5-031. Trackside view, Southern Railway Combined Depot, west side of Belton Public Square, Belton, Anderson County, South Carolina. Jack Boucher, photographer, March 1967. P&P,HABS,SC,4-BELT,1A-2.

A Southern Railway staff architect designed this station for the town of Belton, which was a booming place when the building opened around 1910.

5-032. Seaboard Railroad Passenger Station, Darlington, South Carolina. P&P,LC-USZ62-65318.

5-034

5-035

5-036

5-033. Panorama of Nashville terminal, Nashville, Tennessee. H. O. Fuller, photographer, ca. 1905. P&P,PAN US GEOG-Tennessee no. 7 (E size),LC-USZ62-125536.

5-034. Detail, west front entrance, Union Station, 1001 Broadway, Nashville, Davidson County, Tennessee. Jack E. Boucher, photographer, August 1970. P&P,HABS,TENN,19-NASH,19-8.

The exterior of the building, with its heavy Richardsonian Romanesque flavor, was built of Tennessee limestone.

5-035. Detail, fireplace on south wall, Union Station, 1001 Broadway, Nashville, Davidson County, Tennessee. Jack E. Boucher, photographer, August 1970. P&P,HABS,TENN,19-NASH,19-12.

5-036. Detail, ornamental stonework, column and pier capitals, west front entrance, Union Station, 1001 Broadway, Nashville, Davidson County, Tennessee. Jack E. Boucher, photographer, August 1970. P&P, HABS,TENN,19-NASH,19-9.

5-037

5-038

5-037. West front, Union Station, 1001 Broadway, Nashville, Davidson County, Tennessee. Jack E. Boucher, photographer, August 1970. P&P,HABS,TENN,19-NASH,19-2.

5-038. Interior, Union Station, 1001 Broadway, Nashville, Davidson County, Tennessee. Jack E. Boucher, photographer, August 1970. P&P,HABS,TENN,19-NASH, 19-11

The main waiting room featured a barrel vault filled with "art glass" panels along its 125-foot length, as well as a pair of ornate marble fireplaces.

5-039. East side, detail, Union Station, 1001 Broadway, Nashville, Davidson County, Tennessee. Jack E. Boucher, photographer, August 1970. P&P,HABS,TENN,19-NASH,19-5.

5-039

5-040

5-041

5-042

5-040. Union Station, Nashville, Tennessee. DETR, ca. 1900. P&P,LC-D4-13559.

Richard Montfort (1854–1921), Chief Engineer for the Louisville & Nashville Railroad, was the architect of record for Nashville's Union Station of 1900. The Union Station head house is 150 feet square and fronted by a 220-foot tower. The tower originally stood twenty feet taller, capped by a bronze statue of Mercury (who apparently fell from grace in the 1950s).

5-041. Train shed from west, Union Station, 1001 Broadway, Nashville, Davidson County, Tennessee. Jack E. Boucher, photographer, August 1970. P&P,HABS,TENN,19-NASH,19-16.

5-042. Detail, bas-relief of "The General," Union Station, 1001 Broadway, Nashville, Davidson County, Tennessee. Jack E. Boucher, photographer, August 1970. P&P,HABS,TENN,19-NASH,19-13.

According to the *Nashville American*, written on opening day, October 9, 1900, this panel depicts "the '1900 Limited,' a full vestibuled passenger train, with the Nashville & Chattanooga bully engine, No. 108, at the head, which annihilates space and enables Nashville to shake hands with Louisville."

5-043

5-043. Southern Railway Station,
Knoxville, Tennessee. DETR, ca. 1906.
P&P, LC-D4-16408.

5-044. Union Station, Memphis, Tennessee.
DETR, ca. 1900. P&P, LC-D4-39528.

5-044

5-045

5-045. New terminal building, Chattanooga, Tennessee. DETR, ca. 1905. P&P,LC-D4-71773.

In 1973 the great domed waiting room of the 1909 Chattanooga Terminal Station became the restaurant for the adjoining Chattanooga Choo-Choo Hilton Inn.

5-046. Aerial view of station, Louisville & Nashville Railroad, Union Station, 1000 West Broadway, Louisville, Jefferson County, Kentucky. Louisville & Nashville Railroad Company/Family Lines Rail System Archives. P&P,HABS,KY,56-LOUVI,23-12.

Six tracks ran beneath the original 450-foot-long train shed.

5-046

5-047

5-048

5-049

5-047. North (front) façade, Louisville & Nashville Railroad. Union Station, 1000 West Broadway, Louisville, Jefferson County, Kentucky. Jack Boucher, photographer, 1979. P&P,HABS,KY,56-LOUVI,23-1.

The limestone exterior of Louisville's Union Station of 1891 was as churchlike as any, with its four corner towers and east-facing rose window. There was even stained glass in the transom windows of the train shed.

5-048. Waiting room from southeast, Louisville & Nashville Railroad, Union Station, 1000 West Broadway, Louisville, Jefferson County, Kentucky. Jack Boucher, photographer, 1979. P&P,HABS,KY,56-LOUVI,23-9.

The architect, English-born F. W. Mowbray (b. 1848), arrived in Philadelphia in 1872 at age twenty-four and set to work on buildings for that city's Centennial Exposition held in 1876.

5-049. Second floor, west wall, Louisville & Nashville Railroad, Union Station, 1000 West Broadway, Louisville, Jefferson County, Kentucky. Jack Boucher, photographer, 1979. P&P,HABS,KY,56-LOUVI,23-10.

5-050

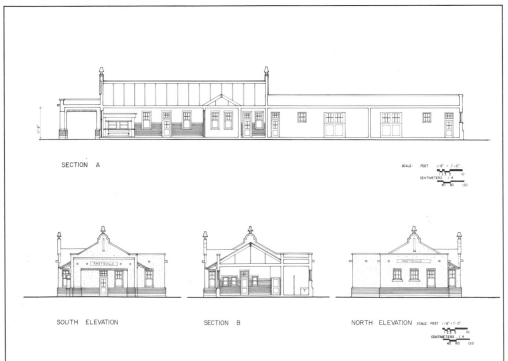

SECTION A

SCALE: FEET 1/8" = 1'-0"
CENTIMETERS 1:4

SOUTH ELEVATION

SECTION B

NORTH ELEVATION SCALE: FEET 1/8" = 1'-0"
CENTIMETERS 1:4

5-051

5-050. New Union Station, Little Rock, Arkansas. DETR, ca. 1905. P&P,LC-D4-71733.

This was the second station on the site, designed by architect Theodore C. Link. The clock tower and front arcade were all that survived a fire in 1920, but both elements were incorporated into the current station building, which opened one year later.

5-051. Elevations and sections, Old Frisco Depot, 550 West Dickson, Fayetteville, Washington County, Arkansas. Paul N. Gajda, delineator, 1995. P&P,no. 4.

5-052. Little Rock & Hot Springs Western
Railroad Depot, Hot Springs, Arkansas.
DETR, ca. 1900. P&P,LC-D4-13148.

5-053. Terminal station, New Orleans,
Louisiana. DETR, ca. 1910. P&P,LC-D4-
72898.

Grand to look at, the Terminal Station
opened in 1908 with a total of four tracks.

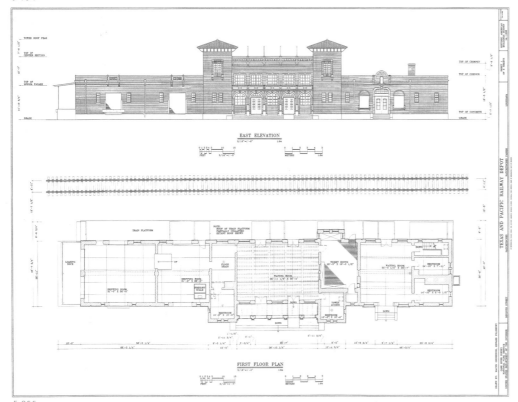

5-054. Close view of front façade, central section to show entrance, with scale, Texas & Pacific Railway Depot, Seventh Street, Natchitoches Parish, Louisiana. Jack E. Boucher, photographer. P&P,HABS,LA-1296-2.

5-055. East elevation and first floor plan, Texas & Pacific Railway Depot, Seventh Street, Natchitoches, Natchitoches Parish, Louisiana. P&P,sheet no. 1.

5-056

5-056. Train standing in depot, Biloxi, Mississippi. P&P,LC-USZ62-93736.

5-057. Railroad station, Mound Bayou, Mississippi. Russell Lee, photographer, January 1939. P&P,LC-USF33-011972-M3.

The Yazoo & Mississippi Valley Line was a major connector through the state.

5-058. Railroad station at Tupelo, Mississippi. Arthur Rothstein, photographer, August 1935. P&P,LC-USF33-002055,LC-USF33-T01-002055-M3.

5-059. Trackside view, Railroad Terminal, 200 Broadway Street, Natchez, Adams County, Mississippi. Jack E. Boucher, photographer, April 1972. P&P,HABS,MISS, 1-NATCH,31-1.

The terminal opened early in the twentieth century as a station on the Yazoo & Mississippi Valley Line.

5-057

5-058

5-059

5-060

5-060. East front, The Depot, 274 Van Dorn Avenue, Holly Springs, Marshall County, Mississippi. Jack E. Boucher, photographer, March 1975. P&P,HABS,MISS,47-HOLSP,4-1.

The Holly Springs Depot dates to 1858, but the bulk of the combined rail station and guesthouse was added about twenty years after the end of the Civil War.

5-061. Northeast façade, Aberdeen Station, Aberdeen, Mississippi. David J. Kaminsky, photographer, August 1978. P&P,HABS,MISS,48-ABDE,12-5.

5-062. Southwest façade, door to baggage room Aberdeen Station, Aberdeen, Mississippi. David J. Kaminsky, photographer, August 1978. P&P,HABS,MISS,48-ABDE,12-7.

Out of service for decades, this depot in Aberdeen seems lost in time.

5-061

5-062

5-063. Trackside view, Southern Railway Depot, 1905 Alabama Avenue, Bessemer, Jefferson County, Alabama. Jet Lowe, photographer, 1993. P&P,HABS,ALA,37-BES,1-1.

5-064. Oblique view of front façade with principal passenger entrance, Louisville & Nashville Railroad Depot, 301 Greensboro Avenue, Tuscaloosa, Tuscaloosa County, Alabama. Jet Lowe, photographer, 1993. P&P,HABS,ALA,63-TUSLO,25-1.

For thirty years this station served train passengers, followed by a quarter-century as a bus depot. The new owners serve meals, according to this photograph.

5-065. Interior view looking north, Union Station, Water Street, Montgomery, Montgomery County, Alabama. Jack Boucher, photographer, 1974. P&P,HAER,ALA,51-MONG,24-1.

5-063

5-064

5-065

5-066

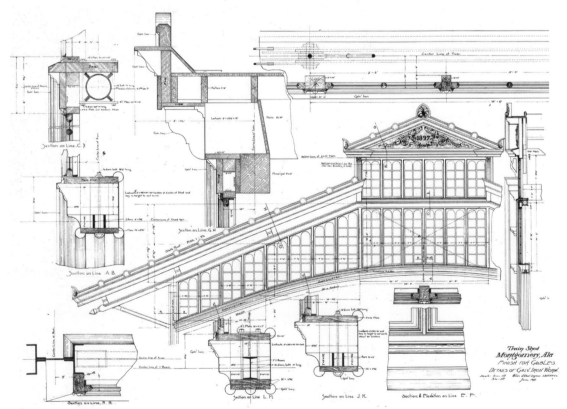

5-067

5-066. Postcard view looking
northwest, Louisville & Nashville
Railroad, Union Station train shed,
Water Street, opposite Lee Street,
Montgomery, Montgomery County,
Alabama. Alabama Archives,
ca. 1915. P&P,HAER,ALA,51-
MONG,23A-16.

5-067. Architectural drawings for
"Finish for Gables, Details of Galv.
Iron Work," Louisville & Nashville
Railroad, Union Station train shed,
Water Street, opposite Lee Street,
Montgomery, Montgomery County,
Alabama. Office of Chief Engineer,
Louisville & Nashville Railroad,
June 1897. P&P,HAER,ALA,51-
MONG,23A-18.

5-068. Street elevation and first floor plan, Union Station, Water Street, Montgomery, Montgomery County, Alabama. Original architect's drawing, 1896. P&P,HAER,ALA,51-MONG,24-10.

5-069. Detail view, Louisville & Nashville Railroad, Union Station train shed, Water Street, opposite Lee Street, Montgomery, Montgomery County, Alabama. Jack Boucher, photographer, April 1974. P&P,HAER,ALA,51-MONG,23A-5.

5-070. Section of train shed showing truss structure, Louisville & Nashville Railroad, Union Station train shed, Water Street, opposite Lee Street, Montgomery, Montgomery County, Alabama. Office of Chief Engineer, Louisville & Nashville Railroad, May 1896. P&P,HAER,ALA,51-MONG,23A-17.

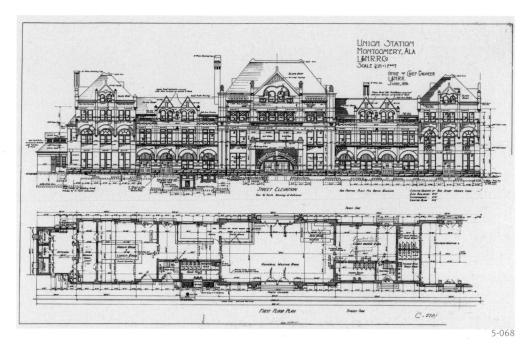

5-068

5-069

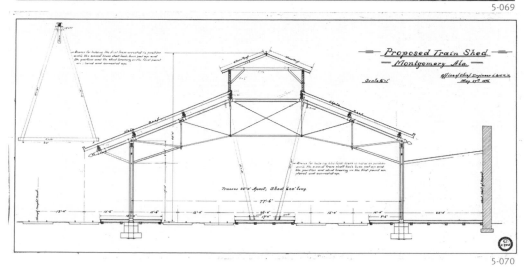

5-070

5-071

5-072

5-071. Southeast façade, Union Station, Water Street, Montgomery, Montgomery County, Alabama. Jack Boucher, photographer, 1974. P&P, HAER, ALA, 51-MONG, 24-6.

5-072. Southeast façade, Union Station, Water Street, Montgomery, Montgomery County, Alabama. Alabama Archives and Historical Commission. P&P, HAER, ALA, 51-MONG, 24-9.

Somewhere along the way Montgomery's polychrome exterior got a whitewash and its train shed became an oversize carport, used as parking for special occasions in the district.

5-073

5-073. South façade, Gulf, Mobile & Ohio Railroad, Passenger Terminal, Beauregard Street & Telegraph Road, Mobile, Mobile County, Alabama. Ray Thigpen, photographer, July 1966. P&P,HABSALA,49-MOBI, 128A-1.

5-074. Decoration above entrance, Gulf, Mobile & Ohio Railroad, Passenger Terminal, Beauregard Street & Telegraph Road, Mobile, Mobile County, Alabama. Ray Thigpen, photographer, July 1966. P&P,HABS,ALA,49-MOBI,128A-2.

Mobile's terminal features a rich Spanish Colonial treatment, visible all along the main façade above its front arcade.

5-074

5-075

5-078

5-079

5-075. East (front) façade
and main entrance, Seaboard
Airline Railway Station, Datura
Street & Tamarind Avenue,
Palm Beach, Palm Beach
County, Florida. Jack E. Boucher,
photographer, April 1972.
P&P,HABS,FLA,50-PALM,3-1.

The principal Seaboard Airline
stockholders, if not the railway
itself, were based in West Palm
Beach. Architect L. Phillips
Clarke designed all three dozen
or so of the line's stations in
Florida.

5-076

5-076. West façade, trackside, Seaboard Airline Railway Station, Datura Street & Tamarind Avenue, Palm Beach, Palm Beach County, Florida. Jack E. Boucher, photographer, April 1972. P&P,HABS,FLA,50-PALM, 3-8.

5-077. East (front) passenger entrance, Seaboard Airline Railway Station, Datura Street & Tamarind Avenue, Palm Beach, Palm Beach County, Florida. Jack E. Boucher, photographer, April 1972. P&P,HABS,FLA,50-PALM,3-4.

5-078. [opposite page] View through entrance porch and loggia, Seaboard Airline Railway Station, Datura Street & Tamarind Avenue, Palm Beach, Palm Beach County, Florida. Jack E. Boucher, photographer, April 1972. P&P,HABS,FLA,50-PALM,3-6.

5-079. [opposite page] Fireplace, north waiting room, Seaboard Airline Railway Station, Datura Street & Tamarind Avenue, Palm Beach, Palm Beach County, Florida. Jack E. Boucher, photographer, April 1972. P&P,HABS,FLA,50-PALM,3-14.

5-077

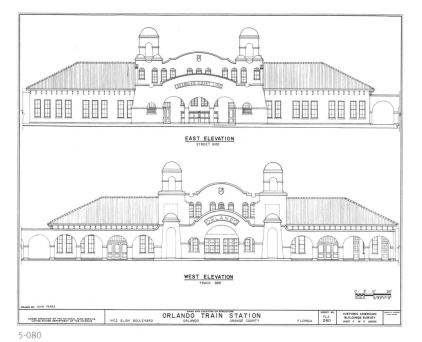

5-080

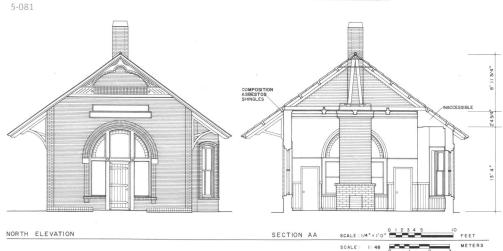

5-081

5-080. East and west elevations, Atlantic Coast Line Railroad Station, 1402 Sligh Boulevard, Orlando, Orange County, Florida. Unidentified delineator, 1972. P&P, sheet no. 4.

5-081. Arcade plan and elevations, Atlantic Coast Line Railroad Station, 1402 Sligh Boulevard, Orlando, Orange County, Florida. Unidentified delineator 1972. P&P, sheet no. 5.

Architect M. A. Griffith designed the Orlando station in 1926.

5-082. Elevation and section, Old Fernandina Depot, 100 Atlantic Avenue, Fernandina Beach, Nassau County, Florida. P&P, sheet no. 4.

After fire destroyed the previous waterfront station and its wharf, this depot was constructed on the other side of the tracks, mostly of brick. The depot sits at the foot of this Victorian-filled resort town on Amelia Island.

5-082

5-083. East Coast Railway Station,
New Smyrna, Florida. DETR, ca. 1904.
P&P,LC-D4-17637.

5-084. Louisville & Nashville Railway
Station, Pensacola, Florida. DETR, ca. 1900.
P&P,LC-D4-71814.

The station was replaced by a more
substantial, if less fanciful, one in 1913.

5-083

5-084

5-085

5-086

5-087

5-085. Main façade from southeast, San Juan Railroad Terminal, Calle Commercio & Calle Harding, San Juan, San Juan County, Puerto Rico. Jack E. Boucher, photographer, January 1967. P&P,HABS,PR,7-SAJU,34-1.

5-086. Clock and tower, San Juan Railroad Terminal, Calle Commercio & Calle Harding, San Juan, San Juan County, Puerto Rico. Jack E. Boucher, photographer, January 1967. P&P,HABS,PR,7-SAJU,34-5.

This terminal saw the end of its railroad business in 1946 and later served as the base for a trucking company.

5-087. South front detail, entry gate, San Juan Railroad Terminal, Calle Commercio & Calle Harding, San Juan, San Juan County, Puerto Rico. Jack E. Boucher, photographer, January 1967. P&P,HABS,PR,7-SAJU,34-2.

5-088

5-088. Terminal Station, Atlanta, Georgia.
P&P,LC-USZ62-61261.

The Terminal Station came down in stages.
First it lost its towers, then its trains in 1970,
and soon thereafter it was gone.

5-089. Union Depot and West Broad Street,
Savannah, Georgia. P&P,LC-USZ62-61262.

5-089

5-090

5-091

5-092

5-090. Railroad depot, Valdosta, Georgia. P&P,LC-USZ62-63809.

5-091. South front and east side, Plains Depot, Hudson & Main streets, Plains, Sumter County, Georgia. Mark Harrell, photographer, July 1989. P&P,HABS,GA,131-PLAIN,15-2.

5-092. Interior, north wall, warehouse section (museum), Plains Depot, Hudson & Main streets, Plains, Sumter County, Georgia. Mark Harrell, photographer, July 1989. P&P,HABS,GA,131-PLAIN,15-9.

The depot gained national fame in 1976 when it served as local headquarters for Jimmy Carter's successful campaign for the U.S. presidency.

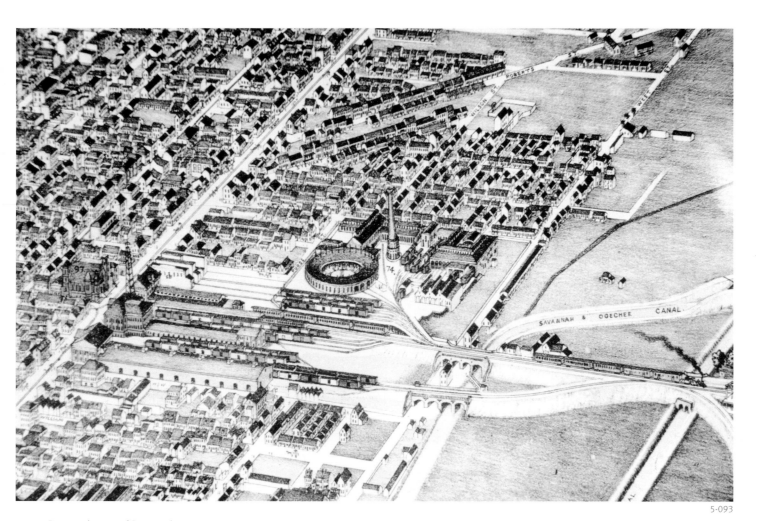

5-093. Panoramic map of Savannah, Georgia, 1891, showing Savannah Repair Shops, Central of Georgia Railway, Savannah Repair Shops & Terminal Facilities, bounded by West Broad, Jones, West Boundary, & Hull streets, Savannah, Chatham County, Georgia. Augustus Koch/Morning News Lithograph, 1891. P&P,HAER,GA,26-SAV,55-2.

CENTRAL OF GEORGIA RAILROAD FACILITIES, SAVANNAH, GEORGIA

This was one set of southern railroad properties, partially built at the time, that Sherman and his armies neglected to flatten on his March to the Sea; yet it still almost did not survive. The head house for the passenger station and the train shed were both begun before the Civil War. The shed, with its famously original tricomposite trusses (of wood, cast iron, and wrought iron), was designed by engineer Augustus Schwab and completed in 1861. The head house remained uncompleted through the war and was virtually deserted by 1874, when the decision was made to salvage it. Salvaging was completed in 1876.

The rest of this National Historic Landmark grouping includes a cotton yard to the north of the passenger station and the railway company headquarters building, as well as a roundhouse with machine shop and locomotive turntable. The great exclamation point for the facilities is a combination smokestack, water tank, and privies. The capacity of the water tank is 400,000 gallons, which must have occasioned more than a few jokes from those making use of the facilities just below.

5-094

5-095

5-094. East front and side to shed,
Central of Georgia Railway, passenger
station & train shed, corner of Louisville
(Railroad) Road & West Broad Street,
Savannah, Chatham County, Georgia. Jack
Boucher, photographer, August 1974.
P&P,HAER,GA,28-SAV,56-4.

5-095. Inscription on portico, Central of
Georgia Railroad, Gray Building, 227 West
Broad Street, Savannah, Chatham County,
Georgia. Louis Schwartz, photographer,
August 1962. P&P,HABS,GA,26-SAV,57A-4.

5-096. South half of gate showing brick detailing, Central of Georgia Railway, cotton yard gates, West Broad Street, Savannah, Chatham County, Georgia. Jack Boucher, photographer, August 1976. P&P,HAER,GA, 26-SAV,59-4.

5-097. View looking down length of Wickersham fence with passenger station in background, Central of Georgia Railway, cotton yard gates, West Broad Street, Savannah, Chatham County, Georgia. Jack Boucher, photographer, August 1976. P&P,HAER,GA, 26-SAV,59-7.

5-098. South half of cotton yard gates, Wickersham fence running parallel to West Broad Street, passenger station in background, Central of Georgia Railway, cotton yard gates, West Broad Street, Savannah, Chatham County, Georgia. Jack Boucher, photographer, August 1976. P&P,HAER,GA,26-SAV,59-3.

5-099. Juncture of head house and train shed, Central of Georgia Railway, passenger station & train shed, corner of Louisville (Railroad) Road & West Broad Street, Savannah, Chatham County, Georgia. Jack Boucher, photographer, August 1974. P&P,HAER,GA,26-SAV,56-8.

5-100. Looking out of train shed through arched opening, Central of Georgia Railway, passenger station and train shed, corner of Louisville (Railroad) Road & West Broad Street, Savannah, Chatham County, Georgia. Jack Boucher, photographer, August 1974. P&P,HAER,GA,26-SAV,56-13.

5-101. Detail of arched opening of train shed, Central of Georgia Railway, passenger station & train shed, corner of Louisville (Railroad) Road & West Broad Street, Savannah, Chatham County, Georgia. Jack Boucher, photographer, August 1974. P&P,HAER,GA,26-SAV,56-16.

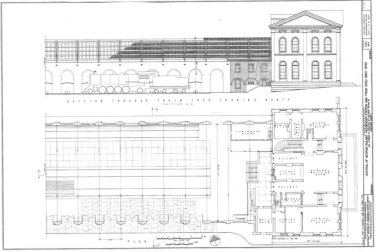

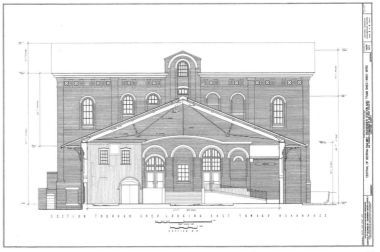

5-102. Detail of truss and wall intersection, Central of Georgia Railway, passenger station & train shed, corner of Louisville (Railroad) Road & West Broad Street, Savannah, Chatham County, Georgia. Jack Boucher, photographer, August 1974. P&P,HAER,GA,26-SAV,56-22.

One of engineer Augustus Schwab's tricomposite trusses is clearly visible below the roofline.

5-103. Interior, south wall, Central of Georgia Railroad, passenger station & train shed, Corner of Louisville (Railroad) Road & West Broad Street, Savannah, Chatham County, Georgia. Jack Boucher, photographer, August 1974. P&P,HABS,GA,26-SAV,56-3.

5-104. Section and plan, Central of Georgia Railway, passenger station & train shed, corner of Louisville (Railroad) Road & West Broad Street, Savannah, Chatham County, Georgia. P&P,sheet no. 1.

5-105. Section/elevation, Central of Georgia Railway, passenger station & train shed, corner of Louisville (Railroad) Road & West Broad Street, Savannah, Chatham County, Georgia. P&P,sheet no. 5.

5-106

5-107

5-106. Roundhouse with gable end of machine shop and smokestack in background, Central of Georgia Railway, Savannah Repair Shops & Terminal Facilities, machine shop, bounded by West Broad, Jones, West Boundary, & Hull streets, Savannah, Chatham County, Georgia. Jack Boucher, photographer, August 1976. P&P,HAER,GA,26-SAV,55A-2.

5-107. View from roundhouse roof showing remains of gable (north) end and clerestory monitor of machine shop, Central of Georgia Railway, Savannah Repair Shops & Terminal Facilities, machine shop, bounded by West Broad, Jones, West Boundary, & Hull streets, Savannah, Chatham County, Georgia. Jack Boucher, photographer, August 1976. P&P,HAER,GA,26-SAV,55B-1.

5-108. Low-level bird's-eye view looking southwest at the Savannah Repair Shops, Central of Georgia Railway, Savannah Repair Shops & Terminal Facilities, bounded by West Broad, Jones, West Boundary, & Hull streets, Savannah, Chatham County, Georgia. Jack Boucher, August 1976. P&P,HAER,GA,26-SAV,55-1.

5-109. Central of Georgia Railroad docks #2, Savannah, Georgia. Haines Photo Company, ca. 1909. P&P,PAN US GEOG-Georgia no. 16 (E size).

5-110. Detail view of electric motor that drove turntable, Central of Georgia Railway, Savannah Repair Shops & Terminal Facilities, machine shop, bounded by West Broad, Jones, West Boundary, & Hull streets, Savannah, Chatham County, Georgia. Jack Boucher, photographer, August 1976. P&P,HAER,GA,26-SAV,55A-15.

5-111. Eastern segment of roundhouse looking straight on locomotive smoke flue, Central of Georgia Railway, Savannah Repair Shops & Terminal Facilities, machine shop, bounded by West Broad, Jones, West Boundary, & Hull streets, Savannah, Chatham County, Georgia. Jack Boucher, photographer, August 1976. P&P,HAER,GA,26-SAV,55A-20.

5-110

5-111

5-112. Looking down on locomotive turntable, Central of Georgia Railway, Savannah Repair Shops & Terminal Facilities, machine shop, bounded by West Broad, Jones, West Boundary, & Hull streets, Savannah, Chatham County, Georgia. Jack Boucher, photographer, August 1976. P&P,HAER,GA,26-SAV,55A-11.

5-113. Locomotive turntable, Central of Georgia Railway, Savannah Repair Shops & Terminal Facilities, machine shop, bounded by West Broad, Jones, West Boundary, & Hull streets, Savannah, Chatham County, Georgia. Jack Boucher, photographer, August 1976. P&P,HAER,GA,26-SAV,55A-13.

5-114

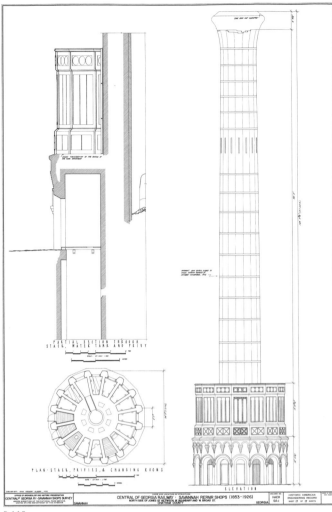

5-115

5-116

5-114. View east to combination smokestack, water tank, and privies, Central of Georgia Railway, Savannah Repair Shops & Terminal Facilities, combination smokestack, water tank, & privies, bounded by West Broad, Jones, West Boundary, & Hull streets, Savannah, Chatham County, Georgia. Jack Boucher, photographer, August 1976. P&P,HAER,GA,26-SAV,55F-1.

5-115. Elevation and details of smokestack, Central of Georgia Railway, Savannah Repair Shops & Terminal Facilities, bounded by West Broad, Jones, West Boundary, & Hull streets, Savannah, Chatham County, Georgia. P&P,sheet no. 17.

5-116. Base of smokestack showing brick privies and cast-iron water tank, Central of Georgia Railway, Savannah Repair Shops & Terminal Facilities, combination smokestack, water tank, & privies, bounded by West Broad, Jones, West Boundary, & Hull streets, Savannah, Chatham County, Georgia. Jack Boucher, photographer, August 1976. P&P,HAER,GA,26-SAV,55F-3.

5-117. Site plan, Savannah Shops Survey, Central of Georgia Railway, Savannah Repair Shops & Terminal Facilities, bounded by West Broad, Jones, West Boundary, & Hull streets, Savannah, Chatham County, Georgia. P&P, sheet no. 1.

5-118. Elevation of machine shop and smokestack, Central of Georgia Railway, Savannah Repair Shops & Terminal Facilities, bounded by West Broad, Jones, West Boundary & Hull streets, Savannah, Chatham County, Georgia. P&P, sheet no. 12.

5-119. Site plan, Central of Georgia Railway, Savannah Repair Shops & Terminal Facilities, bounded by West Broad, Jones, West Boundary, & Hull Streets, Savannah, Chatham County, Georgia. P&P, sheet no. 2.

5-120. Roundtable plan, Central of Georgia Railway, Savannah Repair Shops & Terminal Facilities, bounded by West Broad, Jones, West Boundary, & Hull streets, Savannah, Chatham County, Georgia. P&P, sheet no. 4.

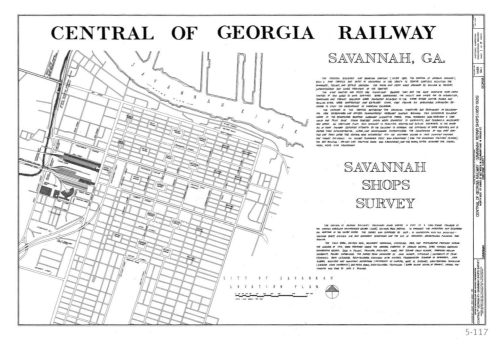

5-117

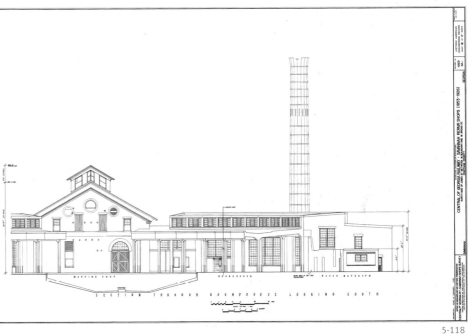

5-118

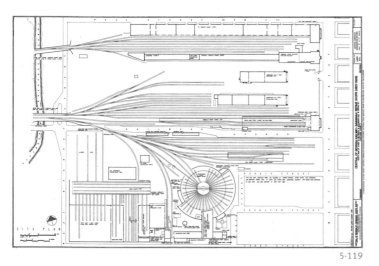

5-119

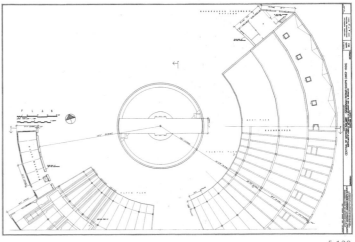

5-120

THE MIDWEST

This region—home to some of the world's great navigable interior waterways—has also been where many of our nation's major railways have crossed and met. Even given Baltimore's pride of place in railroad history, nowhere are the tracks more concentrated than in the Midwest. For all the fame attached to the magnificent train terminals of America's East and West coasts, the nation's hub remains Chicago. At one point nearly two dozen railroad companies operated trains through Chicago. At present, however, only two of the city's major rail stations, Dearborn Street Station and Union Station, are still standing. Neither one is fully intact.

Other midwestern stations for a time rivaled Chicago's dominance. Detroit, Indianapolis, Minneapolis, and especially St. Louis all had heavy traffic in their heydays, each with a grand-scale station to match. All still operate, but in diminished capacities.

Milwaukee's two old-style stations were emblematic of the city's rich railroad history, both its rise and fall. Its lakefront station, built for the Chicago & North

6-001. Steamboat landing and Union Station, St. Paul, Minnesota. DETR, ca. 1908. P&P,LC-D4-70671.

6-002

6-002. Union Station, Detroit, Michigan.
DETR. P&P,LOT 9126,LC-USZ62-128593.

Also known as the Fort Street Union Depot,
the building was dominated by its corner
clock tower—100 feet tall but made thick by
its doubling as an office block.

Western Railroad in 1899, was closed down in 1966 and sacrificed for a proposed
elevated highway that eventually took another route. A short distance to the west was
the Everett Street Depot (1885), the home station of the Chicago, Milwaukee & St.
Paul Railroad. More popularly known as the Milwaukee Road, the line featured a fleet
of Hiawatha Streamliners, beloved in the city and all around the system. Despite the
significance of the depot to the Milwaukee Road, as the rail line's prospects declined
the station building became expendable. It was replaced by a modern box of a station in
1965.

By the 1970s both the Indianapolis Union Station (1888) and the even more massive
St. Louis Union Station (1894) were essentially out of the passenger train business.
New operators in each case found a suitable mix of hotel and retail uses to save the
properties. This was less of a stretch for the St. Louis station, as it was designed by
European-born architect Theodore C. Link with a substantial portion allocated for hotel
accommodations from the start.

6-003. Grand Central Railway Depot, Detroit, Michigan. Unidentified engraver, 1850. P&P,LOT 4129-1,LC-USZ62-61269.

The engraver took liberties when rendering the roundhouse looming behind the depot, which seems rounded out of proportion.

6-004. North and east sides, Michigan Central Railroad, Capitol Avenue, Battle Creek, Calhoun County, Michigan. Allon Strous, photographer, 1965. P&P,HABS,MICH,13-BATCR,1-1.

The station exterior had a unified color theme, with red brick and red stone for the walls and red tiles for the roof.

6-005. Original waiting room, Michigan Central Railroad, Capitol Avenue, Battle Creek, Calhoun County, Michigan. Allon Strous, photographer, 1965. P&P,HABS,MICH,13-BATCR,1-5.

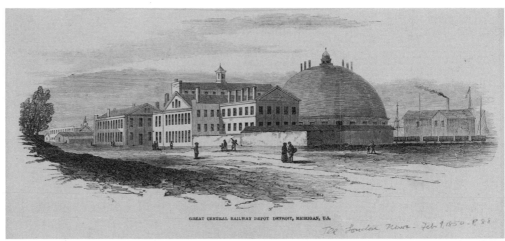

6-003

6-004

6-005

6-006

6-007

6-006. Michigan Central Railroad Station, Ann Arbor, Michigan. DETR, ca. 1910. P&P,LC-D4-39658.

Ann Arbor's Michigan Central Station was a well-known pioneer in the adaptive reuse movement. It was one of the first to be converted to a restaurant.

6-007. Railroad station and steamer dock, Muskegon, Michigan. DETR. P&P,LC-D418-2200.

6-008

6-008. Michigan Central Station,
Ypsilanti, Michigan. DETR, ca. 1906.
P&P,LC-D4-13614.

6-009. Pere Marquette Railroad Station and
Railroad Park, Petoskey, Michigan. DETR, ca.
1908. P&P,LC-D4-70739.

6-009

6-010

6-011

6-012

6-013

6-010. North (front) façade and west side, Union Station, Jackson Place & Illinois Street, Indianapolis, Marion County, Indiana. Unidentified photographer, ca. 1889. P&P,HABS,IND,49-IND,20-2.

6-011. Detail of upper portion of east side from northeast, Union Station, Jackson Place & Illinois Street, Indianapolis, Marion County, Indiana. Jack E. Boucher, photographer, August 1970. P&P,HABS,IND,49-IND,20-9.

6-012. Train gates from west, main floor, Union Station, Jackson Place & Illinois Street, Indianapolis, Marion County, Indiana. Jack E. Boucher, photographer, August 1970. P&P,HABS,IND,49-IND,20-13.

This concourse dates to 1914, when the station was modified with elevated train tracks.

6-013. View of building from northeast, Union Station, Jackson Place & Illinois Street, Indianapolis, Marion County, Indiana. Jack E. Boucher, photographer, August 1970. P&P,HABS,IND,49-IND,20-3.

6-014

6-015

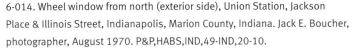

6-014. Wheel window from north (exterior side), Union Station, Jackson Place & Illinois Street, Indianapolis, Marion County, Indiana. Jack E. Boucher, photographer, August 1970. P&P,HABS,IND,49-IND,20-10.

On April 1, 1850, Indianapolis took steps toward becoming the first American city to consolidate its rail traffic, and in September 1853 it opened its first Union Station. The current Union Station dates to 1888, with its great Richardsonian Romanesque design by Thomas Rodd (1849–1929), "Engineer and Architect, Pittsburgh, Pennsylvania." The cathedral-like exterior features rose windows at either end, but on closer inspection both indicate their railroad roots with wheel motifs.

6-015. Wheel window from south (interior), Union Station, Jackson Place and Illinois Street, Indianapolis, Marion County, Indiana. Jack E. Boucher, photographer, August 1970. P&P,HABS,IND,49-IND,20-15.

6-016. General view of interior, Union Station, Jackson Place & Illinois Street, Indianapolis, Marion County, Indiana. Jack E. Boucher, photographer, August 1970. P&P,HABS,IND,49-IND,20-11.

The 100-foot-long skylight that centers the main waiting room was blacked out during World War II as a defense measure, but it was uncovered during a 1980s transformation of the station into a hotel and festival marketplace.

6-016

6-017

6-018

6-019

6-017. Erie Railroad depot, Decatur, Indiana. Unidentified photographer, September 1935. P&P,LC-USF342-000120-A,LC-USF342-T01-000120-A.

6-018. Front façade from south, Beverly Shores South Shore Railroad Station, Broadway Avenue & north side of U.S. Highway 12, Beverly Shores, Porter County, Indiana. Jack E. Boucher, photographer, 1994. P&P,HABS,IND,64-BEVSH,12-1.

6-019. Trackside façade, Beverly Shores South Shore Railroad Station, Broadway Avenue & north side of U.S. Highway 12, Beverly Shores, Porter County, Indiana. Jack E. Boucher, photographer, 1994. P&P,HABS,IND,64-BEVSH,12-4.

Most of the Beverly Shores station served as a residence for the stationmaster (the ticket seller) for what was mainly the light-rail line of its day. The station is located near the Indiana Dunes district along the shore of Lake Michigan. Leo W. Post, President of the Beverly Shores Construction Company, built nine stations with similar Mission Style appearances for the President of the South Shore Railroad, Samuel Insull, giving rise to a new architectural category: Insull Spanish.

6-020. Side view of station, New Albany & Salem Railroad, North Street, Gosport, Owen County, Indiana. P&P,HAER,IND,60-GOSP,2A-3.

6-021. Plan and sections, New Albany & Salem Railroad, North Street, Gosport, Owen County, Indiana. P&P,sheet no. 2.

The station in Gosport is a rare survivor from the days when trains actually passed through the station building proper.

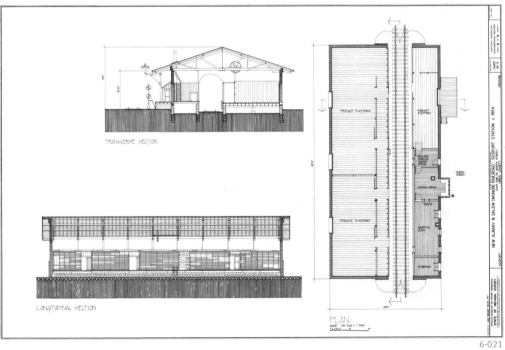

6-022

6-023

6-022. Passenger terminal, Chicago & North Western Railway, Chicago, Illinois. Unidentified photographer, ca. 1912. P&P,PAN US GEOG-Illinois no. 70 (E size).

Known colloquially as the North Western Terminal, the building was designed by Frost & Granger, a firm whose principals had each married a daughter of the President of the Chicago & North Western Railway. The terminal opened in 1911.

6-023. Madison Street vestibule, Chicago & North Western Railway, Chicago, Illinois. DETR, ca. 1912. P&P,LOT 9088,LC-USZ62-101585.

The terminal building is as gloriously overstyled as the great Chicago movie palaces of the decade that followed—except here the marble was real, unlike many of the theatrical counterparts.

6-024. Train concourse, Chicago & North Western Railway, Chicago, Illinois. DETR, ca. 1912. P&P,LOT 9088,LC-USZ62-101583.

6-024

6-025

6-025. Main waiting room, Chicago & North Western Railway, Chicago, Illinois. DETR, ca. 1912. P&P,LC-D4-72525.

6-026. Passenger terminal, Madison Street entrance, Chicago & North Western Railway, Chicago, Illinois. DETR, ca. 1912. P&P,LOT 9088,LC-USZ62-101582.

6-026

6-027

6-028. Train sheds, Chicago & North Western Railway, Chicago, Illinois. DETR, ca. 1912. P&P,LC-D4-72530.

The terminal had sixteen platforms, all sheltered by an 894-foot-long set of Bush sheds.

6-027. Lobby stairs to waiting room and concourse, Chicago & North Western Railway, Chicago, Illinois. DETR, ca. 1912. P&P,LOT 9088,LC-USZ62-101584.

6-028

6-029. In the waiting room of the Union Station, Chicago. Illinois. Jack Delano, photographer, January 1943. P&P,LC-USW3-015486.

6-030. Union Station train concourse, Chicago, Illinois. Jack Delano, photographer, January 1943. P&P,LC-USW3-015456-E.

6-029

6-030

6-031

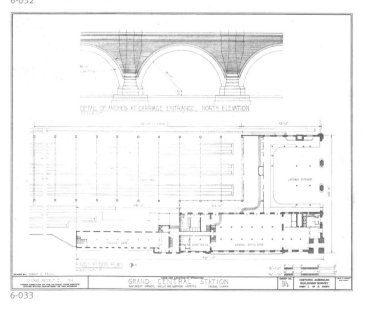

6-032

6-031. Exterior from northwest, Grand Central Station, 201 West Harrison Street (corner of West Harrison & South Wells), Chicago, Cook County, Illinois. Cervin Robinson, photographer, July 1963. P&P,HABS,ILL,16-CHIG,18-1.

The Grand Central Station opened in 1890 to the designs of Solon Spencer Beman (1853–1914). The architect had apprenticed for eight years in New York City with Richard Upjohn, before arriving in Chicago at the end of 1879 to help George Pullman design the planned community for his Pullman-Standard Sleeping Car Company.

6-032. Waiting room, Grand Central Station, 201 West Harrison Street (corner of West Harrison & South Wells), Chicago, Cook County, Illinois. Cervin Robinson, photographer, July 1963. P&P,HABS,ILL,16-CHIG,18-3.

Beman's inclusion of rows of stained-glass windows brightened the stolid waiting room.

6-033. Plan and detail, Grand Central Station, 201 West Harrison Street (corner of West Harrison & South Wells), Chicago, Cook County, Illinois. P&P,sheet no. 2.

6-034. North elevation, Grand Central Station, 201 West Harrison Street (corner of West Harrison & South Wells), Chicago, Cook County, Illinois. P&P, no. sheet 4.

6-033

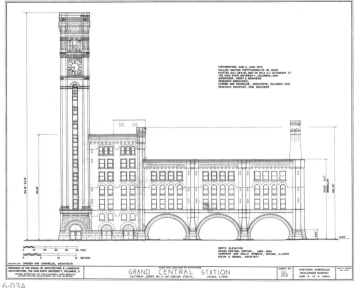

6-034

6-035

6-035. Dearborn Street Station, Chicago, Illinois. DETR, ca. 1910. P&P,LC-D418-72294.

Dearborn Street Station, which opened in 1885 as the Polk Street Depot, was designed by a New Yorker, Cyrus Eidlitz (1853–1921). Portions of the station survive at the south end of Printers Row.

6-036. West façade of center bay with west wing demolished, Chicago & Western Indiana Railroad, Dearborn Station Trainshed, 47 West Polk Street, Chicago, Cook County, Illinois. Hedrich-Blessing, photographer, May 1976. P&P,HAER,ILL,16-CHIG,104A-6.

6-036

6-037

6-037. Chicago & North Western Railroad Station, Chicago, Illinois. DETR, ca. 1898. P&P,LC-D4-4857.

6-038. Illinois Central Railway Station, Chicago, Illinois. Unidentified photographer, possibly Hans Behm/DETR, ca. 1900. P&P,LC-D4-70181 B.

6-039. View of north (front) and west side, Illinois Central Railroad Station, Michigan & Roosevelt streets, Chicago, Cook County, Illinois. Jack E. Boucher, photographer, February 1971. P&P,HABS,ILL,16-CHIG,99A-1.

The Illinois Central was rushed into business in the spring of 1893 to serve the crowds attending the great 1893 World's Columbian Exposition on the south side.

6-038

6-039

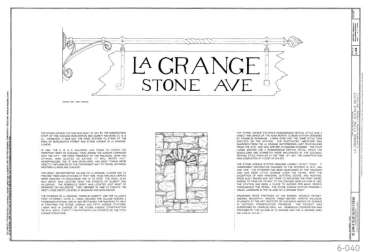

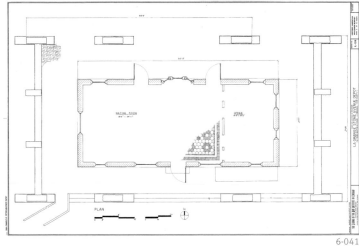

6-040 6-041

6-040. Title sheet, La Grange Stone Avenue Depot, 701 Burlington Avenue, La Grange, Cook County, Illinois. P&P,HABS,IL-1218,sheet no. 1.

6-041. Plan, La Grange Stone Avenue Depot, 701 Burlington Avenue, La Grange, Cook County, Illinois. P&P,sheet no. 2.

6-042. North elevation, La Grange Stone Avenue Depot, 701 Burlington Avenue, La Grange, Cook County, Illinois. P&P,sheet no. 4.

6-043. Details, La Grange Stone Avenue Depot, 701 Burlington Avenue, La Grange, Cook County, Illinois. P&P,sheet no. 6.

This depot, which opened in 1901, was the work of the engineering staff of the Chicago, Burlington & Quincy Railroad.

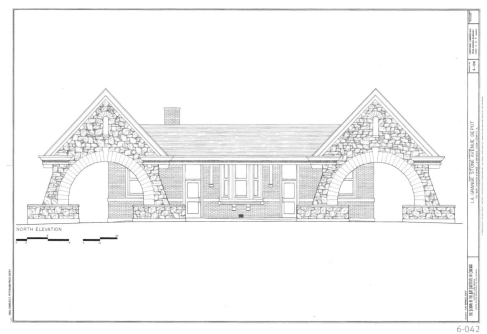

6-042

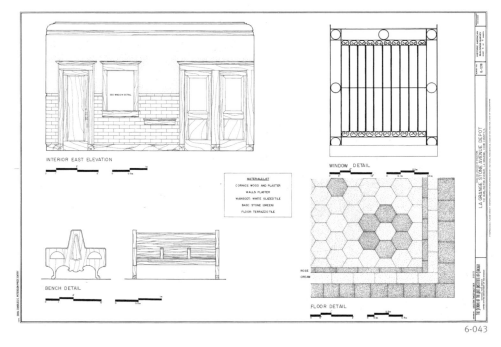

6-043

6-044

6-045

6-046

6-044. Center façade of station, Union Station, 50 East Jefferson Street, Joliet, Will County, Illinois. Martin Stupich, photographer, 1988. P&P,HAER,ILL,99-JOL,2-1.

As with most union stations, the one that opened in Joliet in 1912 was designed as much to relieve traffic congestion on the city streets as heavy traffic on the rails. Architect Jarvis Hunt (1863–1941) designed a two-level track, as the station had to deal with both grade-level and elevated tracks.

6-045. Detail of entry, upper façade, Union Station, 50 East Jefferson Street, Joliet, Will County, Illinois. Martin Stupich, photographer, 1988. P&P,HAER,ILL,99-JOL,2-8.

The stonework was left rough for Joliet's freight station, but it was fully dressed for the passengers at Union Station downtown.

6-046. South façade, Santa Fe Railroad, Joliet Freight Depot, Cass & Scott Streets, Joliet, Will County, Illinois. Martin Stupich, photographer, 1988. P&P,HAER,ILL,99-JOL,9-2.

6-047. Original passenger depot, Illinois
Central Railroad, Passenger Depot No. 1,
north of First Street, east of Union Street, La
Salle, La Salle County, Illinois. Unidentified
photographer, 1894. P&P,HAER,ILL,50-
LASAL,4C-1.

Twenty years after this photo was taken, the
depot lost its upper story to modernization.

6-048. South façade of station, Rock Island
Railroad, Marseilles Passenger Depot, east
of Main Street, Marseilles, La Salle County,
Illinois. Martin Stupich, photographer,
1988. P&P,HAER,ILL,50-MARS,7-1.

6-047

6-048

6-049

6-050

6-051

6-049. Michigan Central Depot, Frankfort, Illinois. Unidentified photographer, ca. 1910. P&P,LC-USZ62-89270.

6-050. An emblem on a Chicago, Milwaukee, St. Paul & Pacific Railroad (Milwaukee Road) freight car, San Bernardino, California. Jack Delano, photographer, March 1943. P&P,LC-USW3-021562-E.

6-051. Chicago & North Western Railway Station, Milwaukee, Wisconsin. DETR, ca. 1898. P&P,LOT 12688,no. 18 (H).

The lakefront location of the Chicago & North Western's station in Milwaukee was to prove its undoing. The station was torn down to make way for a lakeside highway, later built elsewhere.

6-052

6-052. Steamboat landing and Union
Station, St. Paul, Minnesota. DETR, ca.
1908. P&P,LC-D4-70671.

6-053. Chicago, Milwaukee & St. Paul
Railway Station, Minneapolis, Minnesota.
DETR, ca. 1908. P&P,LC-D4-70635.

The lantern and cupola atop this 1899
station building were lost to a tornado in
1941.

6-053

6-054

6-054. Duluth & Iron Range Railroad Locomotive #46 (built in 1888) with log train at Endion Depot, Endion Passenger Depot, 1504 South Street, Duluth, St. Louis County, Minnesota. Unidentified photographer, ca. 1910. P&P,HAER,MINN,69-DULU,6-15.

6-055. View of east front, Endion Passenger Depot, 1504 South Street, Duluth, St. Louis County, Minnesota. Dale R. Tresler and David R. Gonzalez, photographers, 1985. P&P,HAER,MINN,69-DULU,6-1.

A local firm, Tenbusch & Hill, designed the station building, which was completed in 1899.

6-055

6-056

6-057

6-056. Detail of center bay (east façade), Union Pacific Station (Transfer Depot & Hotel), Twenty-first Street, Council Bluffs, Pottawattamie County, Iowa. J. Chris Jensen, photographer, February 1934. P&P,HABS,IOWA,78-COUB,2-4.

6-057. Detail of center bay (east façade) 2nd story, Union Pacific Station (Transfer Depot & Hotel), Twenty-first Street, Council Bluffs, Pottawattamie County, Iowa. J. Chris Jensen, photographer, February 1934. P&P,HABS,IOWA,78-COUB,2-5.

6-058. East elevation, Union Pacific Station (Transfer Depot & Hotel), Twenty-first Street, Council Bluffs, Pottawattamie County, Iowa. P&P,sheet no. 7.

A little piece of French Royal architecture found its way to Pottawattamie County. Council Bluffs had already made its name in the 1870s. Once the rails linked in Utah, the town was the point of departure for travelers headed to the West by rail.

6-058

6-059

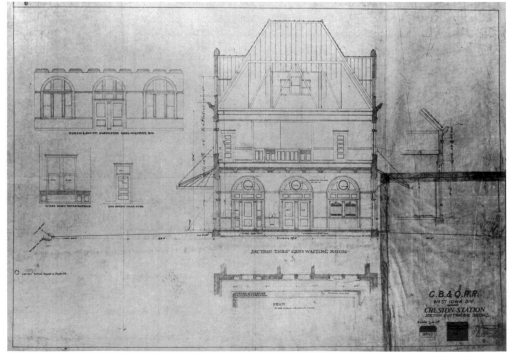

6-060

6-059. North and west façades, Chicago,
Burlington & Quincy Railroad, West Iowa
Division, Creston Station, 116 West Adams,
Creston, Union County, Iowa. Ted Wall,
photographer, 1981. P&P,HABS,IOWA,88-
CREST,1-1.

The station's is attributed to the firm of
Burnham & Root. John Wellborn Root, in
any case, was long dead by the time the
building went into service in 1899.

6-060. Section through general waiting
room, Chicago, Burlington & Quincy
Railroad, West Iowa Division, Creston
Station, 116 West Adams, Creston, Union
County, Iowa. Architect's original drawing,
1898. P&P,HABS,IOWA,88-CREST,1-12.

6-061

6-061. Illinois Central Railroad Station, Dubuque, Iowa. John Vachon, photographer, April 1940. P&P,LC-USF34-060576.

6-062. Chicago, Milwaukee & St. Paul Railroad Station, Dubuque, Iowa. John Vachon, photographer, April 1940. P&P,LC-USF33-001681-M4,LC-USF33-T01-001681-M4.

6-062

6-063

6-063. Chicago Great Western Railroad Station, Dubuque, Iowa. John Vachon, photographer, April 1940. P&P,LC-USF33-001699-M3,LC-USF33-T01-001699-M3.

6-064. Chicago, Rock Island & Pacific Railroad Depot, Independence, Iowa. Unidentified photographer, ca. 1909. P&P,LC-USZ62-118645.

6-065. Mississippi River, Keokuk, Iowa. F. J. Bandholtz, photographer, ca. 1907. P&P,PAN US GEOG-Iowa no. 38 (E size), LC-USZ62-71771,LC-USZ62-71772.

Keokuk's Union Station was the work of the Chicago firm of Burnham & Root. The station opened in 1891, just as the designers were beginning work on the 1893 Exposition back in Illinois.

6-064

6-065

6-066

6-067

6-066. General exterior, St. Louis Union Station, Market Street between Eighteenth & Nineteenth, Saint Louis, St. Louis City County, Missouri. P&P,HABS,MO,96-SALU,126-1.

The head house of the St. Louis Union Station ran a length of 606 feet and enclosed its Grand Hall, a room that surely deserved its name. The architect of the station, which opened in 1894 at a cost of $6.5 million, was Theodore C. Link, who won a $10,000 prize for his troubles. Part of the cost went to the solid Indiana limestone of the exterior.

6-067. General view showing east entrance, St. Louis Union Station, Market Street between Eighteenth & Nineteenth, Saint Louis, St. Louis City County, Missouri. Jack E. Boucher, photographer, April–May 1986. P&P,HABS,MO,96-SALU,126-5.

6-068. Detail showing top of clock spire, St. Louis Union Station, Market Street between Eighteenth & Nineteenth, Saint Louis, St. Louis County, Missouri. Jack E. Boucher, photographer, April–May 1986. P&P,HABS,MO,96-SALU,126-9.

6-068

6-069

6-070

6-071

6-069. View along east side of building, St. Louis Union Station, Market Street between Eighteenth & Nineteenth, Saint Louis, St. Louis City County, Missouri. Jack E. Boucher, photographer, April–May 1986. P&P,HABS,MO,96-SALU,126-6.

6-070. Detail showing granite downspout support loops and stone work, east façade, St. Louis Union Station, Market Street, between Eighteenth & Nineteenth, Saint Louis, St. Louis City County, Missouri. Jack E. Boucher, photographer, April May 1986. P&P,HABS,MO,96-SALU,126-7.

6-071. Grand Hall showing ceiling, skylights, and arched mural at west end, St. Louis Union Station, Market Street between Eighteenth & Nineteenth, Saint Louis, St. Louis City County, Missouri. Jack E. Boucher, photographer, April–May 1986. P&P,HABS,MO,96-SALU,126-13.

The Grand Hall was converted to use as a restaurant and a hotel lobby during the rescue operations performed in the mid-1980s.

6-072

6-073

6-072. South side of Grand Hall, St. Louis Union Station, Market Street between Eighteenth & Nineteenth, Saint Louis, St. Louis City County, Missouri. Jack E. Boucher, photographer, April–May 1986. P&P,HABS,MO,96-SALU,126-10.

6-073. North side of Grand Hall, St. Louis Union Station, Market Street between Eighteenth & Nineteenth, Saint Louis, St. Louis City County, Missouri. Jack E. Boucher, photographer, April–May 1986. P&P,HABS,MO,96-SALU,126-12.

6-074. Detail showing arch over north entrance of Grand Hall, St. Louis Union Station, Market Street between Eighteenth & Nineteenth, Saint Louis, St. Louis City County, Missouri. Jack E. Boucher, photographer, April–May 1986. P&P,HABS,MO,96-SALU,126-15.

The stained glass depicts female figures that symbolize the cities of New York, St. Louis, and San Francisco. The hometown heroine links the other two.

6-074

6-076

6-075

6-075. Detail showing iron column of train shed, St. Louis Union Station Train Shed, 1820 Market Street, Saint Louis, St. Louis City County, Missouri. Jack E. Boucher, photographer, April–May 1986. P&P,HAER,MO,96-SALU,81-4.

The train shed was also a work of art in the category of engineering. The design by engineer George H. Pegram (1855–1937) featured five bays covering a total of 378,000 square feet. In the early twentieth century this was all necessary space, as St. Louis housed operations for twenty-two different lines—more than anywhere else in the world, even Chicago.

6-076. Interior detail showing entrance to offices off of grand hall, St. Louis Union Station, Market Street between Eighteenth & Nineteenth, Saint Louis, St. Louis City County, Missouri. Jack E. Boucher, photographer, April–May 1986. P&P,HABS,MO,96-SALU,126-16.

6-077. The Knickerbocker Special leaving St. Louis Union Station, St. Louis, Missouri. Unidentified photographer, ca. 1906. P&P,LC-USZ62-101996.

6-077

6-078

6-079

6-078. Trackside view, Missouri-Pacific Railroad Station, Kirkwood, St. Louis County, Missouri. Paul Piaget, photographer, July 1967. P&P,HABS,MO,95-KIRK,2-1.

A witch's cap marks the center of this 1893 station in Kirkwood.

6-079. Railroad station, Jefferson City, Missouri. John Vachon, photographer, May 1940. P&P,LC-USF33-001903-M5,LC-USF33-T01-001903-M5.

6-080. Union Station, Kansas City, Missouri. DETR. P&P,LC-D419-132.

6-081. Union Station and loading dock, Kansas City, Missouri. DETR. P&P,LC-D419-26.

This massive limestone station, which opened in 1914, was the work of Jarvis Hunt. The complex included Harvey House facilities by Mary Jane Colter (1869–1958), an architect who frequently designed for the Santa Fe line in the American Southwest.

6-080

6-081

THE NORTHERN PLAINS AND THE NORTHWEST

7-001. Entrance and clock tower, Union Pacific Passenger Station, 121 West Fifteenth Street, Cheyenne, Goshen County, Wyoming. Unidentified photographer, 1974. P&P,HABS,WYO,11-CHEY,5-6.

The clock tower rises to a height of more than 120 feet from the broad expanse of the station building.

As competing rail lines raced across the northern plains to the Pacific Ocean in the late 1800s, the stations and depots they built tended to be less than imposing. The mineral wealth of the region brought about a quick change to the situation, as seen in the number of turn-of-the-century station buildings created by famous architects. Cass Gilbert (1859–1934) designed a station for Fargo, North Dakota, which was completed in 1898 for the Northern Pacific. The line's 1901 depot in Bismarck was put up by Reed & Stem, shortly before the firm began work on New York City's Grand Central Terminal. The firm went on to build a string of stations across Montana, ending up in Washington State with Seattle's King Street Station (1906) and the Tacoma Union Station (1911).

The architectural firm of Van Brunt & Howe moved from Boston to Kansas City, Missouri, in the 1880s. Once resettled, they built such gems as Cheyenne's Union Pacific Station (1887) in Wyoming and Union Station (1896) in Portland, Oregon. Another western wonder with eastern roots was the Union Pacific Railroad Depot (1925) in Boise, Idaho, produced by the New York firm of Carrère & Hastings.

7-002

The Alaska Railroad, government operated into the 1980s, was never the beneficiary of such world-renowned architectural expertise. What mattered more was that the station buildings could withstand the tests of time and climate. Two that have, and that are nearing their centenary birthdays, survive in the towns of Seward and Wasilla.

7-002. Starkweather, North Dakota. John Vachon/FSA, photographer, November 1940. P&P,LC-USF34-061463-D.

7-003. Bird's-eye view, Dickinson, North Dakota. Doubleday & Myers, ca. 1914. P&P, PAN US GEOG-North Dakota no. 8 (E size).

The roundhouse that formed part of the station in Dickinson is visible at far left.

7-003

7-004

7-004. Railroad station, Fargo, North Dakota. Arthur Rothstein, photographer, 1939. P&P,LC-USF33-003066-M2.

The Great Northern Depot in Fargo was the work of staff architect Samuel L. Bartlett (dates unknown).

7-005. Railroad station, Bismarck, North Dakota. P&P,LC-USZ62-116330.

The new Northern Pacific Station of 1901 seemed a luxury job for the firm of Reed & Stem. Just two years later they were brought in to design the new Grand Central Terminal in New York. (Reed died in 1911, two years before Grand Central opened.)

7-006. People of Deadwood, South Dakota, celebrating completion of a stretch of railroad. John C. H. Grabill, photographer, 1888. P&P,LOT 3076-5,no. 1459,LC-DIG-ppmsc-02566,LC-USZ62-46193.

7-005

7-006

7-007

7-008

7-007. Main street façade, Union Pacific Passenger Station, 121 West Fifteenth Street, Cheyenne, Goshen County, Wyoming. Unidentified photographer, 1974. P&P,HABS,WYO,11-CHEY,5-2.

Even from a distance the Union Pacific emblem shows clearly on the face of the tower.

7-008. Long view of station, Union Pacific Passenger Station, 121 West Fifteenth Street, Cheyenne, Goshen County, Wyoming. Unidentified photographer, 1974. P&P,HABS,WYO,11-CHEY,5-1.

7-009. Trackside façade, Union Pacific Passenger Station, 121 West Fifteenth Street, Cheyenne, Goshen County, Wyoming. Unidentified photographer, 1974. P&P,HABS,WYO,11-CHEY,5-8.

Architects Van Brunt & Howe gave even the track side a very formal character in Cheyenne.

7-010. Trackside entrance to station, Union Pacific Passenger Station, 121 West Fifteenth Street, Cheyenne, Goshen County, Wyoming. Unidentified photographer, 1974. P&P,HABS,WYO,11-CHEY,5-18.

7-011

7-012

7-013

7-011. Station property, Rock Creek Station, junction of Rock Creek & Union Pacific Railroad, Rock River, Albany County, Wyoming. P&P,HABS,WYO,1-ROCRI,V,1-3.

7-012. Station property, Rock Creek Station, junction of Rock Creek & Union Pacific Railroad, Rock River, Albany County, Wyoming. P&P,HABS,WYO,1-ROCRI,V,1-21.

Part of this ghost town station looks as windblown as any tumbleweed.

7-013. South façade of the railway s general offices, Anaconda Historic District, Butte, Anaconda & Pacific Railway, General Offices, 300 West Commercial Avenue, Anaconda, Deer Lodge County, Montana. Jet Lowe, photographer, May 1979. P&P,HABS,MONT,12-ANAC,1-P-1.

This 1898 office block was once the depot for the Butte, Anaconda & Pacific, the brainchild of Anaconda's favorite son, copper magnate Marcus Daly. The line hauled in materials mined in Butte to go into the mix at the Anaconda smelter.

7-014

7-014. Grain elevator at railroad station, Fairfield, Montana. Arthur Rothstein/ FSA, photographer, 1939. P&P,LC-USF33-003107.

As was often the case on the central and northern plains, the grain elevator was the dominant feature on the landscape, with the railroad station left to play second fiddle.

7-015. View of south front, Great Northern Depot, 100–110 Neill Avenue, Helena, Lewis and Clark County, Montana. Paul Anderson, photographer, November 1987. P&P,HAER,MONT,25-HEL,13-2.

7-016. Railroad station, Froid, Montana. Marion Post Wolcott/FSA, photographer, August 1941. P&P,LC-USF34-057967-D.

7-015

7-016

7-017

7-018

7-019

7-017. North view of campanile with garden area in foreground, Union Pacific Railroad Depot, 1701 Eastover Terrace, Boise, Ada County, Idaho. Duane Garrett, photographer, March 1974. P&P,HABS,ID,1-BOISE,21A-2.

This capital-city depot sits on a rise above its own landscaped garden.

7-018. Detail of west end of depot, Union Pacific Railroad Depot, 1701 Eastover Terrace, Boise, Ada County, Idaho. Duane Garrett, photographer, March 1974. P&P,HABS,ID,1-BOISE,21A-5.

The work of Carrère & Hastings, architects for the main branch of the New York Public Library, the 1925 Union Pacific Depot in Boise is a masterwork in its own right. Its exterior is coated in whitewashed stucco and capped by a red tile roof.

7-019. Track side, Union Pacific Railroad Depot, 1701 Eastover Terrace, Boise, Ada County, Idaho. Duane Garrett, photographer, March 1974. P&P,HABS,ID,1-BOISE,21A-6.

The track side of the depot is stark by comparison with the other faces.

7-020

7-021

7-020. View of waiting hall looking west, Union Pacific Railroad Depot, 1701 Eastover Terrace, Boise, Ada County, Idaho. Duane Garrett, photographer, March 1974. P&P,HABS,ID,1-BOISE,21A-9.

One could easily mistake the waiting hall for a modern version of a Mission Style church, with pews instead of passenger benches. The painted roof trusses add to the effect.

7-021. View of painted roof trusses, Union Pacific Railroad Depot, 1701 Eastover Terrace, Boise, Ada County, Idaho. Duane Garrett, photographer, March 1974. P&P,HABS,ID,1-BOISE,21A-10.

7-022. Trackside (south) arched entrances to waiting hall, Union Pacific Railroad Depot, 1701 Eastover Terrace, Boise, Ada County, Idaho. Duane Garrett, photographer, March 1974. P&P,HABS,ID,1-BOISE,21A-8.

7-022

7-023

7-024

7-025

7-023. Exterior, south side and east front, Idaho Northern Railroad, tool shed, North Broadway Street, west side, Montour, Gem County, Idaho. Hans Muessig, photographer, April 1979. P&P,HABS,ID,23-MONT,5B-1.

7-024. Exterior, east front, Idaho Northern Railroad, tool shed, North Broadway Street, west side, Montour, Gem County, Idaho. Hans Muessig, photographer, April 1979. P&P,HABS,ID,23-MONT,5B-2.

This glorified tool shed marks the site of the original Montour depot, and it certainly lacks for nothing in terms of signage.

7-025. Detail of old railroad station, Irrigon, Oregon. Dorothea Lange/FSA, photographer, October 1939. P&P,LC-USF34-021131-E.

7-026. Railroad station, Irrigon, Oregon, population 108. Dorothea Lange/FSA, photographer, October 1939. P&P,LC-USF34-021094-C.

Lange lends a formal eye to her recordkeeping of this station in rural Oregon. Her notes for the Farm Security Administration say, "Population: 108. Land was opened to settlers here in 1914."

7-026

7-027

7-028

7-027. Detail view of date stone at northwest corner of the porte cochere, Bend Railroad Depot, 1160 Northeast Division Street (at foot of Kearney Street), Bend, Deschutes County, Oregon. P&P,HABS,ORE,9-BEND,2-22.

7-028. General view from southwest, Union Depot, 1713 Pacific Avenue, Union Depot Study Area, Tacoma, Pierce County, Washington. Jet Lowe, photographer, July 1979. P&P,HABS,WASH,27-TACO,6-10.

The 90-foot-high, copper-covered dome makes a modest and stylish nod in the direction of Mount Rainier to the east (not visible in image). The building, designed by architects Reed & Stem, now houses a museum.

7-029. Station and downtown Tacoma looking northeast, Union Passenger Station Concourse, 1713 Pacific Avenue, Tacoma, Pierce County, Washington. Bolland Collection/Tacoma Public Library Northwest Collection, 1922. P&P,HABS WASH,27-TACO,6C-24.

As the depot sits on a slope between the center of town and Commencement Bay below, the tracks are a full 27 feet below the street-level entrance. Elevators in addition to stairs enable passengers to reach their trains.

7-030. Drawing No. 10—track elevation, Union Passenger Station Concourse, 1713 Pacific Avenue, Tacoma, Pierce County, Washington. Burlington Northern Collection, June 1909. P&P,HABS,WASH, 27-TACO,6C-31.

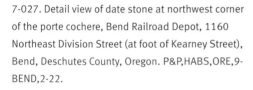

7-029

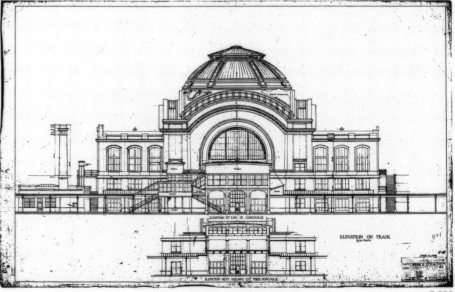

7-030

7-031

7-032

7-033

7-031. The first depot at Anchorage, Alaska. P&P,LOT 11453-1,no. 272,LC-DIG-ppmsc-01827.

7-032. Government railway office building, Seward, Alaska. Unidentified photographer, 1916. P&P,LOT 11453-1,no. 537,LC-DIG-ppmsc-02092.

7-033. Tanana Valley Railroad at Chatanika Station, Chatanika, Alaska. Unidentified photographer, 1916. P&P,LOT 11453-1,no. 119,LC-DIG-ppmsc-01674.

7-034. South front, Alaska Railroad Depot, 411 First Avenue, Anchorage, Greater Anchorage Area Borough, Alaska. Jet Lowe, photographer, 1991. P&P,HABS,AK,2-ANCH,15-1.

7-034

7-035. Front view, Alaska Railroad Depot, Seward, Kenai Peninsula Borough, Alaska. Walter Smalling Jr., photographer, 1982. P&P,HABS,AK,9-SEW,1-E-2.

The depot in Seward was completed in 1917 as the terminus in this all-weather port.

7-036. White Pass & Yukon Route Railroad Depot, looking south, City of Skagway, Skagway, Skagway-Hoonah-Angoon Census Area, Alaska. Jet Lowe, photographer, July 1982. P&P,HABS,AK,18-SKAG,1-65.

The depot and the adjoining White Pass & Yukon Office Headquarters Building were both completed in 1898, as the starting point of the narrow-gauge rail line to Whitehorse.

7-037. Ocean terminus of Copper River Railroad, Cordova, Alaska. Unidentified photographer, 1916. P&P,LOT 11453-1,no. 642,LC-DIG-ppmsc-02197.

The terminal in Cordova appears to be as remote a facility as any imaginable.

7-035

7-036

7-037

THE CENTRAL PLAINS AND THE ROCKIES

While trains in the plains reached their stations mainly out on flat ground, the Rocky Mountain depots perched on more rugged landscapes. The precarious nature of these latter buildings, and the tracks that led to them, caused a preference among regional carriers for narrow-gauge rail. The undersized tracks did not necessarily result in diminished station buildings. However, sparse population in the region, combined with the boom-and-bust economies of many towns, did mean that even well-built depots might suddenly be abandoned.

Rail companies in Denver and Salt Lake City bracketed the Rockies with major facilities. Just after the turn of the century Denver Union Station (orig. 1881, revisions 1894, 1914) was a mild misnomer, as it did not quite unify all the lines. The Denver, Northwestern & Pacific, operated by transplanted New Yorker David Moffatt, was not permitted use of the central station. As a result Moffatt built his own small but stylish station a short distance away.

Union Station (1931) in Omaha, Nebraska, features an Art Deco treatment by Gilbert Stanley Underwood (1890–1960). He was best known for a number

8-001. Railway station, Ophir, Colorado. Russell Lee/FSA, photographer, September 1940. P&P,LC-USF34-037642-D.

8-002

8-002. Gateway, Union Depot, Denver, Colorado. A. C. Roebuck, ca.1908. P&P,LOT 4939,LC-USZ62-107800.

of national park lodges that were commissioned by the Union Pacific Railroad and built at Bryce Canyon, at Zion, and at the North Rim of the Grand Canyon. Underwood's masterwork was the Awahnee, the rustic but luxurious lodge at the heart of Yosemite National Park. It opened a few years prior to his very different work in Omaha for the railroad.

8-003

8-003. New Union Station, Omaha, Nebraska. John Vachon/FSA, photographer, November 1938. P&P,LC-USF34-008894-D.

The heavily ornamented exterior of the station in Omaha is clad with white terra cotta.

8-004. Santa Fe Station and Hotel, Dodge City, Kansas. P&P,LC-USZ62-117035.

The station in Dodge City has the look of a standard Fred Harvey concession.

8-005. Railroad station, Wellington, Kansas. Russell Lee, photographer, August 1939. P&P,LC-USF34-034055-D.

8-006. Abandoned railway station, now used for a church, in the oil ghost town of Slick, Oklahoma. Russell Lee, photographer, February 1940.

8-004

8-005

8-006

8-007

8-008

Santa Fe Depot, Perry, Okla.

8-009

8-010

8-007. Aerial view, St. Louis/San Francisco Railroad Station, Perry, Noble County, Oklahoma. Frederick D. Schirrmacher, photographer, July 1975. P&P,HABS,OKLA,52-PERRY,2-1.

8-008. Detail with baggage cart, Atchison, Topeka & Santa Fe Railroad Station, Perry, Noble County, Oklahoma. Frederick D. Schirrmacher, photographer, July 1975. P&P,HABS,OKLA,52-PERRY,1-3.

8-009. Postcard view of Santa Fe Depot, Atchison, Topeka & Santa Fe Railroad Station, Perry, Noble County, Oklahoma. Unidentified photographer, 1903. P&P,HABS,OKLA,52-PERRY,1-7.

8-010. Exterior of modified station, Atchison, Topeka & Santa Fe Railroad Station, Perry, Noble County, Oklahoma. Frederick D. Schirrmacher, photographer, July 1975. P&P,HABS,OKLA,52-PERRY,1-2.

8-011. Welcome arch and Union Depot, Denver, Colorado. DETR, ca. 1908. P&P,LC-USZ62-118057.

Both the Welcome gateway and the clock tower dating from 1894, visible here, were taken down in the course of enlargements to the station made in 1914.

8-012. Union Station, Denver, Colorado. C. L. McClure, photographer. P&P,LC-USZ62-62259.

The central block of 1914 has a crown clock face encircled by a neon sign spelling out "UNION STATION, TRAVEL BY TRAIN" in bright orange letters.

8-011

8-012

8-013

8-014

8-013. View of exterior, Moffatt Station, 2101 Fifteenth Street, Denver, Denver County, Colorado. Troy Ostendorf, photographer, May 1991. P&P,HABS,COLO,16-DENV,61-1.

8-014. Front, looking northeast, Moffatt Station, 2101 Fifteenth Street, Denver, Denver County, Colorado. Troy Ostendorf, photographer, May 1991. P&P,HABS,COLO,16-DENV,61-6.

MOFFAT STATION

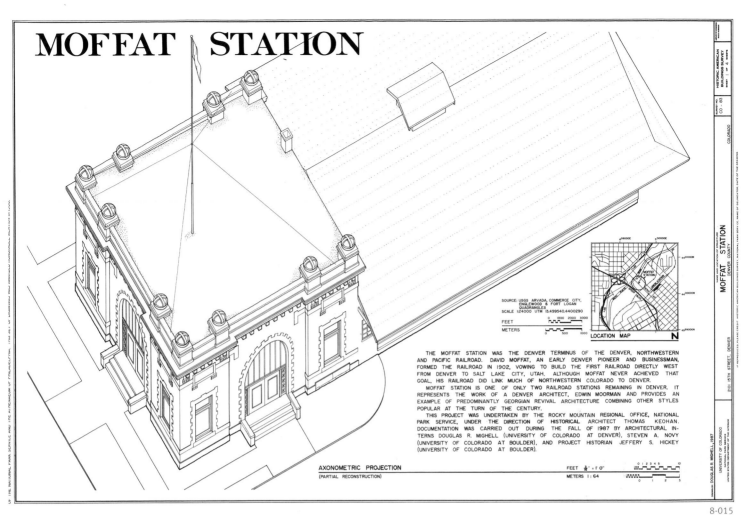

SOURCE: USGS ARVADA, COMMERCE CITY,
ENGLEWOOD & FORT LOGAN
QUADRANGLES
SCALE 1:24000 UTM 13.499540.4400290

FEET

METERS

LOCATION MAP

N

MOFFAT STATION
DENVER COUNTY

2101 15TH STREET, DENVER

THE MOFFAT STATION WAS THE DENVER TERMINUS OF THE DENVER, NORTHWESTERN
AND PACIFIC RAILROAD. DAVID MOFFAT, AN EARLY DENVER PIONEER AND BUSINESSMAN,
FORMED THE RAILROAD IN 1902, VOWING TO BUILD THE FIRST RAILROAD DIRECTLY WEST
FROM DENVER TO SALT LAKE CITY, UTAH. ALTHOUGH MOFFAT NEVER ACHIEVED THAT
GOAL, HIS RAILROAD DID LINK MUCH OF NORTHWESTERN COLORADO TO DENVER.
    MOFFAT STATION IS ONE OF ONLY TWO RAILROAD STATIONS REMAINING IN DENVER. IT
REPRESENTS THE WORK OF A DENVER ARCHITECT, EDWIN MOORMAN AND PROVIDES AN
EXAMPLE OF PREDOMINANTLY GEORGIAN REVIVAL ARCHITECTURE COMBINING OTHER STYLES
POPULAR AT THE TURN OF THE CENTURY.
    THIS PROJECT WAS UNDERTAKEN BY THE ROCKY MOUNTAIN REGIONAL OFFICE, NATIONAL
PARK SERVICE, UNDER THE DIRECTION OF HISTORICAL ARCHITECT THOMAS KEOHAN.
DOCUMENTATION WAS CARRIED OUT DURING THE FALL OF 1987 BY ARCHITECTURAL IN-
TERNS DOUGLAS R. MIGHELL (UNIVERSITY OF COLORADO AT DENVER), STEVEN A. NOVY
(UNIVERSITY OF COLORADO AT BOULDER), AND PROJECT HISTORIAN JEFFERY S. HICKEY
(UNIVERSITY OF COLORADO AT BOULDER).

AXONOMETRIC PROJECTION
(PARTIAL RECONSTRUCTION)

FEET ⅛" = 1'-0"

METERS 1 : 64

DRAWN BY: DOUGLAS R. MIGHELL, 1987

UNIVERSITY OF COLORADO
NATIONAL PARK SERVICE
UNITED STATES DEPARTMENT OF THE INTERIOR

8-015

8-015. Axonometric projection, Moffatt
Station, 2101 Fifteenth Street, Denver,
Denver County, Colorado. P&P, sheet no. 1.

8-016. Southeast elevation, Moffatt Station,
2101 Fifteenth Street, Denver, Denver
County, Colorado. Unidentified delineator,
1991. P&P, sheet no. 3.

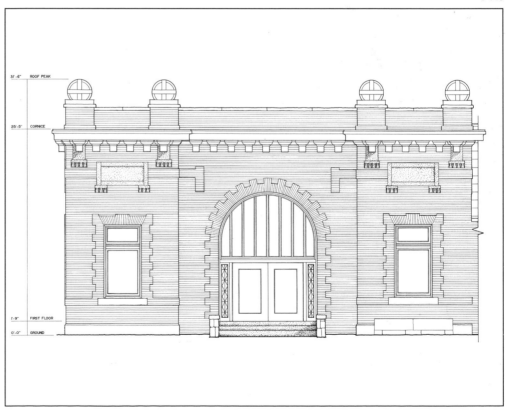

31'-6" ROOF PEAK

25'-5" CORNICE

1'-9" FIRST FLOOR

0'-0" GROUND

8-016

8-017

8-017. Railroad station, Golden, Colorado. P&P,LC-USZ6-1340.

8-018. Cog Road Depot, Manitou, Colorado. A. C. Roebuck, photographer, ca. 1908. P&P,LOT 4939,LC-USZ62-107802.

8-018

8-019

8-019. Denver & Rio Grande Western Station, Glenwood Springs, Colorado. P&P,LC-USZ62-100224.

With the Colorado River across its tracks to the north, the south side of the station featured a staircase built into the hillside to lead down to the street.

8-020. Railroad station of the Denver & Rio Grande Western Railroad, Ouray, Colorado. Russell Lee/FSA, photographer, September 1940. P&P,LC-USF34-037589-D.

The line through Ouray was narrow gauge, as was the case with many mountainside stations in Colorado.

8-020

8-021

8-022

8-021. North and west (track) sides, Union Passenger Station, Third West & South Temple, Salt Lake City, Salt Lake County, Utah. Louise T. Taft, photographer, July 1985. P&P,HABS,UTAH,18-SALCI,25-2.

8-022. Waiting room looking northwest, Union Passenger Station, Third West & South Temple, Salt Lake City, Salt Lake County, Utah. Louise T. Taft, photographer, July 1985. P&P,HABS,UTAH,18-SALCI,25-4.

The barrel-vaulted waiting room featured murals painted by California artist John A. MacQuarrie at either end. To the north the painting was of Brigham Young and the arrival of his cohort in Utah; the south wall showed a depiction of the 1869 golden spike ceremony in Promontory Point.

8-023. East front, Union Passenger Station, Third West & South Temple, Salt Lake City. Salt Lake County, Utah. Louise T. Taft, photographer, July 1985. P&P,HABS,UTAH,18-SALCI,25-1.

The exterior of Salt Lake City's Union Station was somewhat ponderous, odd in both scale and the mix of materials.

8-024. Elevations, Union Passenger Station, Third West & South Temple, Salt Lake City, Salt Lake County, Utah. P&P,sheet no. 4.

8-025. Elevations and sections, Union Passenger Station, Third West & South Temple, Salt Lake City, Salt Lake County, Utah. P&P,sheet no. 5.

8-023

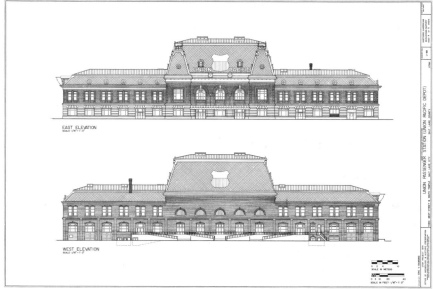

8-024

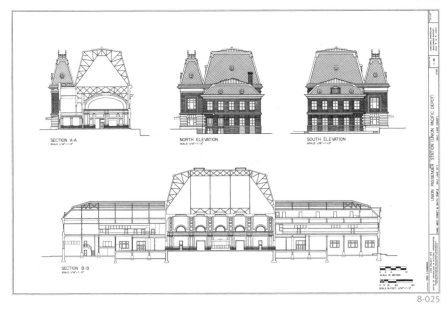

8-025

8-026

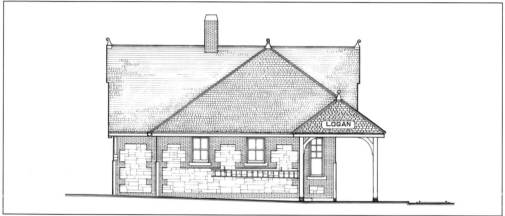

8-027

8-026. Union Pacific Passenger Depot, Logan, Utah. P. Kent Fairbanks, photographer, August 1967. P&P,HABS,UTAH,3-LOG,1-3.

8-027. North elevation and detail, Union Pacific Passenger Depot, Logan, Utah. P&P,sheet no. 4.

The central sandstone block of the depot appears to have corners of dressed stone quoins but they in fact are made of dark red pressed brick.

8-028. South and east sides, Oregon Short Line Railroad Depot, Highway 23, Cache Junction, Cache County, Utah. P&P,HABS,UTAH,3-CAJU,1-1.

The railroad company built this depot to go with the town it hoped would grow here.

8-028

8-029

8-029. Salt Lake Railway Depot at Las Vegas, Nevada. West Coast Art Company, ca. 1910. P&P,PAN US GEOG-Nevada no. 19 (E size),LC-USZ62-137463.

8-030. Depot Hotel, Reno, Washoe County, Nevada. Britton & Rey, lithographers, 1881. Gen. Coll.,Illus in F841,A5 1881,LC-USZ62-61312.

8-031. Railroad station, Carson City, Nevada. Arthur Rothstein, photographer, March 1940. P&P,LC-USF34-029972-D.

DEPOT HOTEL, RENO, WASHOE CO NEVADA.
W.R.CHAMBERLAIN, PROPRIETOR.

8-030

8-031

THE SOUTHWEST

Two major rail lines dominated the American Southwest: the Southern Pacific

and the Atchison, Topeka & Santa Fe. The stations of the Southern Pacific

were often quite fanciful in design, even when erected by in-house architects.

The Brownsville, Texas, station building (1929), designed by Southern Pacific

staffer Leonard B. McCoy (dates unknown), was primarily a stucco concoction,

trimmed with fancy ironwork and cast-stone ornament. Equally attractive is the

anonymously designed Southern Pacific Station (1913) in Berkeley, California,

with a Mission Style stucco exterior.

The Atchison, Topeka & Santa Fe came to be linked in the public mind with

Harvey House hospitality operations, which often featured hotels designed

by architect Mary Jane Colter. She was famous in the Grand Canyon area for

a number of Hopi- and Navajo-inspired buildings. For the Atchison, Topeka &

Santa Fe, Colter teamed with Charles Whittlesey (architect of El Tovar Lodge at

the Grand Canyon) to build a great station complex for Albuquerque, New Mexico

(1902). Unfortunately all their work there has been lost to fire and urban renewal.

9-001. The Atchison, Topeka & Santa Fe Railroad streamliner "Super Chief" stopping for five minutes servicing at the depot, Albuquerque, New Mexico. Jack Delano, photographer, March 1943. P&P,LC-USW3-020415-D.

Albuquerque's Atchison, Topeka & Santa Fe station was always a full-service stop for all trains on its line.

9-002

9-003

9-002. Southwest (front) façade, Southern
Pacific Railroad Passenger Station, 601
East Madison Street, Brownsville, Cameron
County, Texas. Bill Engdahl/Hedrich-
Blessing, photographer, February 1979.
P&P,HABS,TEX,31-BROWN,15-2.

Brownsville's Southern Pacific Station was
almost domestic in scale. Its ivory-colored
walls featured all sorts of openings and
decorative features.

9-003. Front central bay window and
balconet (a vestigal balcony), Southern
Pacific Railroad Passenger Station, 601
East Madison Street, Brownsville, Cameron
County, Texas. Bill Engdahl/Hedrich-
Blessing, photographer, February 1979.
P&P,HABS,TEX,31-BROWN,15-7.

9-004. Cast-stone ornament, east end bay,
Southern Pacific Railroad Passenger Station,
601 East Madison Street, Brownsville,
Cameron County, Texas. Bill Engdahl/
Hedrich-Blessing, photographer, February
1979. P&P,HABS,TEX,31-BROWN,15-11.

The portal openings to the open-air
platforms at the north and south ends of the
station had been enclosed at the time of the
photographs.

Colter's Navajo Hotel at Gallup, New Mexico, is also gone, but her La Posada Hotel
survives, along with its adjoining station built in Winslow, Arizona, in 1930.

Oddly enough, the Atchison, Topeka & Santa Fe did not run its main line to Sante Fe
itself, allocating the town only a spur line for reasons that are unclear. The line had no
problem reaching as far as San Diego, where the Mission Revival style once again was
the dominant theme for railroad buildings. The arcaded station building was the work of
the San Francisco firm of Bakewell & Brown, best known for designing the San Francisco
and Pasadena City Halls.

9-004

9-005. Trademark of the Santa Fe showing map of America on globe and train routes with a lion on top of globe. Unidentified illustrator, ca. 1895, W. A. White. P&P,LOT 2639,LC-USZ62-105406.

9-006. Atchison, Topeka & Santa Fe Railroad at Black, Texas to Clovis, New Mexico. Jack Delano, photographer, March 1943. P&P,LC-USW3-020452-D.

9-007. Burkburnett, Texas, April 24th, 1919. W. H. Raymond, photographer, April 1919. P&P,PAN US GEOG-Texas no. 70 (E size).

There appear to be far more oil wells than people around the station in Burkburnett.

9-005

9-006

9-007

9-008

9-009

9-008. Railroad station, Algoa, Texas. Unidentified photographer, ca. 1907. P&P,LC-USZ62-43023.

9-009. Elevations, Tulia Railroad Depot, State Highway 87, Tulia, Swisher County, Texas. John Jennings, delineator. P&P,HABS,TEX,219-TUL,2-,sheet no. 1.

9-010. Santa Fe Railroad Depot, San Angelo, Texas. Unidentified photographer, March 1908. P&P,LC-USZ62-61266.

9-010

9-011

9-011. The Alvarado Hotel, panoramic view of railroad station, Albuquerque, New Mexico. DETR, ca. 1903. P&P,LOT 9148,LC-USZ62-46258.

The combined effort of architects Mary Jane Colter and Charles Whittlesey was lost to a fire and the city's subsequent encroachments on the derelict railroad properties.

9-012. Central patio, Alvarado Hotel, First Street, Albuquerque, Bernalillo County, New Mexico. Fred Mang Jr., photographer, October 1963. P&P,HABS, NM,1-ALBU.5-5.

9-013. Santa Fe Railroad Station, Albuquerque, New Mexico. DETR, ca. 1903. P&P,LOT 9148,LC-USZ62-50691.

9-012

9-013

9-014

9-014. "This is the crowd that met me when I came to Rockport, Texas." P&P,LC-USZ62-61267.

9-015. South façade from Santa Fe Railroad tracks, Castaneda Hotel, Las Vegas, San Miguel County, New Mexico. P&P,HABS,NM,24-LAVEG,2-1.

9-016. Railroad station, Gallup, New Mexico. P&P,LC-USZ62-103260.

9-015

9-016

9-017

9-017. Passing the depot on the Atchison, Topeka & Santa Fe, Laguna, New Mexico. Jack Delano, photographer, March 1943. P&P,LC-USW3-021147-E.

9-018. Passing the Southern Pacific Railroad Station along the Atchison, Topeka & Santa Fe Railroad, Vaughn, New Mexico. Jack Delano, photographer, March 1943. P&P,LC-USW3-020718-E.

Located far away from any sizable town, the station in Vaughn mainly features a water tower and a coaling chute, rather than any passenger services.

9-019. Southern Pacific Railroad Station, Maricopa, Arizona. P&P,LC-USZ62-136283.

9-018

9-019

9-020

9-020. View to north, Arizona & New Mexico Railroad Passenger Station, Coronado Boulevard, Clifton, Greenlee County, Arizona. Robert G. Graham, photographer, 1993. P&P,HABS,ARIZ,6-CLIFT,34-1.

9-021. View across river to southwest, Arizona & New Mexico Railroad Passenger Station, Clifton, Coronado Boulevard, Greenlee County, Arizona. Robert G. Graham photographer, 1993. P&P,HABS,ARIZ,6-CLIFT,34-3.

The station in Clifton sits alongside the San Francisco River out in the Arizona copper country. It opened in 1913 with an assortment of waiting rooms and offices, including some set aside for Wells Fargo, the stagecoach transportation company that the railroads were steadily replacing.

9-021

9-022

9-023

9-022. Railroad tracks, Beardsley, Arizona.
California Panorama Company, ca. 1908.
P&P,PAN US GEOG-Arizona,no. 54 (E size).

9-023. Hotel Escalante, Ash Fork, Arizona.
DETR, ca. 1908. P&P,LC-USZ62-87475.

9-024. Fray Marcus Hotel, Williams, Arizona.
William Henry Jackson/DETR, ca. 1908.
P&P,LOT 3748,LC-USZ62-89202.

Both the Hotel Escalante and the Fray
Marcus Hotel (a Harvey House operation)
welcomed weary travelers with rooms just
a short walk from their trains. The Italian
Renaissance look of the Fray Marcus was a
bit of a departure from the Harvey House
norm.

9-024

9-025

9-025. South façade, railroad depot, Grand Canyon National Park, Coconino County, Arizona. Jack E. Boucher, photographer, September 1975. P&P,HABS,ARIZ,3-GRACAN,2-5.

9-026. "Station to be built at Grand Canyon, Ariz. for the Grand Canyon Railroad Company," front elevation and foundation plan, railroad depot, Grand Canyon National Park, Coconino County, Arizona. Francis W. Wilson, architect, ca. 1905. P&P,HABS,ARIZ,3-GRACAN,2-1.

9-026

9-027.

9-028.

9-027. Detail of brass doorknob with "Grand Canyon" insignia, railroad depot, Grand Canyon National Park, Coconino County, Arizona. Jack E. Boucher, photographer, September 1975. P&P,HABS,ARIZ,3-GRACAN,2-13.

9-028. Grand Canyon Railroad Terminal, facing northwest, Village Loop Drive, Grand Canyon Village, Grand Canyon National Park, Coconino County, Arizona. Brian C. Grogan, photographer, 1984. P&P,HAER,ARIZ,3-GRACAN,10-7.

9-029. Detail of log wall showing leather strips tacked between logs, railroad depot, Grand Canyon National Park, Coconino County, Arizona. Jack E. Boucher, photographer, September 1975. P&P,HABS,ARIZ,3-GRACAN,2-10.

9-029.

9-030. "North and west elevation, plus details of doors, & wall and gutter construction," railroad depot, Grand Canyon National Park, Coconino County, Arizona. Francis W. Wilson, architect, ca. 1905. P&P,HABS,ARIZ,3-GRACAN,2-3.

The station at the South Rim terminus of the Santa Fe's spur line was built of slabs and logs cut from local stands of Ponderosa pine. When the Santa Fe gave up the line in 1929 the National Park Service took over operations, running trains 40 miles to the station in Williams. The latter was also designed by Francis W. Wilson (1870–1947), though far more elaborate.

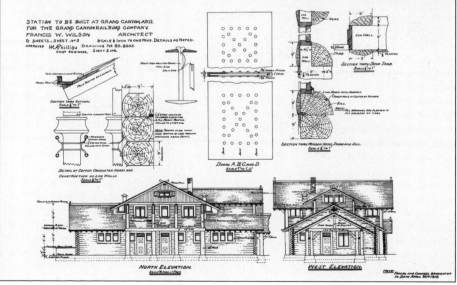

9-030.

9-031

9-032

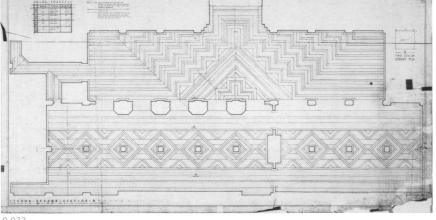
9-033

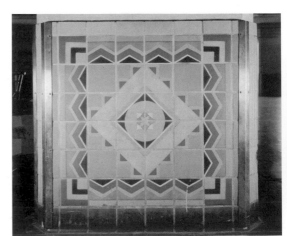
9-034

9-031. Loggia to/from reception hall, from south patio looking east, Los Angeles Union Passenger Terminal, tracks & shed, 800 North Alameda Street, Los Angeles, Los Angeles County, California. Mark A. Bookspan, photographer. P&P,HABS,CAL,19-LOSAN,64-A-48.

9-032. Reception hall and arrival lobby, Los Angeles Union Passenger Terminal, Tracks & Shed, 800 North Alameda Street, Los Angeles, Los Angeles County, California. Mark A. Bookspan, photographer. P&P,HABS,CAL,19-LOSAN,64-A-32.

9-033. Floor design, section III (with color schedule), Los Angeles Union Passenger Terminal, tracks & shed, 800 North Alameda Street, Los Angeles, Los Angeles County, California. P&P,HABS,CAL,19-LOSAN,64-A-59.

9-034. Detail, faience tile, column wainscot pattern, arrival lobby, Los Angeles Union Passenger Terminal, tracks & shed, 800 North Alameda Street, Los Angeles, Los Angeles County, California. Everett Weinreb, photographer. P&P,HABS,CAL,19-LOSAN,64-A-31.

9-035

9-035. Northeast (track) side, San Francisco & San Jose Railroad Station, 1100 Merrill Street, Menlo Park, San Mateo County, California. Jack E. Boucher, photographer, August–September 1975. P&P,HABS,CAL,41-MENPA,4-1.

9-036. Southeast side, San Francisco & San Jose Railroad Station, 1100 Merrill Street, Menlo Park, San Mateo County, California. Jack E. Boucher, photographer, August–September 1975. P&P,HABS,CAL,41-MENPA,4-4.

This domestically scaled station, operating since 1867, is the oldest still in business in California.

9-036

9-037

9-038

9-039

9-040

9-037. Front arcade and tower upon completion, Santa Fe Railroad Station, 1050 Kettner Boulevard, San Diego, San Diego County, California. Marion Rand, photographer, 1971. P&P,HABS,CAL,37-SANDI,22-15.

9-038. South front and west side, Santa Fe Railroad Station, 1050 Kettner Boulevard, San Diego, San Diego County, California. Marion Rand, photographer, 1971. P&P,HABS,CAL,37-SANDI,22-2.

Although the arcaded front plaza of the station was sacrificed for parking in 1954, the steel-framed building has held up well.

9-039. Door to stair hall, Santa Fe Railroad Station, 1050 Kettner Boulevard, San Diego, San Diego County, California. Marion Rand, photographer, 1971. P&P,HABS,CAL,37-SANDI,22-6.

Santa Fe logos figure prominently throughout the station interior and as signage outside as well.

9-040. Waiting room, Santa Fe Railroad Station, 1050 Kettner Boulevard, San Diego, San Diego County, California. Walter Smalling, photographer, November 1980. P&P,HABS,CAL,37-SANDI,22-7.

9-041

9-042

9-041. Construction photo showing towers, August 17, 1914, Santa Fe Railroad Station, 1050 Kettner Boulevard, San Diego, San Diego County, California. Title Insurance Company/San Diego Historical Society, August 1914. P&P,HABS,CAL,37-SANDI,22-9.

9-042. General view prior to demolition of old station, September 3, 1914, Santa Fe Railroad Station, 1050 Kettner Boulevard, San Diego, San Diego County, California. Title Insurance Company/San Diego Historical Society, September 1914. P&P,HABS,CAL,37-SANDI,22-12.

9-043

9-043. General view after demolition of old station, October 1, 1914, Santa Fe Railroad Station, 1050 Kettner Boulevard, San Diego, San Diego County, California. Title Insurance Company/San Diego Historical Society, October 1914. P&P,HABS,CAL,37-SANDI,22-13.

Construction of the towers was a steady process in the late summer of 1914. Demolition of the old station tower was a more dramatic event.

9-044. Demolition of old station tower (between September 3 and October 1, 1914), Santa Fe Railroad Station, 1050 Kettner Boulevard, San Diego, San Diego County, California. Title Insurance Company/San Diego Historical Society, September 1914. P&P,HABS,CAL,37-SANDI,22-14.

9-044

9-045

9-046

9-047

9-045. Road side looking north, Southern Pacific Railroad Station, Burlingame Avenue & California Drive, Burlingame, San Mateo County, California. Morley Baer, photographer, May 1971. P&P,HABS,CAL,41-BURL,1-5.

9-046. Road side, detail of tower, Southern Pacific Railroad Station, Burlingame Avenue & California Drive, Burlingame, San Mateo County, California. Morley Baer, photographer, May 1971. P&P,HABS,CAL,41-BURL,1-6.

9-047. Arcade west of station, Southern Pacific Railroad Station, Burlingame Avenue & California Drive, Burlingame, San Mateo County, California. Morley Baer, photographer, May 1971. P&P,HABS,CAL,41-BURL,1-18.

The Burlingame Country Club commissioned this station, which explains in part its genteel appearance. The architects, George H. Howard, Jr. (dates unknown) and J. B. Mathison (dates unknown), were both club members in good standing.

9-048. [opposite page] East side of waiting room, detail, Southern Pacific Railroad Station, Burlingame Avenue & California Drive, Burlingame, San Mateo County, California. Morley Baer, photographer, May 1971. P&P,HABS,CAL,41-BURL,1-9.

9-049. [opposite page] Garden north of stationmaster's house, Southern Pacific Railroad Station, Burlingame Avenue & California Drive, Burlingame, San Mateo County, California. Morley Baer, photographer, May 1971. P&P,HABS,CAL,41-BURL,1-7.

9-048

9-049

9-050

9-050. Track side, false-front gable, Southern Pacific Railroad Station, Burlingame Avenue & California Drive, Burlingame, San Mateo County, California. Morley Baer, photographer, May 1971. P&P,HABS,CAL,41-BURL,1-3.

9-051. Track side, interior of arcade, Southern Pacific Railroad Station, Burlingame Avenue & California Drive, Burlingame, San Mateo County, California. Morley Baer, photographer, May 1971. P&P,HABS,CAL,41-BURL,1-4.

9-051

9-052

9-053

9-052. Trackside façade, Union Pacific Railroad Depot, intersection of Kelbaker & Kelso Cima roads, Kelso, San Bernardino County, California. P&P,HABS,CAL,36-KELSO,1-1.

9-053. Elevation and emblem, Union Pacific Railroad Depot, intersection of Kelbaker & Kelso Cima roads, Kelso, San Bernardino County, California. P&P,sheet no. 1.

Kelso was a watering station for Union Pacific trains passing through the Mojave Desert.

9-054. Northeast façade, Southern Pacific Depot, 559 El Camino Real, San Carlos, San Mateo County, California. Don Tateishi, photographer, September 1987. P&P,HABS,CAL,41-SACR,1-32.

9-054

9-055

9-056

9-055. Oblique view from lift-bed truck showing deteriorated slate roof, general appearance of passenger platform area and setting, Southern Pacific Depot, 559 El Camino Real, San Carlos, San Mateo County, California. Don Tateishi, photographer, August 1984. P&P,HABS,CAL,41-SACAR,1-3.

The depot building at San Carlos was the first permanent structure of a speculative community developed in 1887 by the San Carlos Land Company. The stone for the station was shipped in on a Southern Pacific spur line from San Jose, at a final cost of $8,000. The architect is uncredited but most likely was Charles Atherton Coolidge (1858–1932). Coolidge was a partner in the firm of Shepley, Rutan, & Coolidge (inheritors of H. H. Richardson's practice in 1886), which was then engaged in designing the campus for nearby Stanford University.

9-056. Detail, northeast façade, operator s bow window and tower, Southern Pacific Depot, 559 El Camino Real, San Carlos, San Mateo County, California. Don Tateishi, photographer, August 1984. P&P,HABS,CAL,41-SACAR,1-16.

Note condition of tower skirt roof, missing section of gutter at left side.

9-057. Detail, northeast façade, operator's bow window and tower, Southern Pacific Depot, 559 El Camino Real, San Carlos, San Mateo County, California. Don Tateishi, photographer, September 1987. P&P,HABS,CAL,41-SACAR,1-45.

The State of California was behind the restoration of the depot building in the mid-1980s.

9-058. Detail, northeast façade, repaired tower skirt roof, knee braces, downspout, Southern Pacific Depot, 559 El Camino Real, San Carlos, San Mateo County, California. Don Tateishi, photographer, September 1987. P&P,HABS,CAL,41-SACAR,1-47.

9-057

9-058

9-059

9-060

9-059. East elevation, National City Depot, 900 West Twenty-third Street, National City, San Diego County, California. P&P,sheet no. 5.

9-060. Street façade, National City Depot, 900 West Twenty-third Street, National City, San Diego County, California. Edward Gohlich, photographer. P&P,HABS,CAL,37-NATCI,5-1.

9-061. Entry door, National City Depot, 900 West Twenty-third Street, National City, San Diego County, California. Edward Gohlich, photographer. P&P,HABS,CAL,37-NATC,5-8.

9-061

9-062. La Grande Station, Los Angeles, California. DETR, ca. 1898. P&P,LOT 9056,LC-USZ62-65773.

9-063. La Grande Station, Los Angeles, California. DETR, ca. 1899. P&P,LOT 9056,LC-USZ62-61705.

9-064

9-065

9-066

9-067

9-064. Panorama of Fresno, California. California Panorama Company, ca. 1909. P&P,PAN US GEOG-California,no. 27 (F size).

9-065. Southern Pacific Depot, Palm Springs, California. P&P,LC-USZ62-61265,

9-066. Railroad depot at Riverside, California. P&P,LC-USZ62-61264.

The oddly proportioned Mission Revival depot in Riverside was built by the San Pedro, Los Angeles & Salt Lake Railroad.

9-067. Steamer landing and Pacific Railroad Depot, Sacramento, California. Lawrence & Houseworth, publisher, 1866. P&P,LOT 3544-31,no. 1976,LC-USZ62-26908.

9-068

9-069

9-070

9-068. Panorama of Kern, California. West Coast Art Company, ca. 1909. P&P,PAN US GEOG-Calsifornia,no. 191 (E size).

9-069. Southern Pacific train at Shasta Springs, Valley of the Sacramento, California. H. C. White Company, ca. 1905. P&P,STEREO SUBJ FILE,LC-USZ62-93783.

9-070. Going through the station on the Atchison, Topeka & Santa Fe Railroad, Bagdad, California. Jack Delano, photographer, March 1943. P&P,LC-USW3-021445.

9-071. The log cabin railroad station, Feather River Inn, California. P&P,LC-USZ62-61256.

9-071

BIBLIOGRAPHY

Alexander, Edwin P. *Down at the Depot: American Railroad Stations from 1831 to 1920*. New York: Clarkson Potter, 1970.

Ballon, Hilary. *New York's Pennsylvania Stations*. New York: Norton, 2002.

Boucher, Jack. E. *A Record in Detail: The Architectural Photographs of Jack E. Boucher*. Columbia: University of Missouri Press, 1988.

Bye, Randolph. *The Vanishing Depot*. Wynnewood, PA: Livingston Publishing, 1973.

Doughty, Jeffrey L. *New York Central's Stations and Terminals*. Lynchburg, VA: TLC Publishing, 1999.

Grant, H. Roger. *Living in the Depot: The Two-Story Railroad Station*. Iowa City: University of Iowa Press, 1993.

Highsmith, Carol M., with Ted Landphair. *Union Station: A History of Washington's Grand Terminal*, 2nd ed. Washington, DC: Union Station Venture, 1998.

Hitchcock, Henry-Russell. *The Architecture of H. H. Richardson and His Times*. Cambridge, MA: MIT Press, 1936.

Holland, Kevin J. *Classic American Railroad Terminals*. Osceola, WI: MBI Publishing/Andover Junction Publications, 2001.

Larson, Erik. *The Devil in the White City*. New York: Random House, 2003.

Lyden, Anne M. *Railroad Vision: Photography, Travel, and Perception*. Los Angeles: J. Paul Getty Museum, 2003.

Maddex, Diane, ed. *Built in the U.S.A.: American Buildings from Airports to Zoos*. Washington, DC: Preservation Press, 1985.

Meeks, Carroll L. V. *The Railroad Station: An Architectural History*. New Haven, CT: Yale University Press, 1956.

Mitchell, Alexander D., IV. *Train Stations: Whistle Stops, Rail Stations, and Train Depots of North America*. Philadelphia: Courage Books, 2001.

Naylor, David. "Old Faithful Inn and Its Legacy: The Vernacular Transformed." Master's thesis, Cornell University, 1990.

O'Gorman, James F. *The Architecture of Frank Furness*. Philadelphia: Philadelphia Museum of Art, 1973.

Potter, Janet Greenstein. *Great American Railroad Stations*. New York: John Wiley & Sons/Preservation Press, 1996.

Waiting room from northwest, Pennsylvania Station, 370 Seventh Avenue, West Thirty-first–Thirty-third streets, New York, New York County, New York. Cervin Robinson, photographer, May 1962. P&P,HABS,NY,31-NEYO,78-6.

An escalator was installed in the middle of the grand staircase down from the retail arcade in the years prior to the demolition, which began late in 1963.

Reinhart, Karen Wildung, with Jeff Henry. *Old Faithful Inn: Crown Jewel of the National Park Lodges*. Emigrant, MT: Roche Jaune Pictures, 2004.

Richards, Jeffrey, with John M. MacKenzie. *The Railway Station: A Social History*. Oxford/ New York: Oxford University Press, 1986.

Riskin, Marci L. *The Train Stops Here: New Mexico's Railway Legacy*. Albuquerque: University of New Mexico Press, 2005.

Schafer, Mike. *Classic American Railroads*. Osceola, WI: MBI Publishing/Andover Junction Publications, 1996.

Schaffer, Kristen. *Daniel H. Burnham: Visionary Architect and Planner*. New York: Rizzoli, 2003.

Schwieterman, Joseph P. *When the Railroad Leaves Town: American Communities in the Age of Rail Line Abandonment*. Kirksville, MO: Truman State University Press, 2001.

Solomon, Brian. *Railroad Stations*. New York: Metro Books, 1998.

Vance, James E., Jr. *The North American Railroad: Its Origin, Evolution, and Geography*. Baltimore: Johns Hopkins University Press, 1995.

Walsh, Joe, with Jim Boyd and William F. Howes Jr. *The American Railroad*. Osceola, WI: MBI Publishing/Andover Junction, 1999.

Wheeler, Keith. *The Railroaders*. New York: Time-Life Books, 1973.

ABOUT THE ONLINE PORTFOLIO

The online portfolio (www.wwnorton.com/npb/loc/railroadstations) includes all of the images in this book and direct links to three of the Library of Congress's most useful online catalogs and sites, which you may choose to consult in locating and downloading high-resolution images included on it or related items. Searching directions, help, and search examples (by text or keywords, titles, authors or creators, subject or location, and catalog and reproduction numbers, etc.) are provided, in addition to information on rights and restrictions, how to order reproductions, and how to consult the materials in person.

1. The Prints & Photographs Online Catalog (PPOC) (http://www.loc.gov/pictures/) contains catalog records and more than 1.25 million digital images representing a rich cross-section of pictures held by the Prints & Photographs Division and other units of the Library. It includes a majority of the images in the online portfolio and many related images, such as those in the HABS, HAER, and HALS collections cited below. At this writing the catalog provides access through group or item records to about 95% of the Division's holdings.

   Although the catalog is added to on a regular basis, it is not an exhaustive listing of the holdings of the Prints & Photographs Division, which consist of more than 14 million items (paper finding aids, card catalogs, and browsing files of pictures available on site supplement descriptions in PPOC); nor does it include all the items in the online portfolio (most books, maps, and manuscripts are covered by the Library of Congress Online Catalog, http://catalog.loc.gov). PPOC does offer direct display of digital images, and links to rights, ordering, and background information about the collections represented. When there are potential rights considerations, only "thumbnail" images (GIF images) will display to those searching outside the Library of Congress, while on-site searchers have access to larger JPEG and TIFF images.

   The Historic American Buildings Survey, Historic American Engineering Record, and Historic American Landscapes Survey collections are part of this catalog and are among the most heavily represented collections in the online portfolio, http://www.loc.gov/pictures/collection/hh/.

For further information about how to search for Prints & Photographs Division holdings, consult the home page, http://www.loc.gov/rr/print/; submit an "Ask a Librarian" query at http://www.loc.gov/rr/askalib/ask-print.html, or contact: Prints & Photographs Reading Room, telephone: 202-707-6394.

2. The American Memory site (http://memory.loc.gov) is a gateway to rich primary source materials relating to the history and culture of the United States. The site offers more than seven million digital items from more than 100 historical collections.

3. The Library of Congress Online Catalog (http://catalog.loc.gov/) contains approximately 14 million records representing books, serials, computer files, manuscripts, cartographic materials, music, sound recordings, and visual materials. It is especially useful for finding items identified as being from the Manuscript Division and the Geography and Map Division of the Library of Congress.

INDEX

Locators that include a section designator followed by a hyphen (e.g., IN-010, 3-152, 5-012) refer to numbered captions. All other locators are page numbers. Individuals who created the original images used in this volume, or the structure depicted, are identified as follows: arch.=architect; art.=artist; del.=delineator; eng.=engineer; engr.=engraver; lith.=lithographer.

accidents and natural disasters, IN-011–013
Alabama
    Bessemer, 5-063
    Mobile, 197, 5-073, 5-074
    Montgomery, 5-065–072
    Tuscaloosa, 5-064
Alaska
    Anchorage, 7-031, 7-034
    Chatanika, 7-033
    Cordova, 7-037
    Seward, 276, 7-032, 7-035
    Skagway, 7-036
    Wasilla, 276
Alaska Railroad, 7-034, 7-035
American Renaissance, 36
Ames, Oakes, 24, IN-034
Amtrak, 63, 4-016, 4-033
Anderson, Paul (ph.), 7-015
Archer, George F. (arch.), IN-073
Arizona
    Ash Fork, 9-023
    Beardsley, 9-022
    Clifton, 9-020
    Douglas, IN-091
    Grand Canyon National Park, 26, IN-035, 9-025–030
    Maricopa, 9-019
    Williams, 9-024
    Winslow, 304
Arizona & New Mexico Railroad, 9-020, 9-021
Arkansas
    Fayetteville, 5-051
    Hot Springs, 5-052
    Little Rock, 5-050
Atchison, Topeka & Santa Fe Railroad, IN-037, 9-005, 9-018
    Albuquerque, New Mexico depot, 9-001
    Bagdad, California station, 9-070

building design for, 303–304
    Laguna, New Mexico depot, 9-017
    Perry, Oklahoma station, 8-008–010
Atlantic Coast Line
    Orlando, Florida station, 5-080, 5-081
    Presidential Special Railroad, IN-004
Atwood, Charles (arch.), 35
Bad Day at Black Rock (film), 43
Baer, Morley (ph.), 9-045–051
baggage handling, IN-084–087
Baker, Ray Standard (ph.), IN-062
Bakewell & Brown (arch.), 304
Baldwin, E. Francis (arch.), 31, IN-042, 64, 1-004, 1-031, 1-049
Baldwin & Pennington (arch.), 63
Baldwin School (Bryn Mawr, Pennsylvania), 32
Baltimore & Ohio Railroad, IN-016, 29–32, IN-041–044
    Baltimore area facilities, 29, IN-038–041, 63–64, 1-002–010, 1-016–020
    Cumberland, Maryland station, 1-035–039
    Harper's Ferry, West Virginia station, 1-046, 1-047, 1-049
    Laurel, Maryland station, 1-031
    Martinsburg, West Virginia facility, IN-088–090, IN-093, IN-094
    Philadelphia Station, 2-021–028
    Point of Rocks, Maryland station, 31, IN-043, 1-001, 64, 1-022–029
    Rockville, Maryland station, 64, 1-030
    Wheeling, West Virginia station, 1-050–052
Baltimore & Potomac Station, IN-005
Bandholtz, F. J. (ph.), 6-065
Bangor & Aroostock Railroad, 4-009
Barnard, George N. (ph.), IN-022–024
Barrett, William Edmund (ph.), IN-039, IN-040, IN-088, IN-093, IN-094, 1-001, 1-003, 1-004, 1-009, 1-010, 1-016, 1-019, 1-023, 1-025, 1-028, 1-035, 1-036, 1-038, 1-039, 1-049, 1-050, 1-052, 4-015, 4-017, 4-030, 4-031
Bartlett, Samuel L. (arch.), 7-004
Baxter, D. C. (engr.), 1-012
Bayless, Charles N. (ph.), 5-027, 5-029, 5-030
Beaux-Arts design, 36
Beman, Solon Spencer (arch.), 6-031

Berghaus & Upham (engr.), IN-005
Berninghaus, O. E. (art.), 38, IN-054
Birrie, Barry A. (art.), 3-076
Black Diamond Express, 2-067
Blue Mountain House (Maryland), 1-033
Bookspan, Mark A. (ph.), 9-031, 9-032
Boston, Massachusetts
    Back Bay Station, 4-035
    North Station, 4-034
    South Station, 4-001, 176, 4-032, 4-033
Boston & Albany Railroad, 33, IN-082, 175–176, 4-035
    Auburndale station, IN-045
    Framingham station, 4-036–039
    Newton station, 4-046
    Palmer station, 4-040, 4-041
    Wellesley station, 4-042, 4-043
Boston & Maine Railroad, 4-044, 4-049, 176
Boston & Providence Railroad
    Boston, Massachusetts Back Bay station, 4-035
    Stoughton, Massachusetts station, 4-051, 4-052
Bostwick, C. O. (ph.), IN-020
Boucher, Jack E. (ph.), IN-043, IN-067, IN-072, IN-073, IN-097, IN-101, IN-106, 55, 1-001, 1-018, 1-021, 1-023, 1-025, 1-028, 1-030, 1-031, 1-045, 1-057, 1-064, 2-007–014, 2-030, 2-033, 2-038–040, 2-055–059, 3-034, 3-035, 3-039, 3-040, 3-053, 3-057–059, 3-067, 3-068, 4-016, 4-018–020, 4-022–024, 4-028, 4-033, 5-002, 5-004, 5-031, 5-034–039, 5-041, 5-042, 5-047–049, 5-054, 5-059, 5-060, 5-065, 5-069, 5-071, 5-075–079, 5-085–087, 5-094, 5-096–103, 5-106–108, 5-110–114, 5-116, 6-011–016, 6-018, 6-019, 6-039, 6-067–076, 9-025, 9-027, 9-029, 9-035, 9-036
Boudelle, Jean (art.), 119
Boudelle, Pierre (art.), 2-104, 2-107
Bradley, Luther Daniels (art.), IN-055
Brady, Matthew B. (ph.), 15, IN-014
Brewster, Robert (ph.), 4-021
Brigham, Charles (arch.), 4-051
Brink, Brian Vanden (ph.), 4-005–007
Britton & Rey (lith.), 8-030
Browne, C. E. (ph.), 3-041
Bryant, William Jennings, IN-002
Burnham, Daniel H. (arch.), IN-050, 35–36, 83–84, 2-009, 2-075

331

Burnham & Root (arch.), 35, 6-059, 6-065
Burns, William George (arch.), 2-006
Bush, Lincoln (arch.), IN-078, 3-068
Bush shed, IN-078, 3-009, 6-028
Butte, Anaconda & Pacific Railway, 7-013
Cabell, F. J. (del.), IN-068
California
    Bagdad, 9-070
    Berkeley, 303
    Burlingame, 9-045–051
    Feather River Inn, 9-070
    Fresno, 9-064
    Kelso, 9-052, 9-053
    Kern, 9-068
    Los Angeles, 43, IN-075, IN-081, 9-031–034, 9-062,
        9-063
    Menlo Park, 9-035, 9-036
    National City, 9-059–061
    Palm Springs, 9-065
    Riverside, 9-066
    Sacramento, 9-067
    San Carlos, 9-054–058
    San Diego, 9-037–044
    Shasta Springs, 9-068
Calvert Station (Baltimore, Maryland), 1-014, 1-015
Camden Depot (Charleston, South Carolina), 5-029,
    5-030
Camden Station (Baltimore, Maryland), 63, 1-008–010
Carpenter Gothic design, 3-057, 4-028
Carrère & Hastings (arch.), 23, 275, 7-018
Carter, Jimmy, 5-092
Cassatt, A. J., 64
Cassatt, Mary (art.), 64
Central of Georgia Railway, Savannah facilities, IN-
    067, IN-097, IN-106, 5-093, 231, 5-094–120
Central Pacific Railroad, 21
Central Railroad of New Jersey
    Bethlehem, Pennsylvania station, 2-038–040
    Elizabeth, New Jersey Station, 3-019
    Jersey City, New Jersey Ferry Terminal, 3-008–014
    Jim Thorpe Station, Pennsylvania, 2-063
Central Union Station (Cincinnati, Ohio), 2-072
Chesapeake & Ohio Railroad
    Newport News, Virginia station, 5-009, 5-010
    Richmond, Virginia station, 5-004
    Shadwell, Virginia station, IN-068
    Thurmond, West Virginia depot, 1-048
Chicago, Burlington & Quincy Railroad, 6-043, 6-059,
    6-060
Chicago, Illinois
    Chicago & Northwestern Railroad Station, 6-037
    coaling station, IN-096
    Dearborn Street Station, 6-035, 6-036
    Grand Central Station, IN-079, IN-080, 6-031–034
    Illinois Central Railroad Station, 6-038, 6-039
    North Western terminal, 6-022–028
    significance of, in national rail system, 243
    Union Station, 43, IN-102, IN-103, 6-029, 6-030
    World's Columbian Exposition, 34–37, IN-049, 6-039
Chicago, Milwaukee, St. Paul & Pacific Railroad, 6-050
Chicago, Milwaukee & St. Paul Railroad
    Dubuque, Iowa station, 6-062
    Milwaukee, Wisconsin station, 244
    Minneapolis, Minnesota station, 6-053

Chicago, Rock Island & Pacific Railroad, 6-064
Chicago & Great Western Railroad, IN-031, 6-063
Chicago & Northwestern Railroad, IN-096
    Chicago North Western terminal, 6-022–028, 6-037
    Milwaukee, Wisconsin station, 243–244, 6-051
Chicago & Western Indiana Railroad, 6-036
City Beautiful Movement, 36
Civil War, 15, IN-015–017, 17, IN-018–024
Clarke, L. Phillips (arch.), 5-075, 198
coal chutes and coaling stations, IN-095, IN-096
Collins, Marjory (ph.), IN-010
Colorado
    Colorado Springs, IN-003
    Denver, 289, 8-011–016
    Glenwood Springs, 8-019
    Golden, 8-017
    Manitou, 8-018
    Ophir, 8-001
    Ouray, 8-020
Colter, Mary Jane (arch.), 6-081, 303–304, 9-011
Connecticut
    New London, 4-022–024
    Southport, 4-028
    Stamford, 4-029–031
    Windsor, 4-025–027
Coolidge, Charles Atherton (arch.), 9-055
Copper River Railroad, 7-037
Coutan, Jules (art.), 3-080
Cret, Paul Philippe (arch.), 119
Crocker, Charles, 21
Currier & Ives (lith.), 15, IN-017, IN-025, IN-047
Cushing, George M. (ph.), 4-052
Daly, Marcus, 7-013
Davis, Jefferson, IN-017
Delano, Jack (ph.), IN-031, IN-096, IN-098, 55,
    IN-102, IN-103, 4-008, 4-009, 6-029, 6-030,
    6-050, 9-001, 9-006, 9-017, 9-018, 9-070
Delaware, Lackawanna & Western Railroad, IN-078,
    IN-101
    Binghamton, New York station, 3-057–060
    Buffalo terminal, 3-067, 3-068
    Vestal, New York station, 3-057
Delaware, Wilmington, IN-061, 64, 1-044, 1-045
Delaware & Hudson Railroad
    Champlain, New York, 3-046
    Plattsburgh, New York, 3-045
    Saratoga Springs, New York station, 3-044
Denver, Northwestern & Pacific, 289
Denver & Rio Grande Western Railroad, 8-019, 8-020
depots, 29
design and construction
    architectural elements, 45
    Carpenter Gothic design, 3-057, 4-028
    Cincinnati Union Terminal, 118–119, 2-108–112
    Cleveland Union Terminal, 118, 2-081, 2-086–088
    Grand Central Terminal (New York), 3-078
    historical development of U.S. railway stations, 9,
        28–37, 197–198, 303–304
    Pennsylvania Railroad Station (New York), 3-090–
        092
    San Diego, California station, 9-041–044
    Union Station, Washington, D.C., 1-054–066, 83–84
Dodge, Grenville, 21
Dowd, Charles, 44

Duluth & Iron Range Railroad, 6-054
East Bay–Seaboard Airline, 5-027, 5-028
East Coast Railway, 5-083
Easy Rider (film), 44
economics
    railroad monopolies, IN-055
    westward expansion of rail system, 21
Eidlitz, Cyrus (arch.), 6-035
Eisenman, George (ph.), 3-006, 3-007
Ellicott Mills Station (Maryland), 29, IN-038, 63–64,
    1-002
El Tovar Lodge, 26, 28
Endahl, Bill (ph.), 9-002–004
Endion Passenger Depot (Duluth, Minnesota), 6-054,
    6-055
Engdahl, Bill (ph.), IN-084
Erie Railway
    Buffalo, New York station, 3-066
    Clifton, New Jersey station, 3-015
    Corning, New York station, 3-061, 3-062
    Decatur, Indiana depot, 6-017
    Jamestown, New York station, 3-053
    Middletown, New York station, IN-072, IN-073,
        3-034, 3-035
    New Milford, New Jersey station, 3-018
    Niagara Falls, New York, 3-065
    Port Jervis, New York station, 3-039, 3-040
    Sparkill, New York station, 3-033
    Suspension Bridge, New York station, 3-064
    Susquehanna, Pennsylvania station & hotel, 2-055–
        062
    Wellsville, New York station, 3-055, 3-056
evangelists and lecturers, 10, 3-102
Fairbanks, P. Kent (ph.), 8-026
Father of the Bride, The (film), 43
Faux, Caleb (ph.), IN-083, IN-099, 2-092–096, 2-103
Fellheimer, Alfred (arch.), 2-099
ferry terminals
    Hoboken, New Jersey, 133, 3-003–007
    Jersey City, New Jersey, 3-008–014
firsts
    architect for station buildings, 31
firsts and mosts
    most train lines served at one station, 6-075
    New England railroad station, 4-048
    oldest station in California, 9-036
    railroad station, IN-038, 63–64
Flagler, Henry, 23
Fleming, Sandford, 44
Florida
    Fernandina Beach, 5-082
    Key West, 23, IN-029
    New Smyrna, 5-083
    Orlando, 5-080, 5-081
    Palm Beach, 198, 5-075–079
    Pensacola, 5-084
    Tampa, IN-008
    tourist travel to, 23
Florida–East Coast Railroad, IN-029
Frank Leslie's Illustrated Newspaper, 15, IN-005, IN-016,
    IN-027
Fred Harvey Company, 26. see also Harvey Houses
Frost & Granger (arch.), 6-022
Fuller, H. O. (ph.), 5-033

Fuller & Hammond (ph.), IN-013
Furness, Frank (arch.), 32, IN-044, 2-023, 64
Gajda, Paul N. (del.), 5-051
Garfield, James, IN-005
Garland, Judy, 28
Garrett, Duane (ph.), 7-017–022
Gaudens, Augustus, 83
Gaudens, Louis St., 83–84
Georgia
    Atlanta, 17, IN-023, IN-024, 197, 5-088
    Plains, 5-091, 5-092
    Savannah, IN-067, IN-097, IN-106, 5-089, 5-093,
        231, 5-094–120
    Valdosta, 5-090
Gilbert, Bradford Lee (arch.), 4-012
Gilbert, Cass (arch.), 275
Glacier National Park, 24, IN-031
Gohlich, Edward (ph.), 9-060, 9-061
Goode, Ned (ph.), 2-046, 2-064
Gosport, New Albany & Salem Railroad, IN-002
Gottscho, Samuel H. (ph.), 3-071
Grabill, John C. H., 7-006
Grafton Machine Shop & Foundry (Virginia), IN-092
Graham, Anderson, Probst, & White (arch.), 2-032, 118
Graham, Robert G. (ph.), 9-020, 9-021
Grand Canyon National Park, 26, IN-035, 9-025–030
Grand Central Depot (New York City), 3-072
Grand Central Railway
    Detroit, Michigan depot, 6-003
Grand Central Station (Chicago, Illinois), IN-079,
        IN-080, 6-031–034
Grand Central Terminal (New York), IN-007, 34, 40,
        IN-057–060, 43, IN-064, IN-076, 3-069, 158–160,
        3-072–088
Grand Trunk Station (Portland, Maine), 4-002
Grant, Cary, 43, IN-063
Grant, Ulysses S., IN-017
Great Northern Railroad, 37, IN-112
    Fargo, North Dakota depot, 7-004
    Helena, Montana depot, 7-015
Great Train Robbery, The (film), 42
Greene, Arthur Smedley (ph.), 3-026
Griffith, M. A. (arch.), 5-081
Grogan, Brian C. (ph.), IN-035, 9-028
Guiteau, Charles J., IN-005
Gulf, Mobile & Ohio Railroad, 5-073, 5-074
Haldeman, A. F. (arch.), 3-028
Hambright, F. Harlan (ph.), IN-077
Harrell, Mark (ph.), 5-091, 5-092
Harriman, Edward Henry, IN-055
Harris & Ewing (ph.), 1-058
Hartford & New Haven Railroad, 4-025–027
Harvey, Frederick Henry, 26–28, 8-004. see also Harvey
        Houses
Harvey Girls, The, 28
Harvey Houses, 26–28, IN-036, 6-081, 9-024, 303
Harwood, Herbert H., Jr., 160
Hedrich-Blessing (ph.), 6-036, 9-002–004
Hiawatha Streamliners, 244
Highsmith, Carol (ph.), 55
Hine, Lewis H. (ph.), IN-085
Hitchcock, Alfred, 43
Hopkins, Mark, 21
Hopper, Edward (art.), 38

Horydczak, Theodor (ph.), 2-001
Howard, George H., Jr. (arch.), 9-047
Huckel Samuel, Jr. (arch.), IN-052, 3-060
Hunt, Jarvis (arch.), 6-044, 6-081
Hunt, Richard Morris (arch.), 36
Huntington, Colis P., 21
Idaho
    Boise, 275, 7-017–022
    Montour, 7-023, 7-024
Idaho Northern Railroad, 7-023, 7-024
Illinois
    East St. Louis, IN-012
    Frankfort, 6-049
    Joliet, 6-044–046
    La Grange Stone Avenue Depot, 6-040–043
    La Salle, 6-047
    Marseilles, 6-048
    see also Chicago, Illinois
Illinois Central Railroad, 36, 6-038, 6-039, 6-061
Indiana
    Beverly Shores, 6-018, 6-019
    Decatur, 6-017
    Gosport, IN-002, 6-020, 6-021
    Indianapolis, 244, 6-010–016
Insull, Samuel, 6-019
Insull Spanish style, 6-019
Iowa
    Council Bluffs, 6-056–058
    Creston, 6-059, 6-060
    Dubuque, 6-061–063
    Independence, 6-064
    Keokuk, 6-065
Irish, Elwood W., IN-049
Ives, J. M. (del.), IN-025
Jackson, William Henry (ph.), 1-033, 3-019, 9-024
Jennings, John (del.), 9-009
Jensen, J. Chris, 6-056, 6-057
Jolliver, Irvin (art.), 38
Jones, Jonnie (ph.), 2-076–080, 2-082–085
Judah, Theodore, 21
Kaminsky, David J. (ph.), 5-061, 5-062
Kansas
    Chanute, IN-036
    Dodge City, 8-004
    Junction City, IN-070
    Wellington, 8-005
Keck, Maxfield (art.), 119, 2-095
Kennedy, John F., IN-007
Kentucky
    High Bridge, 5-001
    Louisville, 5-046–049
King, Moses (art.), 3-070
Knickerbocker Special, 6-077
Koch, Augustus (lith.), 5-093
Lackawanna Railway
    Buffalo, New York terminal, IN-078
    Hoboken, New Jersey station, 3-003–007
    Mt. Pocono, Pennsylvania station, 2-066
La Grande Station (Los Angeles, California), 9-062, 9-063
Lang, Leonard (ph.), 4-025–027
Lange, Dorothea (ph.), 7-025, 7-026
Lanier, Emmet F. (ph.), 1-060
Lee, Russell (ph.), IN-066, IN-108, 5-057, 8-005, 8-006,
        8-020

Lehigh Valley Railroad, 2-067, 3-063
Lexington & West Cambridge Railroad, 4-047, 4-048
Lincoln, Abraham, IN-006, IN-017, 21
Link, Theodore C. (arch.), 2-003, 5-050, 244, 6-066
Little Rock & Hot Springs Western Railroad, 5-052
Livingston, Maurice, IN-085
Loewy, Raymond (designer), IN-061, 2-032
Long Island Railroad
    Brooklyn station, 3-023
    Port Jefferson station, 3-026
Louisiana
    Natchitoches, 5-054, 5-055
    New Orleans, 5-053
    New Roads, IN-108
Louisville & Nashville Railroad
    Louisville, Kentucky station, 5-046–049
    Montgomery, Albama train shed, 5-066, 5-067,
        5-069, 5-070
    Nashville, Tennessee station, 5-040
    Pensacola, Florida station, 5-084
    Tuscaloosa, Alabama depot, 5-064
Lowe, Jet (ph.), 55, 1-007, 1-048, 2-048–051, 2-063,
        4-051, 5-063, 5-064, 7-013, 7-028, 7-034, 7-036
MacQuarrie, John A. (art.), 8-022
Maine
    Bath, 4-005–007
    Caribou, 4-008, 4-009
    Portland, 4-002–004
Maine Central Railroad, 4-007
Main Street Station (Richmond, Virginia), 197-198,
        5-002–006
Major and the Minor, The (film), 43
Mang, Fred, Jr. (ph.), 9-012
Martz, J. (ph.), IN-095
Maryland
    Aberdeen, 1-040–043
    Annapolis Junction, IN-016
    Baltimore area rail buildings, 29, IN-038–041,
        63–64, 1-002–021
    birth of American railroad in, 63
    Blue Mountain House, 1-033
    Cumberland, 1-035–039
    Ellicott City, 29, IN-038, 63–64, 1-002
    Hagerstown, 1-034
    Laurel, 1-031
    Point of Rocks, IN-043, 1-001, 64, 1-022–029
    Rockville, 64, 1-030
    Silver Spring, 1-032
Massachusetts
    Auburndale, IN-045, 4-045
    Framingham, IN-082, 4-036–039
    Lexington, 4-047, 4-048
    Lowell, 4-049
    Newton, 4-046
    North Adams, 4-054
    Palmer, 4-040, 4-041
    Salem, 4-044
    Springfield, 4-050
    Stockbridge, 33, IN-046
    Stoughton, 4-051, 4-052
    Wellesley, 4-042, 4-043
    Williamstown, 4-053
    Worcester, IN-051, IN-052, 37, 176
    see also Boston, Massachusetts

Mathison, J. B. (arch.), 9-047
Mayre, P. Thornton (arch.), 197
McClellan, George B., IN-017
McClure, C. L. (ph.), 8-012
McCoy, Leonard B. (arch.), 303
McKim, George (arch.), 159
McKim, Mead, & White (arch.), 33, 118, 3-001
Michigan
    Ann Arbor, 6-006
    Battle Creek, 6-004, 6-005
    Detroit, IN-011, 6-002, 6-003
    Muskegon, 6-007
    Petoskey, 6-009
    Ypsilanti, 6-008
    see also Detroit, Michigan
Michigan, Detroit, IN-011
Michigan Central Railroad
    Ann Arbor, Michigan station, 6-006
    Battle Creek, Michigan station, 6-004, 6-005
    Detroit, Michigan depot, IN-011
    Ypsilanti, Michigan station, 6-008
military uses of rail system, 10, IN-008–010
    Civil War, 15, IN-015–017, 17, IN-018–024
Minnesota
    Duluth, 6-054, 6-055
    Minneapolis, 6-053
    St. Paul, 6-001, 6-052
Mississippi
    Aberdeen, 5-061, 5-062
    Biloxi, 5-056
    Holly Springs, 5-060
    Mound Bayou, 5-057
    Natchez, 5-059
    Tupelo, 5-058
Missouri
    Jefferson City, 6-079
    Kansas City, 6-080, 6-081
    Kirkwood, 6-078
    Mountain Grove, IN-085
    St. Louis, 244, 6-066–077
Missouri-Pacific Railroad, 6-078
Miyamato, Lanny (ph.), 1-020
Moffatt, David, 289
Moffatt Station (Denver, Colorado), 8-013–016
Mona Lisa Smiles (film), 4-042
Monangahela Incline Plane (Pennsylvania Pittsburgh),
    55, IN-109–111
Montana
    Anaconda, 7-013
    Fairfield, 7-014
    Froid, 7-016
    Gardiner, 24, IN-032, 26
    Helena, 7-015
Montfort, Richard (arch.), 5-040
Mount Clare Station (Baltimore, Maryland), 29,
    IN-038–041, 63, 1-003–007
Mount Royal Baltimore & Ohio Station (Baltimore,
    Maryland), 1-016–020, 63
Mowbray, F. W. (arch.), 5-048
Muessig, Hans (ph.), 7-023, 7-024
Murchison, Kenneth M. (arch.), 2-050, 3-003, 3-068,
    63, 1-021
My Architect (film), 43
narrow-gauge rail, 289

national park system, 24–28
Nebraska
    Grand Island, IN-065
    Omaha, 289, 8-003
    Wymore, IN-095
Nevada
    Carson City, 8-031
    Las Vegas, 8-029
    Reno, 8-030
New Albany & Salem Railroad, 6-020, 6-021
New England rail system, 175–176
New Hampshire
    Laconia, 4-012
    Manchester, 4-010
    North Conway, 4-011
    White Mountains, 4-013
New Haven Railroad, 4-052, 176
New Jersey
    Atlantic City, 3-017
    Beaver Lake, 3-016
    Clifton, 3-015
    Elizabeth, 3-019
    Hoboken, 133, 3-003–007
    Jersey City Ferry Terminal, 3-008–014
    Newark, 3-001, 3-020–022
    New Milford, 3-018
    rail network, 133
New Mexico
    Albuquerque, 9-001, 303, 9-011–013
    El Ortiz station, 38, IN-054
    Gallup, 304, 9-016
    Laguna, 9-017
    Las Vegas, 9-015
    Vaughn, 9-018
New Oriental Limited, IN-112
New Union Station (Little Rock, Arkansas), 5-050
New Union Station (Omaha, Nebraska), 8-003
New York, New Haven & Hartford Railroad, IN-107,
    3-110, 4-022–024, 4-028–031
New York, West Shore & Buffalo Railroad, 3-032
New York Central & Hudson River Railroad, 3-002
New York Central Railroad, 175–176
    Albany station, 3-042
    Garrison station, 3-051
    Rochester station, 3-054
    Saranac Lake station, 3-050
    Scarsdale station, 3-031
    Syracuse depot, 3-052
New York City
    Brooklyn, 3-023
    Grand Central Depot, 3-072
    Grand Central Terminal, IN-007, 34, 40, IN-057–060,
        43, IN-064, IN-076, 3-069, 158–160, 3-072– 088
    Pennsylvania Railroad Station, IN-010, 33, 43, IN-
        100, 158, 3-071, 159–160, 159–160, 3-089–109, 327
    regional rail network, 133, 3-002
New York state
    Albany, 3-042
    Binghamton, 3-057–060
    Bronxville, 3-027, 3-028
    Buffalo, IN-078, 3-066–068
    Champlain, 3-046
    Corning, 3-061, 3-062
    Forest Hills, 3-024

Fulton, 3-048
Garrison, 3-051
Great Neck, 3-025
Haines Corners, 3-049
Hartsdale, 3-029, 3-030
Highland, 3-041
Ithaca, 3-063
Jamestown, 3-053
Middletown, IN-072, IN-073, 3-034, 3-035
New Rochelle, IN-107, 3-032, 3-110
Niagara, IN-028, 3-065
Plattsburgh, 3-045
Port Jefferson, 3-026
Port Jervis, 3-039, 3-040
rail network, 133
Rochester, 3-054
Saranac Lake, 3-050
Saratoga Springs, 3-044
Scarsdale, 3-031
Sparkill, 3-033
Suspension Bridge Station, 3-064
Sylvan Beach, 3-047
Syracuse, 3-052
Troy, 3-043
Vestal, IN-101, 3-057
Wellsville, 3-055, 3-056
West Point, 3-036–038
see also New York City
North by Northwest (film), 43, IN-063
North Carolina
    Asheville, 5-023
    Newton station, 5-024
North Dakota
    Bismarck, 275, 7-005
    Dickinson, 7-003
    Fargo, 275, 7-004
    Starkweather, 7-002
Northern Pacific Railway, 24, IN-030, 275
Northwestern (B&O) Railroad, IN-092
Oanassis, Jacqueline Kennedy, 3-087
Ohio
    Cincinnati, IN-083, IN-099, 91, 2-072, 118–119,
        2-089–112
    Cleveland, 2-001, 91, 2-076–088
    Columbus, 2-075
    Dayton, 2-073
    Delaware, IN-013
    rail lines, 91
    Toledo, 2-074
Oklahoma
    Perry, IN-071, 8-007–010
    Slick, 8-006
Old Faithful Inn, 24, 26
Old Frisco Depot (Fayetteville, Arkansas), 5-051
Olmsted, Frederick Law, 35
Oregon
    Bend, 7-027
    Irrigon, 7-025, 7-026
    Portland, 275
Orgel, Celia (ph.), 3-005
Ostendorf, Troy (ph.), 8-013, 8-014
Overseas Railroad, 23
Oyster Bar at Grand Central Terminal, 3-087
Pacific Railroad, 9-067

Palmer, F. F. (art.), IN-025
Peabody & Stearns (arch.), 3-012
Pegram, George H. (eng.), 6-075
Penn Central Railroad, 2-052–054
Pennsylvania
    Bethlehem, 2-038–040
    Bryn Mawr, 32, 2-041
    Cedar Hollow, 2-064
    Connellsville, 2-065
    Easton, 2-070
    Erie, 2-071
    Greensburg, 2-047, 2-048
    Hanover Junction, IN-014
    Harrisburg, IN-077, 2-034–037
    Jim Thorpe Station, 2-063
    Johnstown, 2-049, 2-050
    Reynoldsville, 2-069
    Sayre, 2-067
    Strafford, 2-052–054
    Susquehanna, 2-055–062
    West Chester, 2-044–046
    Wynnewood, 2-042, 2-043
    see also Philadelphia, Pennsylvania; Pittsburgh,
      Pennsylvania
Pennsylvania Railroad, 32, 40, IN-056, 91, 2-002
    Baltimore station, 63, 1-021
    Bryn Mawr station, 2-041
    Calvert Station (Baltimore, Maryland), 1-014, 1-015
    Harrisburg, Pennsylvania station, IN-077, 2-034–
      037
    Johnstown, Pennsylvania station, 2-049, 2-050
    Newark, New Jersey station, 3-001, 3-020–022
    Philadelphia station, 2-015–020
    Pittsburgh station, 35–36, 2-007–014
    S-1 locomotive, IN-061
    West Chester station, 2-044–046
    see also Pennsylvania Station (New York)
Pennsylvania Station (New York), IN-010, 33, 43,
    IN-100, 158, 3-071, 159–160, 3-089–109, 327
Pere Marquette Railroad Station (Petoskey, Michigan),
    6-009
Philadelphia, Pennsylvania
    Baltimore & Ohio Railroad Station, 2-021–028
    Pennsylvania Railroad Centennial Depot, IN-048
    Pennsylvania Railroad Station, 2-015–020
    Philadelphia & Reading Railroad Terminal Station,
      2-029–031
    Reading Station, 2-068
    Thirtieth Street Station, 2-032, 2-033
    Twenty Fourth and Chestnut Street station, IN-044
Philadelphia, Wilmington & Baltimore Railroad, 63,
    1-011–013
Philadelphia & Reading Railroad Terminal Station,
    2-029–031
Philadelphia World's Fair, IN-047
Piaget, Paul (ph.), 6-078
Pickering, E. H. (ph.), 1-011, 1-014, 1-015, IN-038
Pittsburgh, Pennsylvania
    Monangahela Incline Plane, 55, IN-109–111
    Pennsylvania Railroad Station, 35–36, 2-007–014
    Pittsburgh & Lake Erie Railroad Station, 2-004–006
    Wabash Station, 2-003
Pittsburgh & Lake Erie Railroad Station (Pittsburgh,
    Pennsylvania), 2-004–006

political figures and events, 10
    Garfield assassination, IN-005
    Kennedy funeral, IN-007
    Lincoln funeral, IN-006
    presidential campaigns, IN-003–004
Popko, Edward (ph.), IN-100, 3-108
Post, Leo W. (builder), 6-019
President Street Station (Baltimore, Maryland), 63,
    1-011–013
Providence & Worcester Railroad, 4-019, 4-020
Puerto Rico, San Juan, 5-085–087
Pullman Company, 42, IN-062, 6-031
Queen City Hotel & Station (Cumberland, Maryland),
    1-035–039
Railroad Act (1862), 21
rail system
    first passenger and freight station, IN-038
    historical and social significance of, 9–10, 10, 15
    historical development of, 15, 28–37, 63, 175–176,
      197, 243–244
    station nomenclature, 29
    see also design and construction
Rand, Marion (ph.), 9-037–039
Rau, William Herman (ph.), 2-070
Raymond, W. H. (ph.), 9-007
Raymond Loewy Associates (arch.), 5-011
Reading Railroad, 32, 2-068
Reamer, Robert C., 24, 26
Reed & Stem (arch.), 34, 3-031, 3-083, 3-086, 275, 7-005,
    7-028
Reiss, Winold (art.), 2-102
Rhode Island
    Pawtucket, 4-018
    Providence, 176, 4-015–017
    Westerly, 4-021
    Woonsocket, 4-019, 4-020
Richardson, Henry Hobson (arch.), 24, 33, IN-045,
    175–176, 4-022–024, 4-033, 4-036
Richmond & Petersburg Railroad Depot, IN-021
Rineer, George (ph.), 1-044
Robinson, Cervin (ph.), IN-045, IN-079, IN-082, 55,
    2-026, 3-103–107, 4-036–043, 4-045, 4-046, 6-031,
    6-032, 327
Rock Creek Railroad, 7-011, 7-012
Rock Creek Station (Rock River, Wyoming), 7-011,
    7-012
Rodd, Thomas (arch.), 6-014
Roebuck, A. C. (ph.), 8-002, 8-018
Rogers, Ginger, 43
Roosevelt, Franklin D., IN-004
Roosevelt, Theodore, IN-003
Root, John Wellborn (arch.), 35, 6-059
Rosenberg, Louis (art.), 2-081
Rosener, Ann (ph.), 1-032
Rosskam, Edwin (ph.), IN-057, IN-060
Rothstein, Arthur (ph.), IN-058, IN-059, 1-034, 4-014,
    5-058, 7-014, 8-031
Rough Riders, IN-008
roundhouses, IN-012, 29, IN-088–094, 5-106, 5-107,
    5-110–113
Royal Limited, IN-001
Russell, Andrew J. (ph.), 15, IN-006, IN-015, IN-018,
    5-008
Saint, Eva Marie, 43, IN-063

Salt Lake Railway, 8-029
San Francisco & San Jose Railroad, 9-035, 9-036
San Juan Railroad, 5-085–087
San Pedro, Los Angeles & Salt Lake Railroad, 9-066
Santa Fe Railroad, 26, IN-066
    Albuquerque, New Mexico station, 9-013
    Chanute, Kansas station, IN-036
    Dodge City, Kansas station, 8-004
    San Angelo, Texas station, 9-010
    San Diego, California station, 9-037–044
Schaffer, Kristen, 35
Schiller, William (ph.), IN-012
Schirmacher, Frederick (ph.), IN-071, 8-007–010
Schwab, Augustus (eng.), 5-102, 231
Schwartz, Louis (ph.), 5-095
Seabiscuit (film), 43
Seaboard Airline Railroad
    Charleston, South Carolina station, 5-027, 5-028
    Darlington, South Carolina station, 5-032
    Palm Beach, Florida station, 198, 5-075–079
    Richmond, Virginia Main Street Station, 5-004
Senigo, Stephen L. (ph.), 3-027–031
Shaw, Alfred (arch.), 2-032
shell interlocking tower, 3-110
Shepley, Rutan, & Coolidge (arch.), 3-042, 4-033, 9-055
Shulman, Julius (ph.), IN-081
Singley, B. L. (ph.), IN-008
S-1 locomotive, IN-061
Smalling, Walter, Jr. (ph.), 7-035, 9-040
Smith, C. Hadley (ph.), 3-063
social and historical contexts
    development of midwestern rail network, 243-244
    development of New England rail network, 175-176
    development of southern rail network, 197
    railroad imagery in artistic expression, 38-44
    rail system development, 15, 28-37, 63
    Rocky Mountain rail facilities, 289
    significance of rail system development, 9, 10, 15
    tourism and vacation travel, 23-28
    westward expansion, 21, IN-025-27, 23, 275
South Carolina
    Aiken, 5-007
    Belton, 5-031
    Charleston, 5-025, 5-027–030
    Darlington, 5-032
    Geisboro, IN-018
    Greenville, 5-026
South Carolina Railroad, 5-029, 5-030
South Dakota, Deadwood, 7-006
Southern Express Company, IN-085
Southern Pacific Railroad
    Berkeley, California station, 303
    Brownsville, Texas station, IN-084, 303, 9-002–004
    building design, 303
    Burlingame, California station, 9-045–051
    Maricop, Arizona station, 9-019
    Palm Springs, California depot, 9-065
    San Carlos, California depot, 9-054–058
    Shasta Springs, California station, 9-069
    Vaughn, New Mexico station, 9-018
Southern Railway
    Asheville, North Carolina station, 5-023
    Belton, South Carolina station, 5-031
    Bessemer, Alabama depot, 5-063

Charleston, South Carolina depot, 5-029, 5-030
Charlottesville, Virginia offices, 5-020
Chatham, Virginia passenger depot, 5-022
Greenville, South Carolina station, 5-026
Knoxville, Tennessee station, 5-043
Spozorsky, Michael (ph.), 3-008–014
St. Louis, San Francisco Railroad, IN-071, 8-007
Standard Time Act (1918), 44
Stanford, Leland, 21
Stott, Peter (ph.), 4-047, 4-048
Strobridge & Company (lith.), 3-074
Strous, Alton (ph.), 6-004, 6-005
stub-end stations, 45
Stupich, Martin (ph.), IN-107, 3-110, 6-044–046, 6-048
Sullivan, Louis (arch.), 37
Sunday, Billy, 3-102
Super Chief streamliner, 9-001
Taft, Lorado Z., 1-061
Taft, Louise T. (ph.), 8-021–023
Tateishi, Don (ph.), 9-054–058
Taylor, Elizabeth, 43
telegraph, IN-038
Tell it to the Marines (film), 42–43
Tenbusch & Hill (ph.), 6-055
Tennessee
    Chattanooga, 5-045
    Knoxville, 5-043
    Memphis, 5-044
    Nashville, IN-022, 5-033–042
terminals, 45
Terminal Station (Atlanta, Georgia), 197, 5-088
Terminal Tower (Cleveland, Ohio), 2-001, 2-076–088
Texas
    Algoe, 9-008
    Black, 9-006
    Brownsville, IN-084, 303, 9-002–004
    Burkburnett, 9-007
    Rockport, 9-014
    San Angelo, 9-010
    San Augustine, IN-066
    Tulia, 9-009
Texas & Pacific Railroad, IN-108, 5-054, 5-055
Thayer & Company (lith.), IN-053
Thelma and Louise (film), 44
Thigpen, Ray (ph.), 5-073, 5-074
through stations, 45
Thum, David (ph.), IN-110, IN-111
ticket windows/counters/booths, IN-073, IN-082,
    IN-083, 4-040, 4-041, 5-018
Tiffany Company, 3-007
time zone system, 44
tourism and vacation travel, 23–28, 3-047
Tracey, Spencer, 43
Tulia Railroad, 9-009
Uncle Sam, IN-047
Underhill, Irving (ph.), 3-032, 3-079, 3-083, 5-025
Underwood, Gilbert Stanley (arch.), 289–290
Union Depot
    Mobile, Alabama, 197
    Norfolk, Virginia, 5-021
Union Pacific Railroad, 21, 24, IN-034, IN-055, 290
    Boise, Idaho depot, 275, 7-017–022
    Cheyenne, Wyoming passenger station, IN-087,
        IN-069, 7-001, 275, 7-007–010

Council Bluffs, Iowa Transfer Depot, 6-056–058
    Kelso, California depot, 9-052, 9-053
    Logan, Utah passenger depot, 8-026, 8-027
    Rock Creek Station, 7-011, 7-012
    Salt Lake City, Utah passenger station, 8-021–025
Union Passenger Station (Salt Lake City, Utah),
    8-021–025
Union Passenger Terminal (Los Angeles), 43, IN-075,
    IN-081, 9-031–034
Union Station
    Atlantic City, New Jersey, 3-017
    Charleston, South Carolina, 5-025
    Chicago, Illinois, 43, IN-102, IN-103, 6-029, 6-030
    Columbus, Ohio, 2-075
    Dayton, Ohio, 2-073
    Denver, Colorado, 289, 8-002, 8-011–016
    Detroit, Michigan, 6-002
    Indianapolis, Indiana, 244, 6-010–016
    Joliet, Illinois, 6-044–046
    Kansas City, Missouri, 6-080, 6-081
    Keokuk, Iowa, 6-065
    Memphis, Tennessee, 5-044
    Montgomery, Alabama, 5-065–072
    Nashville, Tennessee, 5-034–042
    Newton, North Carolina, 5-024
    Omaha, Nebraska, 289
    Portland, Maine, 4-004
    Portland, Oregon, 275
    Providence, Rhode Island, 4-017, 176, 4-015
    St. Louis, Missouri, 244, 6-066–077
    Tacoma, Washington, 34, 275, 7-028–030
    Toledo, Ohio, 2-074
    Washington, D.C., IN-009, 35–36, IN-074, IN-086,
        IN-105
    Worcester, Massachusetts, IN-051, 37, IN-052, 176
union stations, 45, 83, 6-044
Union Terminal
    Cincinnati, Ohio, IN-083, IN-099, 2-072, 118–119,
        2-089–112
    Cleveland, Ohio, 118, 2-076–088
Upjohn, Richard (arch.), 6-031
Utah
    Cache Junction, 8-028
    Logan, 8-026
    Promontory Point, 21, IN-026, IN-027
    Salt Lake City, 8-021–025
Vachon, John (ph.), IN-065, 2-065, 6-061–063, 6-079,
    7-002, 8-003
Van Brunt & Howe (arch.), 275, 7-009
Vanderbilt, William, 34
Vermont, Randolph, 4-014
Virginia
    Alexandria, IN-006
    Charlottesville, 5-019, 5-020
    Chatham, 5-022
    Grafton Machine Shop & Foundry, IN-092
    Hopewell, 5-008
    Newport News, 5-009, 5-010
    Norfolk, 5-021
    Petersburg, IN-015
    Richmond, Richmond & Petersburg Railroad
        Depot, IN-021
    Richmond Main Street Station, 197–198, 5-002–
        006

Roanoke, 1-043, 5-011–018
    Shadwell, IN-068
Virginia & Western Railroad, 1-043, 5-011–018
Waddy & Wood (ph.), 5-019, 5-020
Wagner, Steward (arch.), 2-099
waiting rooms, IN-071, IN-072, 1-020, 1-063, 1-064,
    2-006, 2-024–026, 3-001, 3-085, 3-097, 3-103,
    4-040, 4-043, 4-045, 5-038, 5-048, 5-065, 6-016,
    6-025, 6-032, 8-022, 9-040, 9-048
Wall, Ted (ph.), 6-059
Walsh, Joe, 29
Ware & Van Brunt (arch.), IN-052
Warren, Whitney (arch.), 34, 3-080
Warren & Wetmore (arch.), 34, 3-030
Washington, D.C.
    Baltimore & Potomac Station, IN-005
    Union Station, IN-009, 35–36, IN-074, IN-086,
        IN-105, 1-053, 83–84, 1-054–066
    Washington Terminal Station, IN-001
Washington state
    Seattle, 275
    Tacoma, 34, 275, 7-028–030
Weinreb, Everett (ph.), 9-034
Weiss, Winold (art.), 119
Western Virginia Foundation for the Arts and Sciences,
    5-011
West Shore Railroad
    Highland, New York station, 3-041
    West Point, New York station, 3-036–038
West Virginia
    Harper's Ferry aerial view, 1-049
    Harper's Ferry railroad bridge, IN-019, IN-020
    Harper's Ferry Station, 1-046, 1-047
    Martinsburg Repair Shops, IN-088–090, IN-093,
        IN-094
    Thurmond, 1-048
    Wheeling, 1-050–52
    White Sulphur Springs, IN-104
White, Howard J. (arch.), 118
White Pass & Yukon Route Railroad, 7-036
Whittington, Dick (ph.), IN-075
Whittlesey, Charles (arch.), 26, 303, 9-011
Williamstown Railroad Station, 4-053
Wilson, Frank W. (arch.), 9-026, 9-030
Wilson, Harris, & Richards (arch.), 5-004
Wisconsin, Milwaukee, 243–244, 6-051
Wolcott, Marion Post (ph.), 55, IN-105, 4-011, 7-016
workers, railroad, IN-018
World's Columbian Exposition (Chicago, Illinois),
    34–37, IN-049, 6-039
Wright, Frank Lloyd (arch.), 37
Wyeth, N. C. (art.), 40, IN-056
Wyoming
    Cheyenne, IN-069, IN-087, 7-001, 275, 7-007–010
    Laramie, 24, IN-034
    Rock River, 7-011, 7-012
Yates, A. P. (ph.), 3-072
Yazoo & Mississippi Valley Line, 5-057, 5-059
Yellowstone National Park, 24, IN-032, IN-033, 26
Yosemite National Park, 290